THE MEDIEVAL SOLDIER

Medieval Life Series
General Editor: J.J. Bagley, MA,
FRHist. Soc. University of Liverpool

Frontispiece: The murder of St Thomas Becket from a Latin Psalter
executed in England about 1200. Two of the helms have face-guards.
Harley Ms. 5102, f. 32. (Reproduced by permission of the
Trustees of the British Museum.)

THE MEDIEVAL SOLDIER

Vesey Norman

Line drawings by Don Pottinger

Arthur Barker Limited
5 Winsley Street London W1

To
my goddaughters
Linnette and Joanna
and my niece
Joanna

ISBN 0 213 76447 4

Filmset by Keyspools Ltd., Golborne, Lancashire
Printed by C. Tinling & Co. Ltd, Prescot & London

Contents

Illustrations

Figures

Preface

The military system of most of Western Europe during the twelfth and thirteenth centuries was feudal; that is, it was based on the holding of land in return for military service given to an overlord. The holder of the land was supported by agricultural labour and food from his peasants, in return for defending them against raiders, for defending the realm in time of war, and for administering justice to them in his courts. The three important components of the organization were; firstly, the count or earl, originally the royal district officer; secondly, the knight, the armoured cavalryman who formed the backbone of any feudal army; and thirdly, the castle. The last lies outside the scope of this book, so it is mentioned here only in relation to the services owed by knights for garrison duty in the castles of their overlords.

The system developed very unevenly. It was more advanced in France than in Germany, for instance, while in Scandinavia, although some of its features are found, others are not. It originated by the blending of the tribal military systems of the Teutonic barbarians who invaded the Roman Empire, with such features of Roman military organization as survived, for instance, in the towns of France and Italy. Long after the collapse of the Western Roman Empire its prestige lived on, and influenced enormously the thought of those who succeeded to its power.

The need to defend the frontiers of broad realms, like those of Charlemagne, at a time when travel was slow and uncertain, and the central organization poorly developed, led to the appointment of royal deputies called counts. These men were given considerable powers so that they could organize the defences of their own districts. In time of general war they had to come to the royal army with their following. Later, under Charlemagne's weaker successors, the office of count and the lands that supported it became hereditary.

Chivalry, the code which governed the life of the medieval aristocracy from the king himself down to the humblest knight, blended the concepts of honour and manhood, inherited from the dark German forests, with the gentler ideals of Christianity. The Church sanctified the oath of homage to the overlord which had originated in the oath to the leader of the Teutonic war band. The Church it was that canalized the vigorous and warlike energies of Western knighthood into the great endeavours of freeing the Holy Land from the hands of the infidel, in many ways the high point of the earlier Middle Ages.

In the first part of this book I have tried to describe the components from which feudalism and chivalry developed; the organization and ideals of the Teutonic tribes, as well as their equipment. The second part deals with the organization, arming, training, equipment, and ideals of the knight and the troops who supported him in action, in the period before the decline of feudalism changed them all into mercenary soldiers pure and simple.

A book of this type, designed to cover the greater part of Europe over a relatively long period, cannot be written without the help and advice of friends and colleagues too numerous to acknowledge individually. It would be extremely churlish, however, not to mention those who have given up a considerable amount of time to helping. I am very grateful to Mrs Leslie E. Webster, Assistant Keeper of the Department of British and Medieval Antiquities, the British Museum, for reading for me the sections on the Franks, Vikings, and Saxons in typescript and for many most helpful suggestions; to Mr

E.H.H. Archibald, Deputy Head of the Department of Pictures, National Maritime Museum, Greenwich, for advice about ships; to Miss Amanda Tomlinson, Conway Librarian, the Courtauld Institute of Art, University of London, and Miss Alison Stones, now of the Department of Art History, the University of Minnesota, for advice over the dating of manuscripts; and to Mr Don Pottinger, Unicorn Pursuivant, for permission to reuse some of his drawings originally prepared for our book *Warrior to Soldier 449–1660* (US edition: *A History of War and Weapons, 449 to 1660*).

There are two people to whom I am particularly grateful. They are my wife, Catherine Barne, for her patience and kindness in reading and correcting my manuscript and for her many suggestions for improving it; and Mr Claude Blair, Deputy Keeper of the Department of Metalwork at the Victoria and Albert Museum, for also reading my manuscript with a kindly but critical eye, and for giving me the benefit of his unparalleled knowledge of the literary source material as well as of actual surviving arms and armour.

Mrs Hilda R.E. Davidson has very kindly allowed me to quote from her invaluable book, *The Sword in Anglo-Saxon England,* the passage on the swords sent to the Emperor Theodoric by the Warni. Penguin Books has also very kindly allowed me to quote from H. Mattingly, *Tacitus on Britain and Germany* and from M.R.B. Shaw, *Joinville & Ville-hardouin: Chronicles of the Crusades.* I am extremely grateful to Dr R. Allen Brown for drawing my attention to the passage in the *Roman de Rou* of Robert Wace, describing the Norman landing at Pevensey.

In a work of this nature the writer must depend heavily on the work of his predecessors in the field, and I should like to acknowledge my debt to all those whose books appear in the bibliography at the end of the book.

Part I

The Beginnings of
Feudalism

I

The Lombards

Of the great German races that overran western Europe in the fifth and sixth centuries, the Franks in the north and the Lombards in the south left the greatest marks. The Visigoths in Spain, always few in number and irrevocably divided by their religion from their subject people, were unable to form a united kingdom and succumbed to the Saracen advance early in the eighth century. For similar reasons the Vandals failed to secure their hold of the North African coast line. They added to their difficulties by their harsh treatment of the natives and persecuting all not of the Arian faith.[1]

The Lombards, or Langobards, had lived for several generations in the Danube plain under Avar influence and, like all the people of this area, had become skilled horsemen. They were Arian Christians and almost untouched by Roman culture or military techniques, since they came into contact with the Empire only after its disintegration. In 552, when 5,500 of them came into Italy as mercenary cavalry of the Byzantine general Narses, they must have seen both its fertility and its vulnerability. In 586 the next Lombard king, Albion, invaded Italy not with an army but with his whole

---

[1] The Arian heresy, named after its first teacher Arius, was based on the idea that Christ, having been created by God, was therefore less divine than God the Father.

race, thus giving to the north Italian plain the name of Lombardy. Only a few cities in which there were Imperial garrisons, like Pavia, and Padua in its marshes, held out for a time. Elsewhere in Italy their progress was spasmodic, conquest being piecemeal by individual dukes, and, as a result, Roman cities and Lombard settlements existed side by side.

In 643 King Rothari codified their traditional laws. This code is important today for what it tells us of the social organization of the tribe, the dukes, the war leaders; the king's *schultheus* or reeves, the administrators in country districts; the king's *castaldus,* the administrators of towns; free Lombards, already called *barones;* men dependent on the king or a duke, *gaisindi,* equivalent to the war-band of Northern Europe; and men known as *aldii,* half-free occupiers of land held by Lombards, presumably the descendants of the original Roman population. Each is carefully distinguished by his *wergild,*[1] the payment which must be made by the murderer to the victim's lord and kinsmen. These and later laws stress the importance of the horse to the Lombards and they are dealt with in many clauses. A horse with its harness is valued at a sum equivalent to twice the wergild of a household slave and two-thirds that of the more humble of the free Lombards. Most graves of male Lombards contain saddlery.

Although they normally fought on horseback, on occasion the Lombards could act as infantry; as they did at Narses's order at Taginae, forming a solid core of spearmen in the centre of the Byzantine line. Paul the Deacon, writing about 790, gives as their armament helm, *lorica* or body armour, and *ocrea* or greaves. A few pieces of armour were found in excavations at Castel Trosino in central Italy which was

---

[1] The word *wergild* is, in fact, Old English but is now used to indicate this type of fine among Teutonic people.

captured by the Lombards in 578. These include parts of a body armour made of many tiny, narrow plates, originally laced together by leather thongs so that each overlapped one of its neighbours. In the same grave was the brow-plate of a helm, and the hemispherical dome which fitted on the very top. This had a narrow tube sticking out of the centre of the top to hold a plume. Also in this grave were the boss and handle of a shield, a sword 92 cm long, four arrow heads, two knives, a spear head 27·5 cm long with a broad leaf-shaped blade, and a pair of spurs. Other warriors in this grave-field were less lavishly armed and no other traces of body armour or helms were found, except for a small piece of mail. Mail is flexible armour made of many small inter-linked rings of iron wire: each ring is passed through its four neighbours and its ends then closed and locked by a tiny rivet passing through both ends of the ring where they overlap (Figure 1). Mail is quite common on Roman sites and certainly goes back to the third or fourth century BC in northern Europe, and has been found in sacrificial deposits of this date at Hjort-spring and Thorsberg in Denmark. The grave in which this

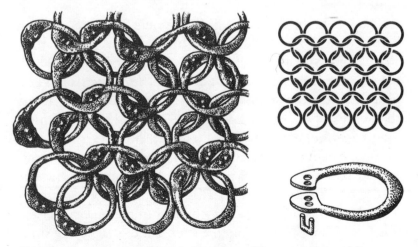

Figure 1 A piece of mail, with diagrams of its construction. More usually a simple straight rivet was used

Lombard mail was found also contained a sword, a knife, an acutely pointed spear-head 35 cm long, and the boss and part of the iron rim of a shield.

In a grave of the second half of the sixth or the early seventh century at Nocera Umbra, were found a brow-plate and, riveted to it, a nasal branching at the top to form a stop-rib along the lower edge of the helm over the eyes. A more or less complete helm of this type was found in an Avar grave at Kertch in the Crimea, and another of similar construction was found in an Alamannic grave at Niederstotzingen in Württemberg.

Warriors, dressed in long-sleeved knee-length coats, apparently made of rows of many narrow vertical plates, and wearing helms with domes on top, are shown on a gold brow-plate of a helm found near Lucca in Italy, inscribed with the name of the Lombard king, Agilulf (590–615). The skulls of these helms seem to be made of many narrow segment-shaped plates, and are fitted with cheek-pieces like the Kertch helm. Plumes, probably of horse-hair, fly from the top of the domes. These men carry round shields with central bosses.

The shield bosses from these cemeteries have an iron hemispherical or conical bowl with a narrower neck and a circular lip which is riveted to the surface of the shield by means of five large rivets. The shield itself was of wood probably covered with leather. A handle was fitted across the hollow inside of the boss and was extended by means of long bars right across the inside of the shield.

A wide variety of spears was found, principally with heads shaped like broad laurel leaves, or with long pointed triangular blades, both with stout central ribs, the second type sometimes with short lugs or wings projecting from the socket on each side. According to Paul the Deacon, these spears were stout enough to lift an enemy from his saddle and hold him aloft.

The hilts of most of the long two-edged swords found in Lombard graves have entirely disappeared, but two gold-mounted examples of about 600 were discovered in the grave-field at Nocera Umbra. Both swords have had a straight cross-guard at each end of the grip made of some perishable material which has now disappeared. The form of the guards is, however, indicated by the gold plates riveted above and below each. Swords of the same general type from other areas have been found with horn or wooden guards protected by similar plates. Horn is surprisingly difficult to cut, but the purpose of the guard may have been as much to prevent the hand from slipping down onto the blade as for protection. The pommel acts both as a counterweight for the blade and to prevent the end of the tang, the narrow part of the blade within the grip, from piercing the wrist. The end of the narrow portion of the blade which passed through the grip was bent over sharply outside the pommel bar to secure it and concealed by a mount shaped like a cocked hat riveted to the pommel bar. Both the Nocera Umbra hilts have a small fixed ring fitted to one end of the pommel, a development of the loose ring similarly attached to Scandinavian hilts and others found in England.

2

The Franks

The Early Franks

The Franks entered the province of Gaul to the north of Trier, Cologne and Mainz in the fourth century, at first as military colonists, or *foederati*, of the Roman Empire to keep out their fellow barbarians. Later, they advanced to fill the gap left both by the withdrawal of the Legions and by the destruction by the Huns of the last Roman garrisons in the Rhineland at Trier and Mainz. To the west of them, and almost completely cut off from Rome and the remainder of the Empire, lay the only surviving Roman district in Gaul, governed from Soissons by a Patrician. Nearly the whole of southern France up to the river Loire was incorporated into the Visigothic kingdom which stretched as far south as Gibraltar and covered the whole Iberian Peninsula, except for the Basque province in the western Pyrenees, and the territory of the Suevi in Galicia and what is now northern Portugal.

The Franks were a loose grouping of heathen German tribes governed by many princelings claiming descent from the house of the Merovings. They were famed for their treachery and perjury. In spite of their long contact with Romans along the Rhine and their employment in the Imperial army, they remained largely uninfluenced by Roman culture or law. It was not until the reign of Chlodovech (Clovis), 481–511, that they were combined under a single king. He

8

succeeded his father Childeric at the age of sixteen and almost at once began his life's work by over-turning the Roman province of Soissons. He then turned on his fellow Franks, and in a series of campaigns incorporated all except the kingdom of Cologne into his own lands, slaying all of the royal line who fell into his hands. He then attacked the Alamanni to the east of the Rhine; and later the Burgundians to his south. In 507 he turned on the Visigoths under their young king, Amalric, choosing as a cause their Arian persecution of their Catholic subjects, to which faith he had meanwhile been converted. The Visigothic power in the south was only saved by the intervention of Theodoric the Ostrogoth, grandfather of Amalric. Finally, Chlodovech seized the last surviving independent Frankish kingdom, Cologne, having encouraged the old king's son to revolt and murder his own father.

Chlodovech was the only one of the great Teutonic founder-kings whose work was to survive, and this was partly because he and his tribe after him were baptised as Catholics and were therefore in religious sympathy with their Roman subjects, unlike the Goths, Lombards, and Vandals, all of whom were Arians. Chlodovech's personal prestige was strengthened in 508 by the gift of a diadem and robe from the Emperor Anastasius, who hoped to make him his ally against the Ostrogoths in Italy. This gave Chlodovech an appearance of legality in the eyes of his Roman subjects.

The earliest surviving written code of Frankish laws, probably of the end of Chlodovech's reign, makes no mention of any military role for the Gallo-Romans, but Procopius in his *History of the Gothic War*, written in the second half of the sixth century, says that in 539 the Gallo-Roman cities sent their contingents to the Frankish army under their ancient banners and equipped as Romans. It is probable that by the end of the sixth century a major part of the Frankish army consisted of Gallo-Romans. The Burgundian allies of the Franks in the sixth century had a Gallo-Roman general, Eunius Mummolus, and by 636 one of the twelve dukes of the Frankish army is described as 'a Roman', possibly a native of Aquitaine. By 605 in fact, the chief officer of the royal household, and therefore of the kingdom, the Mayor of the Palace, was a Gallo-Roman, Protadius.

When the Franks first settled in what is now northern France and the Rhineland, they seem to have been little advanced from the German tribes described by Tacitus in AD 97–8: 'Only a few use swords or lances. The spears they carry – *framae* is the native word – have short and narrow heads, but are so sharp and easy to handle, that the same weapon serves at need for close or distant fighting. The horseman asks no more than his shield and spear, but the infantry have also javelins to shower, several per man, and can hurl them to a great distance; for they are either naked or only lightly clad in their cloaks. There is nothing ostentatious in their turn-out. Only the shields are picked out with carefully selected colours.' He goes on to say that few have body armour *(loricae)*; 'only here and there will you see a helmet of metal or hide *(cassis et galea)* . . . They choose their kings for their noble birth, their leaders for their valour. . . . As for the leaders, it is their example rather than their authority that wins them special admiration – for their energy, their distinction, or their presence in the van of fight.' When a youth came of age he was armed with shield and spear by one of the chiefs, by his father or a kinsman. Then he could join the war-band of a chief, either of his own or a neighbouring tribe, where he would compete against his companions to be in the front rank. For the chief 'dignity and power alike consist in being continually attended by a corps of chosen youths. . . . Nor is it only in a man's own nation that he can win name and fame by the superior number and quality of his companions but in neighbouring states as well.'

'On the field of battle it is a disgrace to the chief to be surpassed in valour by his companions, to the companions not to come up to the valour of their chief. As for leaving a battle alive after your chief has fallen, *that* means lifelong infamy and shame. To defend and protect him, to put down one's own acts of heroism to his credit – that is what they really mean by "allegiance". The chiefs fight for victory, the companions for their chief. . . . '

'The companions are prodigal in their demands on the generosity of their chiefs. It is always "give me that warhorse", or "give me that bloody and victorious spear". As for meals with their plentiful, if homely, fare, they count simply as pay. . . . A man is bound to take up the feuds as well as the friendships of father or kinsmen. But feuds do not go unreconciled. Even homicide can be atoned for by a fixed number of cattle or sheep, and the satisfaction is received by the whole family.'[1]

The evidence of what documents and descriptions by contemporaries there are, suggest that the Franks were not much advanced by the fifth century.

Sidonius Apollinaris, Bishop of Auvergne (about 430–87/8), says 'The Franks are a tall race, and clad in garments which fit them closely. A belt encircles their waist. They hurl their axes and cast their spears with great force, never missing their aim. They manage their shields with great agility, and rush on their enemy with such speed, that they seem to fly more swiftly than their spears.'

Agathias of Myrna, the Byzantine poet (536–82), writing

[1] H. Mattingly, *Tacitus on Britain and Germany*, Penguin Books, 1948, pp. 105, 106, 112–3, and 118.

his *Historiae* about 570, says that the arms of the Franks were very simple and they wore neither body armour nor greaves, their legs being covered only by linen or leather. The majority were bare-headed and a helmet was very rare. Breast and back were naked to the waist. In fact, Gregory of Tours (538–94) mentions Franks wearing body armour on several occasions, as when Count Leudast shocked him greatly by entering the church-house fully armed and wearing helm and body armour. He also criticised the Bishops Salonius and Sagittarius who armed themselves, not with the heavenly cross, but with the helm and body armour *(lorica)* of the world. Agathias goes on to say that they only served mounted on rare occasions, for it was their national custom to fight on foot, which they did very well. They carried a sword, and a shield hung on their left hip. The Emperor Leo vi in his *Tactica,* perhaps here copying a lost version of the *Strategicon* of 580, says that the Germanic people carried their sword in a shoulder belt but that some carried it on a waist-belt. Agathias goes on to say that the Franks had neither bows nor slings, nor any missile weapon, except double axes and *angons* which they used a great deal. These angons he describes as spears of moderate length which could be used like a dart, or for thrusting in hand-to-hand combat, as required. The greater part of the shaft was covered in iron and the head was barbed. When hurled, if the angon struck home it was almost impossible to remove from a wound, because of its barbs, and these caused terrible wounds, usually proving fatal. If it struck in the shield, it hung there, its end dragging on the ground. The man struck could not pull out the angon because of its barbs, nor cut it with his sword because 'he cannot reach the wood through its covering of iron'. When he saw his adversary in this state, the Frank swiftly put his foot on the trailing butt of the spear, thus pressing down on the shield and uncovering the enemy's head and breast. He then, seizing his chance, killed his defenceless adversary either by a blow on the skull with his axe, or by a thrust through the throat with a second spear. Procopius, who was military secretary to the Byzantine general Belisarius, describing the Frankish force led into Italy by Theodebert in 539, says that 'there were but few horsemen, and these the king kept about him: they alone carried spears. The remainder were infantry who had neither spear nor bow, but were armed only with sword, shield and a throwing axe'. He describes the blade of the axe as large, the handle of wood and very short.

Although both Agathias and Procopius comment on the scarcity of cavalry in the Frankish army, the *Notita Dignitatum*, as early as about the year 400, lists two squadrons of Frankish cavalry in Roman pay, one stationed in Egypt, the other in Mesopotamia. Writing of the year 507, Gregory of Tours states that Chlodovech, when crossing the territory of Tours to attack the Visigoths, made a strict rule that no man should take anything from the land except forage and water, which certainly suggests the presence of horses in the army.

What is presumably the angon is known from many Frankish graves and is probably a descendant of the Roman *pilum*. The barbed head is made in one with an iron shaft, usually 80 to 90 cm long but occasionally much longer, with a socket at the other end for a short wooden haft. The statement of Agathias that the shaft was of wood covered in iron is not borne out by grave finds. The heads usually have two long thin barbs.

The second spear mentioned by Agathias, and described by Procopius as a cavalry weapon, is probably represented by the heavy leaf-shaped spear heads found in Frankish graves alongside the angon. A complete spear found in a grave at Oberflacht in Germany was over two metres long.

The full equipment of a Frankish chieftain of the early sixth century can be reconstructed from a grave at Krefeld-Gellep, in the Rhineland. This contained, among other things, a helm with ear-flaps and a mail neck-guard, based probably on an East Roman model and almost certainly imported, since several have been discovered outside the Frankish area. The weapons were a short sword, a heavy spear, an angon, two knives in separate sheaths but in one hanger, and a light throwing axe (francisca). There were also the remains of a hilt for a long sword set with garnets. An iron boss and hand-grip indicated that there had been a shield as well.[1]

The domed helm consists of six inverted T-shaped sections of bronze, riveted round a brow-band, and with the uprights of the T's curved inwards to meet at the top of the skull, where the joint is covered by a plume-holder. The gaps between these sections are filled by iron plates riveted onto the inside of the frame. There are two ear-flaps and the traces of a neck-guard made of mail, hanging from the lower edge. The ear-flaps retain parts of their leather lining held in by a leather thong around the edge, and the skull was probably once similarly lined. It has been suggested that this type of helm with its gilt and decorated surface and weak construction was more of a symbol of rank than a true piece of armour. A helm for a small boy of about this period, found in a grave in Cologne Cathedral, was made entirely of horn segments with narrow strips of brass covering the joins: it retains parts of its lining, horn cheek-pieces and a mail neck-guard. The remainder of the equipment was the same as in the last grave described. On the other hand, a helm found at Bretzenheim near Mainz was of more robust construction. It consisted of

[1] R. Pirling, Germania, XLII, 1964, pp. 188–216.

two strips of iron crossing on top of the skull and bent down to meet a broad iron brow-band; the interspaces were filled with iron plates (the helm was destroyed in the Second World War). This type is without the plume-holder on the top 'or the cheek-pieces and is presumably the precursor of very similar helms depicted, for instance, in the Codex Perizoni 17 of Leiden University (a manuscript illuminated at the Abbey of St Gallen about 950), which have some form of neck-guard but apparently no independent cheek-pieces.

Another helm of the Bretzenheim type, entirely of iron, was found in a grave at Trivières in Hainault, together with a sword, spear, angon, a small knife, and a francisca. In a grave at Lavoye near Saint Germain-en-Laye in France, dateable by a coin of AD 474–91, there was a group of three light spear heads, as well as a sword, a *scramasax* (a long single-edged knife), and a shield boss.

As far as the writer is aware, no trace of body armour has so far been found even in the richest Frankish graves. This would seem to confirm the statements by some early writers that it was not worn but, in fact, we know from others that it was. It may mean that it was too valuable to be buried. Even in the eighth century, when armour was probably becoming more common, the laws of the Ripuarian Franks value a *brunia,* probably a shirt of mail, at twelve *solidi*, equivalent to the price of two horses or two helms. The Gallo-Romans of Imperial days are very often represented in mail shirts; for instance, the stone warrior from Vachèras now in the Museum at Avignon. The Alamanni, the Lombards, and the Avars, all people with whom the Franks were in contact, are known to have worn lamellar armour.

St Gregory describes Count Leudast of Tours as appearing *'cum toracibus et loricis'*. If this is more than the repetition of a time-honoured phrase, an echo of Livy, it must suggest body armour in addition to the '*lorica*' which Gregory elsewhere indicates as being made of mail, when he says that a weapon is turned '*a circulis loricae*'; by the rings of his body armour. Thorax in Greek means a breast-plate or cuirass.

Frankish shield bosses of the fifth and sixth centuries are conical on a short cylindrical base with a broad lip riveted to the surface of the shield; as, for instance, one found in a very rich grave at Vermand in France, in which the boss was plated with silver-gilt and decorated with imitation chalcedony studs on the flange. Later, they are either hemispherical with a narrower neck, like Lombard ones but with a button on a short stalk on top of the dome, or have a flattened conical dome with a similar button. The traces of carbonised wood in the Vermand grave suggests that the diameter of this shield was about 80 cm. By the late seventh century, bosses with tall sugar-loaf-shaped domes are normal. An iron bar, riveted vertically right across the centre of the shield inside, formed the hand grip. The hole for the hand in the centre of the boy's shield found under Cologne Cathedral, was shaped like a key-hole placed sideways. The vertical grip crossed the narrow neck of the hole. The hand passed in through the shank-end of the key-hole and the tips of the fingers emerged from round the grip through the bit end. The shield itself was of wood covered in leather.

The Merovingian two-edged sword had an average blade-length of 85 cm and an average width immediately below the hilt of 5 cm. The edges are parallel for almost the whole length and the point relatively blunt. The hilts are more or less similar to those described for the Lombards, but on several the complete guards have survived because they were of gold set with jewels; as on the sword of King Childeric (d. 481), found in 1653 in his grave, together with a ring bearing the king's name and image. The method of suspending Merovingian swords was by a strap passing under two short metal bars fitted to the front of the wooden scabbard some inches below its mouth. The tip of the scabbard was protected by a short projection mounted on a U or J-shaped rim.

Cassiodorus, the secretary of Theodoric the Ostrogoth, (AD 493–526), thanking a chief of the Warni, a Teutonic tribe, for a present of musical instruments, slave boys, and swords, describes these weapons:

'Your Fraternity has chosen for us swords capable even of cutting through armour, which I prize more for their iron than for the gold upon them. So resplendent is their polished clarity that they reflect with faithful distinctness the faces of those who look upon them. So evenly do their edges run down to a point that they might be thought not shaped by files but moulded by the furnace. The central part of their blades, cunningly hollowed out, appears to be grained with tiny snakes, and here such varied shadows play that you would believe the shining metal to be interwoven with many colours. The metal is ground down by your grindstone and vigorously burnished by your shining dust until its steely light becomes a mirror for men; the dust is granted you by the natural bounty of your land, so that its possession may bestow singular renown upon you'.[1]

It seems possible that the Warni at this time were inhabiting the Elbe basin, an area where a mild abrasive called *kieselguhr* is found naturally and was worked at an early date. This may be the 'shining dust' referred to in the letter. The 'cunningly hollowed out' blade 'grained with tiny snakes' accurately describes the pattern-welded swords found in many barbarian

---

[1] H.R.E. Davidson, *The Sword in Anglo-Saxon England*, Oxford 1962, pp. 105–9.

graves. The hollow, called the fuller by many modern writers, is the groove running down the centre of each face of the blade almost to the point, while the 'snakes' are the wriggly pattern formed by the different quality of the twisted iron used to make the central section of the blade. Modern experiments have shown how these blades were made. The core is made of a number of parallel bars of iron welded together by hammering them when they are hot. Each of these bars is itself made up of several case-hardened iron strips placed, like the filling of a sandwich, between two rods of similar iron. The case-hardening, which produces a core of soft malleable iron within a skin of iron with a higher carbon content and therefore harder, can be done by repeated heating in a charcoal (i.e. carbon) fire. One end of the 'sandwich' of rods and strips is welded together and the other end placed in a vice. The welded end is gripped with tongs and the iron is then heated to a yellow heat, a section at a time, and twisted tightly thus welding all the component parts together. The rods on each side serve to fill the grooves of the spiral formed by the twisted strips. Two such twisted bars can be welded to the sides of a third to form the centre of the blade, while another bar of case-hardened iron is welded on all the way up each side and round the point to form the cutting edge. The blade is now filed into shape, and then, in the majority of cases, quenched and tempered. Quenching consists of cooling the metal rapidly from a high temperature by dipping it into water or oil, to make it hard and brittle. Tempering is the reheating of the blade to a chosen temperature, judged by the colour of the metal, and then allowing it to cool slowly. This reduces the internal strains and brittleness caused by the quenching and makes the blade flexible. The blade would then be sharpened and polished and the surface in the hollow etched with a mild acid in order to bring out the twisted pattern by eating away a little of the surface of the softer parts of the iron.

This complicated method of construction, which was certainly in use by the end of the second century, was probably developed because of the difficulty of finding large pieces of iron of uniform quality throughout, and the need to mix any inferior metal used with the better iron so as to minimise the effect of the former. The result was a blade exceedingly sharp, tough, and flexible. Many graves contain the sharpening stone necessary to keep the edge in good condition. The laws of the Ripuarian Franks give the value of a sword and scabbard as seven *solidi,* while a sword without a scabbard was valued at only three. A scabbard found at Klein-Hüningen was of decoratively carved wood both covered and lined with leather. Traces of woollen lining have been found elsewhere, and a Frankish grave at Orsoy produced a sheath lined with sheep's fleece with the wool next to the blade. Presumably the natural grease in the wool would help to prevent the blade from rusting. Scabbards were occasionally covered with decorative metal plates, as on a seventh-century one found at Gutenstein, Baden.

During the course of the fifth century a large single-edged knife, probably what Gregory of Tours called a *'scramasax',* begins to appear in graves together with the sword. For instance, one was found in the grave of King Childeric (d. 481) as well as a francisca. By the seventh century the scramasax had become more or less universal, replacing the throwing axe. The scabbard of this type of knife appears to have consisted of a fold of leather with the edges riveted together on the side nearer the cutting edge. Scabbards of this type appear in carvings throughout most of northern Europe, and in some graves the rivets have been found in position. Childeric's knife had a heavy jewelled gold top-mount to its scabbard with an extension down the front of the cutting

edge, but few others have more than a thin metal rim covering the join of the leather. The sheath of the scramasax in the
boy's grave under Cologne cathedral contained a small
knife placed in front of the main weapon.

The francisca, the characteristic throwing axe of the early
Franks, has a small iron head about 16 cm long with a short
curved cutting edge with the upper point more prominent
than the lower. The narrow body of the axe curves down
towards the socket giving its top edge a slight S-line. Later
examples have cutting edges longer in proportion to their
length than early ones, the lower point finally becoming
more prominent than the upper. The head was secured to the
shaft by driving an iron wedge into the end of the shaft causing
it to expand and fit the socket tightly, and in a few cases there
is a long rivet passing transversely through the shaft below
the head into the back of the socket. A few examples are
decorated with silver and brass inlay (Plate 1).

None of the earliest descriptions of the Franks mentions
the use of the bow in warfare, but arrow heads are very
common in graves. The early Frankish laws mention poison
arrows which clearly cannot be hunting weapons, and
Gregory of Tours describes their use by the Franks fighting

Plate 1 Throwing axe of Frankish type *(francisca)* probably of sixth
century date. Found in France, this axe is now in the British Museum.
(Reproduced by permission of the Trustees)

against the Romans in much earlier times than his own.

Little is known of Frankish tactics but Agathias twice describes the Franks taking up their positions on foot in a wedge-shaped formation. They seem to have learnt something from the Romans, since St Gregory several times mentions tents being used on campaigns. The Saint says that during the siege of Convenae, the Franks used 'waggons fitted with rams covered with wattle-work and planks, under which troops could go forward to destroy the walls'. This engine is clearly of Roman origin. The defenders, also Franks, hurled down on them showers of stones; vessels of pitch, presumably hot; and grease, perhaps to make their enemies' feet slip. The attackers later vainly filled up the ditch with fascines but were still repulsed.

Organization

During the first period of Frankish expansion and continuous warfare, the kings had grown increasingly powerful, since they and their personal war-bands took the brunt of the fighting and therefore the greater part of the rewards. The exaggerated respect of the Gallo-Romans for the Imperial authority was transferred to the conquerors and eventually affected the Franks' own feelings about their kings. As the Frankish lands spread wider, the calling of the old assembly of the nation in arms became more difficult. Meeting less often, its effect as a check on the royal authority was gradually diminished, and within a few generations there was no sign of the voice of the people in government. The gathering itself survived only as an annual assembly in March, the Marchfield, whence many campaigns started.

Government eventually passed entirely into the hands of the king and was administered by his household, his personal followers, known as *antrustiones*, bound to him by an oath of fidelity; the war-band of former times, but now ministers and officials as much as warriors. The chief of these was the Mayor of the Palace, the Marshal (count of the stable), the Counts of the Palace who acted as advisors to the king, the Treasurer, and the Secretary, the last almost always a Gaul, since an educated Frank was very exceptional. The Salic Laws make it clear that the *antrustiones* included Romans and freed men, as well as free Franks, since they lay down the wergild of each of these.

Provincial government was by counts *(comes)* each chosen and appointed by the king to rule over either a single tribal district *(pagus)* in the Frankish area, or a single *civitas,* a city and its dependant district in the Gallo-Roman area – an administrative territory surviving from Imperial times. The counts were responsible for the collection of taxes within their district, the raising and leading of military forces, and the administration of justice with the assistance of assessors appointed by themselves. Their deputy was the *vicarius* (later viscount), while minor administration was done by hundred-men *(centenarii)* each from one of the divisions of the county known as a 'hundred', perhaps from its originally having represented the land of one hundred households. The hundred-men presided in the local courts and led the local forces. Particularly in the border provinces several counts would be placed under the authority of a duke *(dux* or *Herzog)* to co-ordinate defence, to over-ride their bickering, and, if necessary, to lead the combined forces from several counties. In the Gallo-Roman area this office was equated with that of the former Patrician.

At first, taxes were apparently levied only in Roman districts. Theudebert (d. 548) is said to have been the first to tax his Frankish subjects, thus driving them to revolt.

In very early times, every free Frank was liable for military service with the king. Later it seems probable that only one man was taken from each household, since a case is known of a son being allowed to volunteer to take his father's place on a campaign. The length of service was theoretically unlimited at the will of the king, but in fact the needs of agricultural life reduced the period of campaigning to the three months between seed-time and harvest. By the eighth century the fine for failure to answer the summons to arms for a free Frank was sixty *solidi*, the price of six horses, and for a Roman, a freed man, or a vassal of the church, thirty *solidi*. Certainly down to the time of Charlemagne, men were expected to bring their own rations and, if foraging proved difficult, discipline soon collapsed and pillaging, even of friendly territory, broke out.

The lack of discipline and organization of Frankish armies is noted by several contemporary writers. The Emperor Leo VI in his *Tactica* mentions that the Franks were especially bad at obeying their leaders and were given to deserting in adverse circumstances. The counts, being royal appointments, were without tribal or family links in their counties, and their personal authority over their followers was therefore slight. The Frankish king Guntrum, when asking for an explanation of the disastrous campaign against the Visigoths in Septimania in 586, received the reply: 'No man feareth the king, none respects duke or count; and if by chance any one dislikes this evil, and ... tries to put it right, immediately sedition and riot break out among the people, and all rage so furiously against their officer, that if he is unwilling any longer to hold his peace he can hardly hope to escape with his life.'

The Beginnings of Feudalism

During the periods of civil war which succeeded the death of each of the Meroving kings and the ensuing struggle between his descendants over the customary subdivision of his kingdom, the state could no longer maintain the peace or protect its subjects from oppression. The dukes and counts, whether to gain more power for themselves or to help keep the peace, required armed retainers. The lower classes, oppressed by constant wars and raids, were glad to obtain the protection of a powerful neighbour in exchange for serving him. In this manner, a few sank down to being slaves but most remained freemen, dependent on a count or duke for protection and bound to serve him in some way in return. The Germanic tribes already had this type of tradition in the 'war-band', which consisted of a group of warriors sworn to follow their chosen lord, to fight in his quarrels and win him wealth and, more important, renown. No tribal link was involved and famous chiefs were followed by men of many races. In return for their service the lord was expected to be generous to his followers with gifts of gold rings, horses, and arms, food and wine in his hall, and protection in their quarrels. The lord must revenge the death of one of his men with the blood of the killer, or by a fine called *wergild* extracted from him or his kinsmen, and divided between the dead man's kin and his lord. On the man's death, except in battle before his lord, the gifts of horses, armour, and weapons were to be returned to his lord and this gradually became a feudal due, comparable to modern death duties, but payable to the man's lord, called in English *heriot,* literally, war gear. Loyalty was to the grave and beyond, since if the lord of the war-band were killed, his men must revenge him or live out their lives dishonoured.

This was paralleled in Gaul where latterly Roman magnates had surrounded themselves with bodyguards, and this system had survived the break up of the Empire, at least in the area south of the Loire, as is shown in laws of the Visigothic king Euric towards the end of the fifth century.

One who placed himself under the protection of another was called a *vassus* (later vassal), originally meaning a slave, but by about 700 meaning a freeman in dependance on another. The act of placing oneself under protection was called commendation *(commendatio)*. The *Formulae Turonenses* of the second quarter of the eighth century gives the earliest known form of commendation. A freeman binds himself to another for his own lifetime without ability to withdraw, in exchange for food and clothing, offering some unstipulated service and respect to his superior but retaining his right as a freeman. The need for food and clothes indicates that a man of the poorest class is involved in this case.

Notice that there is an equal obligation on each party of the contract. The essence of the feudalism which developed from these beginnings can be summed up as 'no privileges without obligations, no duties without rights'. The count had a duty to defend his vassal against enemies, and the vassal in return must serve him in war or with agricultural labour according to his rank. Commendation by someone of higher station than the example mentioned above would be in exchange for military service.

The simplest way for a lord to maintain a vassal was to grant him sufficient land to support him. Sections of the great Roman estates had been let to tenants in return for labour and a fixed rent in late Imperial days, and this continued into Frankish times. In Merovingian times another form of land grant existed, called a *benefice,* in which the tenant owed only nominal services or a very small rent or even no rent at all.

These grants were for the life of the tenant only. One possible reason for this type of grant was the need to encourage the development and improvement of unprofitable land. A benefice might be granted in exchange for another estate, or to win the support of the man to whom it was granted, or to acknowledge the usurpation of the land while retaining the right of ownership for the future.

In the earliest times, the two institutions of the benefice and vassalage were entirely separate. By the middle of the eighth century, however, there is some evidence that vassals were occasionally rewarded by the grant of a benefice, in order to maintain them and to give them sufficient wealth to be able to support armed retainers, but it was unusual and was not yet being used by the king to reward his antrustiones. The vassal might in fact own land outright as well as holding a benefice or, in some cases, benefices.

During the reigns of the great Mayors of the Palace, Pepin of Herstal and his son Charles Martel, a period of civil war and expeditions along many frontiers followed. The necessity for an efficient military force caused both to make many vassals. While many of these were probably granted land outright from the royal domains, many others were given benefices from the already wide lands of the church. They owed military service to the Crown and at the same time a nominal rent to the Church, thus ensuring the Church's actual ownership of the land on the vassal's death. If the national need was such, the king could again re-grant the land to a vassal.

By the reign of Charlemagne, the vassals of the king, as well as those of the magnates, normally received a benefice. The virtual union of the two institutions raised the status of vassalage by making them wealthy. Vassalage became a coveted state, and the nobility and royal officials like the counts began to seek the position. The derogatory earlier meaning of the word entirely disappeared. The antrustiones, as such, also disappeared, since their position as the remains of the sworn war-band of the king gave them no advantage, and they were in fact in much the same position as an unbeneficed vassal.

The Later Franks

The Frankish kingdom, after its first unification under Chlodovech, passed through a century and a half of anarchy, due above all to the civil wars following the partition of the kingdom on the death of each king. The need to keep their supporters loyal forced the kings to give them estates taken from the royal lands. As a policy this was only practical when the kingdom was expanding and the supply of royal land increasing. In fact, the kings impoverished themselves and lost their influence. Their rule was no longer absolute; the laws of Chlotar II of about 620 are endorsed by the council of the nobles consisting of bishops, dukes and counts. Kings are now recorded as assenting to the petitions of the nobility. A series of young and weak kings allowed the power of the nobles, and particularly of the Mayor of the Palace, to increase enormously. Whereas early Frankish kings led their people in battle, latterly the army was led by the Mayor of the Palace. Under Chlotar II this official began to be appointed for life, and the king could no longer remove him. The kingdom itself became more or less permanently divided in half: Austrasia, the older and more Teutonic area to the east of the Meuse and Scheldt; and Neustria, the newer area west of these rivers and north of the Loire where the Franks were not so thickly settled.

The greatness of the Frankish kingdom was restored by a

succession of able and ambitious Mayors of the Palace, descended from Count Pepin the Elder, Mayor of the Palace of Austrasia to Dagobert I, the son of Chlotar II. When Pepin died, his son Grimoald waged three years of war to gain the succession to his father's post, a war in which the king was powerless to intervene. It was Pepin's grandson, Charles Martel (the Hammer) (719–41), who began the reclamation of the old Frankish kingdom, not only with the sword but also by sending missionaries to the Frisians and Hessians. He was Mayor of the Palace of both Neustria and Austrasia but, relying on the loyalty of the nobles of his own country, gave many of the most important posts to Austrasians.

Although Neustria did revolt against him, it was unsuccessful. He reconquered the Swabians and Bavarians, and later the Aquitanians, all of whom had won virtual independence under the Merovings. He was also forced to subdue the Frisians and Saxons. Most important of all, he turned back the Saracen expansion which had already eaten up Visigothic Spain and was beginning to threaten the Duchy of Aquitaine on its northern frontier. For the last few years of his life Charles Martel reigned without a king even as a figurehead, and on his death his sons divided the kingdom as though their father had, in fact, been king. Unlike the Merovings, however, the two elder sons acted in unison to put down the numerous revolts that followed and to pacify the whole land. In 751, Charles's son, Pepin III, was able to make himself king of all the Franks by election at the national council. The Pope's approval was asked and he, hoping to enlist the aid of the Franks against the Lombards, gladly gave it. Pepin's intervention in Italian politics and his defeat of the Lombards began the movement of the Franks towards the centre of the world stage, and set the scene for his greater son, Charlemagne.

Charlemagne united the greater part of the lands which

are now France, Germany west of the Elbe, northern and central Italy, Belgium, Holland, Switzerland, Austria, and the northern march of Spain, and gave them firm government under their customary laws, modified as necessary by his edicts *(capitularies)*. In spite of the break up of this empire after his death, he had stamped upon it a uniformity which these lands never entirely lost.

His coronation as Roman Emperor on Christmas Day 800 by the Pope may only have recognized the fact that the Eastern Emperor, or actually at that moment Empress, was powerless in the West, and that a German king held almost the entire western half of the old Empire, but it revived in Western Europe the idea of a political unity greater than any single race.

During the period of the great Mayors of the Palace, little is known about the military organization of the Franks. Cavalry seems to have become more common. Although there are some earlier references to cavalry engagements, the first record of a battle decided by a cavalry charge is during the Saxon war of 626. Charles Martel does not yet seem to have found his horsemen sufficient, perhaps in number or discipline, to face the Saracen cavalry at Poitiers in 732. Isidorus Pacensis tells us that the Franks 'stood like a wall motionless; they were like a belt of ice frozen together.' However, by 755 Pepin found it necessary to put off the traditional gathering, the Marchfield, to the first of May, in order that there should be sufficient growth on the grass for the horses.

Charlemagne is important militarily, not only for his conquests and his pacification of wide territories, but for his military reforms carried out by a long series of capitularies issued throughout his reign. He improved the standard of arming, forbade the export of shields and byrnies, and made

strong efforts to halt indiscipline, forbidding drunkenness
in the army, reasserting the penalty for failure to answer the
summons to the army at sixty *solidi,* and fixing the penalty
for desertion as death and the confiscation of all property.
The penalty for failing to attend the army was later reduced
for the less well-to-do. A capitulary, probably of the year
805, states that the full fine is only to be exacted from those
having six pounds in gold, goods and livestock, and even
then, 'the women and children shall not be deprived of their
garments for this fine.' Those who had less were fined less
accordingly. In 811, the confiscation was ordered of any
royal benefices held by anyone who had been unwilling to
go with his peer to the army or to remain there with him.

The '805' capitulary, in a chapter concerning the equipment of the army, states that 'the same shall be observed as
we have previously commanded in another capitulary, and
in particular, every man who possessed twelve *mansi*[1] shall
have a byrnie; he who has a byrnie and shall not have brought
it with him shall lose his whole benefice, together with the
byrnie'. Unfortunately, this other earlier capitulary is lost. It
is not certain that this man was to be mounted, although it is
probable. The capitulary to the Frisians refers to the service
of beneficed vassals 'and all the horsemen in general' without
defining the status of the latter. It has been suggested that
they represent independent freemen. A letter of Charlemagne's to Abbot Fulrad, written probably in 806, summon-
ing him and his men to the army seems to suggest that all the
Bishop's vassals are expected to serve mounted. Charlemagne
now had a very large cavalry force available in the Lombard
kingdom. The capitulary of 786 implies that all those Lombards who are to take the oath of allegiance to him habitually
served on horseback and in armour. It was this Lombard

[1] A *mansus* is equivalent to the English virgate, or a quarter of a hide.

army led by Pepin, Charlemagne's son, and Erick, Duke of Friuli, which eventually completely defeated the Avars, the nomadic light cavalry of Pannonia. The change of the traditionally infantry Franks into a race of cavalrymen was probably more or less completed by the reign of Charles the Bald, grandson of Charlemagne (843–77), who decreed '*ut pagenses Franci qui caballos habent, vel habere possunt, cum suis comitibus in hostem pergant*'. ('that those Franks who inhabit the *pagi* who have horses, or can obtain them, should be allowed to proceed to the host with their followers.')[1] By 891, the *Annales de Fulda* remarked that the Franks did not know how to fight on foot. Thus developed the mounted knight, one of the most characteristic features of feudalism in Western Europe.

The Capitulary of Aachen states that the bishop, count or abbot himself must see how his men were prepared. They were to be armed with spear, shield, bow with two strings, and twelve arrows. They must have a byrnie (almost certainly a shirt of mail), and a helm. Nothing is known about how the bow and arrows were carried at this time but, although most illustrations show it in use by infantry, it is occasionally shown being used by a horseman.

Since, for his protracted campaigns beyond the Frankish frontiers and against war-like foes, Charlemagne required an army less numerous but better equipped than the full call-up of available man-power, he introduced selective service for the poorer classes. It was decreed by a capitulary of 808 that 'Every freeman who have four *mansi* of his own property, or as a benefice from anyone, shall equip himself and go to the army, either with his lord, if the lord goes, or with his count. He who has three *mansi* of his own property shall be

---

[1] A. Boretius and V. Krause, *Capitularia Regum Frankorum*, II, Hanover 1890, p. 321, Edict of Pitres, AD 864.

joined to a man who has one *mansus,* and shall aid him so that he may serve for both. He who has only two *mansi* of his own property shall be joined to another who likewise has two *mansi,* and one of them with the aid of the other, shall go to the army. He who has only one *mansus* of his own shall be joined to one of three who have the same and shall aid him, and the latter shall go alone; the three who have aided him shall remain at home'. The counts were charged with organizing the grouping. Unfortunately nothing is said of the equipment to be provided. It almost certainly did not include a byrnie, since this is only demanded of those holding twelve *mansi.*

An earlier capitulary which introduced selective service for those holding only half a *mansus,* and even for those without land at all but with a certain value in goods, is now thought to have only been issued temporarily and locally in a year of great need.

A count must take with him all his beneficed vassals, except two, who were excused service and the fine in order to guard the count's wife, and two more to guard each of his territories. This ensured the peace at home and limited the number of exemptions. If the count remained on duty at home, he must send his men with whoever went as his replacement. A bishop or abbot might leave only two of his vassals at home. A capitulary of AD 811 stated that any royal vassal who remained at court serving in the royal household, and was known to have benefices, should not keep his vassals with him but send them to the army with the count to whose district they belonged. If a lord or count allowed any freeman to stay at home during a summons, except those actually exempted, he must pay the fines on his behalf. This capitulary also restated the ancient custom that men coming to the army must bring with them rations for a march of three months, and clothing and arms for six months. Furthermore, the three month march was to be calculated as beginning at the frontier, and the implication is that additional rations must be carried to cover the march to the frontier. A capitulary issued at Aachen shows that these supplies, consisting among other things of flour, wine and pork, were carried in carts, with mills (for corn), adzes, axes, augers, slings (*fundibuli*, probably in this case light siege-engines), and men skilled in their use. The king's marshals were, if necessary, to bring stones carried on packhorses for these slings. The summons to Abbot Fulrad also lists the equipment to be carried on the campaign carts, and adds planes, boards, spades and iron-shod stakes. The Capitulary *de Villis Dominicis* gives the capacity of these carts as twelve bushels of corn or twelve small barrels of wine. They were to have leather covers which could be laced together and stuffed, presumably with hay, to act as pontoons for crossing rivers. The capitularies of AD 802 and AD 811 made naval service in maritime provinces obligatory, even for the magnates.

The result of this reorganization was that Charlemagne, after repeated campaigns, was at last able to conquer the Saxons. This entailed spending a whole winter on campaign, that of 785–6, a hitherto unthinkable task for a Frankish army. He also built permanent forts (burgs) connected to each other by roads, in order to overawe the Saxons once and for all. It was presumably to make stockades for these forts that the iron-shod stakes were carried on the carts. Here, he was probably using the example of Imperial Rome. His library certainly contained a number of Roman military books, including *Caesar* and *Tacitus;* and the military skill and prestige of the Empire were clearly deeply impressed on the barbarian mind. Charlemagne must have been particularly affected by this feeling now that the title of Emperor had been resurrected for him personally.

The army under his son, Louis, invaded Catalonia in
800/1 and was able to besiege Barcelona while lying safely
behind a rampart built all around the city. It was covered by
a third of its force under William, Count of Toulouse, some
miles to the west, while another third covered the lines of
communication through the Pyrenees. This was a highly
developed strategy of which a pre-Carolingian army would
almost certainly not have been capable.

Unfortunately, the custom of burying arms with the dead
having waned with the spread of Christianity, we know a
good deal less about the armour of Carolingian times than
about Merovingian equipment. Illuminated manuscripts
become fairly common but at this period have to be interpreted with great care, since they are often strongly influenced
by Byzantine illuminations and ivory carvings. Many illustrations of soldiers show them wearing late Roman armour; a
wide brimmed crested helmet, and a cuirass formed like the
muscles of the torso with a kilt-like skirt. This is not now
generally thought to represent the actual appearance of
Frankish warriors of the day, but it has recently been suggested
that the gold hinged clasps in the Saxon memorial ship at
Sutton Hoo represent the remains of such a cuirass, the actual
body being made of leather.

Probably the great majority of Carolingian manuscript
illustrations show warriors, even those as famous as Goliath,
without body armour. For instance, the early ninth-century
Psalter from the Abbey of Corbie, now at Amiens (Bibliothèque Communale, Ms. 18), shows the Philistine with
round convex shield, winged spear, sword, and what is
probably a conical helm. On the other hand, a number do
show armoured figures. The *Stuttgart Psalter* (Württembergische Landesbibliothek, Biblia Folio 23) illuminated at
Corbie early in the ninth century, shows Goliath wearing a

hemispherical helm with a narrow band around the lower edge and two others crossing on the top, but without ear- or neck-guards. His short-sleeved tunic is clearly of scale; that is, armour consisting of small pieces of metal or horn riveted to a fabric or leather lining and placed so as to overlap each other like the scales on a fish. The famous *Psalterium Aureum* begun before 883, in the Abbey Library at St Gallen (Codex 22) shows both cavalry and infantry wearing a short-sleeved, flexible body-defence to mid-thigh. It is covered with a series of curved pen-strokes, which look rather more like a conventional representation of scale armour than of mail. This interpretation is perhaps confirmed by the fact that the illuminations depict the inside of the armour without the curved pen-strokes and in a different colour. The warriors in all these manuscripts carry convex round shields with a central boss, behind which is the hand-grip; in some cases, they are slung on the back by means of a strap. In the *Psalterium Aureum,* the helms have a rib running fore and aft across the top of the head and appear to have a brim rather deeper at the back than at the front. So far, no actual helm of this type has been discovered, and it is probably only a convention of the manuscript illuminators. Its development from the brimmed and crested type mentioned above can be seen by comparing the version of the *Psychomachia* of Prudentius in the Bibliothèque Nationale, Paris (Ms. lat. 8085), which shows the brimmed crested helm, with the version at Valenciennes (Bibliothèque Publique, Ms. 563), which is apparently copied from the Paris manuscript, where the copyist has simplified his model by rounding off the brim and omitting the crest altogether to give a helm exactly like those in the *Psalterium Aureum.* Neither the legs nor the fore-arms of the figures in the *Psalterium Aureum* are armoured but the laws of the Ripuarian Franks of the eighth century give the value

Plate 2 A Frankish archer of the early ninth century, apparently
wearing a shirt of scale and thigh-defences of similar material. From
the *Stuttgart Psalter* in the Württembergische Landesbibliothek, Biblia
Folio 23. (Reproduced by permission of the authorities of the
Landesbibliothek, Stuttgart)

of *bainbergae,* that is armour for the shins, as six *solidi*. The
often quoted description of Charles's appearance at Pavia in
773, written some sixty years after his death, states that he and
all his men wore iron greaves and that he himself wore some
kind of separate thigh defence, possibly of scales. One figure
in the *Stuttgart Psalter* seems to wear scale thigh defences of
some sort made separately from the body armour (Plate 2).

No Frankish representation of greaves is known at present; but a warrior decorating the side of a gold flask of mid-ninth century date, from Nagy-Szent-Miklos in Hungary, has greaves and fore-arm defences apparently made of long strips of some stiff material, metal or perhaps whale-bone. Similar strips of iron, found in a grave at Valsgärde in Sweden, have been reconstructed to form two shin-guards and a fore-arm defence, held together by transverse leather straps going round the limbs. The warriors depicted on the decorative plates of helms belonging to the Swedish Vendel culture have gauntlet cuffs, or wrist guards, apparently made of strips of this type.

The ivory situla of about the year 1000, now at Aachen, which was formerly used in the Imperial coronation ceremony, is surrounded by a series of small warriors holding winged spears. They are dressed in short-sleeved shirts of mail from under which appear the sleeves and skirts of their tunics. On their heads are hemispherical helms with a raised rib running fore and aft over the skull from which mail fringes hang down over their ears, presumably covering the backs of their necks. Their shields are represented as nearly flat and slightly oval instead of round, and some are made without the central boss. Their legs are apparently covered by hose with criss-cross binding.

By the end of the tenth century a new shape of shield had appeared, still rounded above the boss but drawn out into a long point below. It has been said that these were particularly suitable for cavalrymen since the long point protected the otherwise vulnerable left leg, but they were certainly also used on foot. Helms of the type found at Bretzenheim near Mainz were probably still in use, since what appear to be very similar ones are illustrated in the mid-tenth-century *Book of Maccabees* at Leiden University (Cod. Perizoni 17).

Plate 3 Two-edged sword with hilt decorated with silver damascening and signed on the guard HI . . . The blade also appears to have been inlaid with an inscription. Probably Frankish ninth or tenth century. (Reproduced by permission of the Trustees of the Wallace Collection)

The characteristic sword in the Frankish lands of Carolingian times has a blade similar to the earlier type although larger. However, by about 900, blades are found tapering slightly from hilt to point. This makes the sword less heavy to wield since the centre of balance is nearer the hilt and the weapon balances better in the hand. The common idea that medieval swords are clumsy is entirely false: a genuine sword fits the hand and is an ideal tool for its job – in the ninth century this was mainly hewing, but a thrust was possible also. Above, the hand was defended by a short cross-guard. The pommel bar, instead of having a separate cocked-hat-like piece outside it, was made in one with a row of three to five small lobes. A line or depression usually indicates where these two parts formerly joined. The tang passes right through the pommel and the end is enlarged by hammering to prevent the pommel coming off. Both pommel and cross-guard were almost invariably made of steel but might be decorated with an overlay of gold or silver plate, sometimes with an engraved or stamped design. A few Frankish hilts are signed by the maker, usually on the cross-guard (Plate 3).

Although the old form of pattern-welded blade was still in use during most of the tenth century, the new type of blade was made entirely of a tough steel and was no longer pattern-welded. Many have the maker's name in large iron letters running down the central hollow just in front of the hilt. These letters were formed out of iron wire laid in grooves cut into the blade and welded to it at white heat. The average length of Carolingian swords is about 94 cm, ten of which form the tang. The average width immediately below the hilt is 5·5 cm.

The Frankish spear usually has a long leaf-shaped blade and, on each side of the socket in the plane of the blade, a projecting lug. The front edge of the lug is almost always at right angles to the socket; the back edge may be straight or concave; and the end of the lug is usually blunt. It is probable that these are boar-spears in origin, and the lugs are intended to stop the onrush of this exceptionally powerful and ferocious beast when impaled. The shaft was sometimes bound with a spiral of leather thongs to improve the grip; as is shown in the *Codex Egberti* in the Town Library at Trier (Codex 24), and is confirmed by earlier grave finds at Niederstotzingen. It was used both as an infantry weapon and on horseback. The mounted warrior still normally used his lance at arm's length, or overhand like the modern pig-sticker, and numerous manuscripts show him doing this. However, the tenth-century *Book of Maccabees* at Leiden does show one man using his spear with the shaft couched under his arm. This method gave much greater force to the blow since the whole weight of horse and rider was behind it and, from the eleventh century onwards, was to become almost the only way in which the lance was used.

The Development of Feudalism

One result of Charlemagne's almost annual campaigns was certainly the depression of large numbers of freemen into dependence on the counts and wealthier class, due to their impoverishment by the cost of keeping one of their number in the field. Vassalage was greatly on the increase in both the Frankish and non-Frankish lands; and sub-vassalage, also with benefices, began to be granted by those who were themselves vassals, in order to provide themselves with fighting men. This was greatly accelerated by the devastation caused by the later civil wars and by the raids of Viking and Magyar, when the count and his armoured horsemen were the only source of protection. In 847 Charles the Bald had directed that all his subjects should choose a lord, either the king himself or one of his vassals.

Charlemagne, in order to spread his personal authority over his newly-conquered empire, granted part of the new lands to royal vassals as benefices, and set up local administrations under counts – almost invariably Franks from Austrasia, since their loyalty was never in doubt. In order to increase his authority over them, he required his counts and other officers to become his vassals and they in turn took into vassalage their own principal officers. In fact, he always found it difficult to control them, since their pay was in the form of royal estates set aside for their use. Their oppressions are frequently mentioned in the capitularies. To a certain extent the royal vassals and great church landowners, both of whom were often immune from the count's jurisdiction and answered to the Emperor only, acted as a counter-balance to the counts. Royal envoys *(missi dominici)* were sent out fairly regularly to hold enquiries into the administration of the counties. In order to strengthen the bond between himself and his subjects, Charlemagne in 792/3 ordered that all the royal vassals, bishops, abbots and counts should take a new oath of fealty to him through his representatives, the *missi dominici;* lesser vassals and all ordinary subjects were to take this oath through the counts.

By this reign a royal vassal would normally be rewarded, sooner or later, by the grant of a benefice, in order that he should be able to carry out his service most efficiently. A benefice would no longer be granted to someone who was not a vassal. Commendation, the act of becoming a vassal, was carried out by the man placing his hands between those of his lord and promising to serve him faithfully. From the second half of the eighth century this was accompanied by an oath of fealty taken on holy relics. This it was hoped made the promise more binding, since the vassal who broke it could be charged with perjury. It also raised an essentially servile act to a plane above that of a man seeking the protection of a lord and rendering some menial service. Vassalage, once created, was completely binding and was only annulled by the death of either party, or by the lord striking or trying to kill his vassal, or seducing his wife or daughter, or depriving him of his patrimony, or failing to defend him. The vassal's most important service was military, but he might also have to carry out administrative or judicial duties. He remained a freeman in law and was therefore tried in the public courts, rather than in those of his lord, and in the case of a royal vassal could only be tried in the King's court.

The capitularies of Charlemagne already show the connection between vassalage and military service. By the ninth century the term vassal only applied to those furnishing military service with horse, lance, shield, and sword, and the Latin *miles* is sometimes used as synonymous with it. In later texts *miles* invariably means a knight.

Before the end of the ninth century, it had become customary for the vassal to be allowed to commend himself to his lord's successor, and thereby retain his benefice, and before long this had begun to be looked on as a right. From the time of Charles Martel onwards, there are cases of a benefice being held from father to son for many generations; by the end of the ninth century this was customary and a son would normally succeed to his father's benefice by commendation. The benefice had now become hereditary in fact if not in law. This was acknowledged by Charles the Bald, preparing for his Italian expedition in 877, when he laid down that a count who died while the king was away should be succeeded by his son, and the same to be done in respect of the royal vassals, who were in turn to treat their own vassals in the same way.

No doubt the fact that officers were granted benefices to support them gave them such an outward resemblance to vassalage that, as the latter became hereditary, so did the former.

Charlemagne had deliberately fostered the system of vassalage in order to spread his personal authority over a wide and largely newly-conquered empire. Under his weaker successors, and as benefices became hereditary, the result was in fact precisely the opposite. The bond linking a vassal to his immediate lord became stronger than those linking him to the king. The theory that vassals need not serve their lord if he was in arms against the king was widely ignored. Once the office became hereditary the king could have little control over his officials. Between the years 852 and 885 no fewer than seven of the great counties of France are recorded as passing to the sons of the previous counts after their deaths. In Austrasia and among the newly conquered Saxons and Frisians the hereditary principle is not traceable until later. By the end of the ninth century, the sub-vassal had become largely independent of the Crown because his lord was interposed between him and the king. He could only be controlled through his lord, and by the middle of the ninth century this was recognized by the Crown, which no longer summoned sub-vassals to justice but expected their lords to deal with them.

3

The Vikings

The name 'Viking' probably comes from an Old Norse word *víkingr* meaning a sea-rover or pirate. The Swedes, Norwegians, and Danes, who, from the eighth century onwards went a-viking, were mainly industrious farmers, fishermen, and, most important, merchant seamen. Some were town-dwellers; others, like the Norwegian Ohthere whose voyage to the White Sea King Alfred records, combined trading with farming. The Scandinavians had certainly been traders in Roman times, since silver and bronze vessels, glass, brooches, and earthernware from inside the Empire have been found in Scandinavian burials and had presumably been exchanged for amber, slaves, and furs. Trading towns like Birka and Hedeby seem to have evolved in the North rather suddenly about the year 800 and had wide contacts. For instance, a censer of Persian type was dug up at Birka. Nevertheless, there was a tradition of raiding; Hygelac, king of the Danes, the kinsman of Beowulf, was killed raiding the lower Rhineland in 514.

No certain reason has been discovered for the sudden expansion, towards the end of the eighth century, which sent these people voyaging and raiding far and wide. By the following century, Swedish traders venturing up the river Volkhov to Novgorod and down the Volga to the Caspian had reached Baghdad, and others by way of the Don and

44

Dneiper had reached Mickelgarth, as they called Byzantium, and founded the kingdom of Rus with its capital at Kiev. These men were originally merchants exporting furs, honey, slaves, and weapons, in exchange for silver and luxury goods. Later, when their settlements became more secure and thickly populated they occasionally turned to raiding, even, it is said, attacking Byzantium in 860 and 941.

In Norway, deeply divided by long fiords and high mountains which made communications extremely difficult, a centralized state was very slow to develop since one tribe could not easily dominate another. These very conditions ensured that a poor but hardy and independent race of superb seamen would develop. The temptation of the rich and unprotected monasteries of the British Isles, often situated on lonely coastal sites or even islands, must have been great. The first period of raids began with the pillaging of the great Northumbrian abbey of Lindisfarne in 793. A defeat at Monkwearmouth in the following year possibly caused the Vikings to look elsewhere; no good trader seeks a hard bargain. Iona itself was raided in 795, and the Scottish Islands and Man were apparently settled shortly after this. Ireland was certainly reached early in the ninth century. The Irish were then a completely tribal society, rent by never-ending feuds, untouched by Roman civilization, but the seedbed of a rich flowering of Christian culture. During the early ninth century Viking raids are recorded in the Irish chronicles for almost every year, but in spite of this the natives continued their own intertribal warfare. A certain Thorgisl was recorded as the first king of all the Norse in Ireland in 830. Dublin was occupied by the Vikings in 836 and fortified in 841. With the help of Danish mercenaries the Irish defeated the Norse in 849 but they quickly re-established themselves. This was the recurring story in Ireland, first the Irish were successful, then

the Vikings, right down to the great battle of Clontarf in
1014 when Brian Boru, uniting almost all the Irish, defeated
a great army drawn from most of the Norse settlements in
Europe. Almost at once, the Irish fell back to their quarrelling
and the Norse remained and prospered in their fortified
towns. Their kings never ruled as more than one among
equals among the native rulers and they were eventually
absorbed by intermarriage.

An exodus from Norway in the reign of Harald Fairhair,
by those who could not accept his authority, led to the setting
up of an aristocratic republic in Iceland, and from here in
896 adventurers under Eric the Red moved on to Greenland,
and a little later, under his son, to North America.

It was probably Norwegian Vikings from Man or Ireland
who raided Aquitaine in 799, following an ancient trade-
route from Ireland. This is confirmed by finds of Carolingian
material among the many Irish objects discovered in ninth-
century graves in Norway. Arab coins from Spain and Tunis
in west Norway are presumably connected with the Viking
expeditions to Spain and Africa in 844 and 860. The *Vest-
faldingi,* who raided Nantes in 843, were men of Vestfold in
Norway and probably came by way of Ireland. In this case
they were apparently helping one local count in a private
feud against another. It has been suggested that this is the
pattern of Viking raids in Francia, and that at first they came
as mercenaries in the civil war over the partition of the realm
by the sons of Louis the Pious.

During Charlemagne's reign, his conquest of Frisia and
Saxony not only brought the Franks into immediate contact
with the Danes, who claimed suzerainty over these lands,
but eliminated the main maritime power in the North Sea,
the Frisians, leaving the way open for the Danes. Godfred
of Jutland built a line of defences across the narrow neck of

Denmark, and in 810 raided Frisia with 200 ships, only being bought off with 700 pounds of silver after three times defeating the defenders. After Godfred's death the Emperor supported a pretender to the throne, presumably to increase internal strife in Denmark as much as to win a friend if the claimant were successful. Lack of strong internal government in Denmark thereafter probably encouraged raiders.

The coastal defence forces set up by Charlemagne and maintained by Louis the Pious were successful in deterring the Vikings for a time. Skilful diplomacy on the part of the Frankish kings, who sent ambassadors to the Danish rulers, helped to keep the raiders away. The Chronicles only record two Norse raids, both in 820 and both unsuccessful, before 834 when serious raiding began at a time when the Empire was distracted by the quarrels of the Emperor's sons. It seems possible that the Vikings were called in by the eldest son Lothar; certainly in 842 the Danish king, Harald, was present in Lothar's army. The great Frisian trading town of Dorestad was pillaged by the Danes in 834. In the following year Flanders was raided and Antwerp burnt; in the next year Walcheren and Nijmegen. The Danish king admitted responsibility to the Emperor's emissaries and said that he had punished the raiders or would do so. In 835 the first major attack by Danes on the English mainland is recorded in the *Anglo-Saxon Chronicle*. After Louis's death in 840 civil war broke out again and the defence organization of the Empire broke down completely in the absence of counts on campaign. Rouen, far up the Seine, was sacked in 841, and in the following year Quentowic, the great Channel port for the English trade, was pillaged by an army of Danes, fresh from the sack of London, who returned to raid Rochester. At the same time the Slavs revolted against Frankish domination and the Moors landed in the south and sacked Arles.

The Norse band which had burnt Nantes overwintered in France for the first time in 843/4, encamped on an island at the mouth of the Loire. In 850 Rorik, a Danish chieftain from Frisia, stormed Canterbury and London with 350 ships and, although defeated by Æthelwulf of Wessex, passed the winter encamped on the Isle of Thanet and later in the Isle of Sheppey. In 860 a force of Norsemen from the Loire sailed into the Mediterranean and overwintered in the island of Camargue at the mouth of the Rhône. The Vikings sited their camps on islands, or in the fork or bend of a river, closing the open side with an earthwork; these formed secure bases for raiding and were only very rarely stormed. During the reign of Charles the Bald (843–77), Viking settlements were formed at the mouth of most of the great rivers of France from which raids spread out over the land along the waterways. By the Edict of Pistres (864), Charles tried to increase the mobility of his own army by ordering all free Franks who owned a horse, or could afford to keep one, to serve mounted. He ordered towns to build fortified bridges across their rivers thus denying the Vikings their main raiding routes. A fortified bridge had already been successfully thrown across the Seine at Pistres just above Rouen. The defences he built at Paris and the bridges linking the island city with the river banks kept the Vikings at bay for eleven months in 885 and 886.

Possibly these measures were successful; at least from 865 the Vikings seem to have turned their attention to England, the main army landing in East Anglia in that year, led according to tradition by Halvdan, Ubbe and Ivar, the sons of Ragnar Lodbrok (Hairy Breeks). They came, no longer as raiders, but as conquerors. Since 854, when the last of the old dynasty was overthrown in Denmark, there was no generally accepted king powerful enough to discourage piracy by his subjects. For the next fifteen years the Vikings rode across England all summer, pillaging and burning, living off the land, and overwintering in a different fortified camp each year.

Opportunists ever, they first rode into Northumbria on their stolen horses, to take advantage of the civil war raging there. York was captured and its rival kings killed. In 876 the *Anglo-Saxon Chronicle* records that part of the army began to settle around York and to partition out and plough the land. Another part later settled in Mercia and founded the Five Boroughs – Derby, Leicester, Nottingham, Lincoln and Stamford – each under its own *jarl* (earl). Finally, after a last attempt to conquer Wessex was defeated by Alfred at Edington (878), the remainder of the Danes, under Guthrun, settled in East Anglia.

In 880, peace having been made in England, the Danes turned once more to Francia, and, completely crushing the forces of Saxony and Thuringia at Lüneburg Heath, in the winter of 881/2 they actually burnt Charlemagne's old capital of Aachen. The only way to win a respite was to buy off the raiders. Of the thirteen known Danegelds levied in France the total of seven is recorded as 39,700 pounds of silver. The first signs of a turning point came with the successful defence of Paris by its count, Odo, between November 885 and the following October, against a savage but scientific attack. Thereafter, Frankish resistance stiffened and the growth of fortified towns replaced easy pillage with hard-fought sieges and small profit. In 891 King Arnulf successfully stormed the great fortified Danish camp at Louvain, and in the following year the army departed for England.

Alfred's Wessex faced the storm in 892 when 250 ships' crews, driven out of the Seine by famine, landed in Kent bringing their own horses. They were joined by the famous

Norseman Haesten, who landed in the Thames with 80 ships from Amiens. From the north came Earl Sigfred with 140 ships. Alfred's reorganization was successful against them and they were constantly harried by the English until, broken up in 896, they returned to France having done little damage to the English.

After 900 a period of peace ensued. Denmark was pacified by Gorm the Elder, and Norway by Harald Fairhair, whose son was in fact educated at the English court. The defences of the northern coast of France were largely in the hands of Norse vassals settled in Normandy by Charles the Simple in 911. The Norse were actually evicted from Dublin for a time, but settled in north-western England and southern Scotland. Gradually the Danelaw was conquered or came to terms with the English, perhaps preferring them to the influx of Irish Norsemen. Once the Vikings settled down on their own plot of land they seem to have lost their cohesion as an army, and to have broken up into small groups owing allegiance to local petty chieftains.

A new series of raids on England began in 980, at first by small war bands apparently rebelling against the strict rule of Harald Gormsson (known as Blue Tooth), who had temporarily united Denmark and Norway and forced Christianity on their unwilling inhabitants. England was unsettled at the time by the murder of King Edward and the succession of a weak king, partially implicated in the murder, his half-brother, Æthelred.

The obvious weakness of the English defences led to more highly organized raids led by great chieftains, like Olaf Tryggvasson who came with 93 ships in 991. Peace was bought at a cost of 10,000 pounds of silver; by 1012 the payment had risen to 48,000 pounds of silver. There were 240 silver pennies in a pound and the price of an ox was 30 pence.

The vast number of English coins of this period found in Scandinavian hoards are presumably relics of these great payments (gelds). Some even found their way to the Scottish islands, but whether as a result of trade or in the hands of returning raiders is, of course, unknown. Although Earl Byrhtnoth and his men fought so bravely at Maldon in 991, the *Anglo-Saxon Chronicle* is not alone in speaking of the cowardice and treachery of other leaders.

The armies that Swein Forkbeard and his son Cnut brought for the conquest of England in 1013 seem to have been forces of a very different type from even the great armies of Alfredian days. Three great forts of this date have been discovered in Denmark. Their carefully measured and systematically laid out plans indicate the presence of a large force of highly organized professional warriors, while their positions within the old royal estates indicate that they served the Danish crown. It has been estimated that the three camps could together permanently house a force of some 3,000 men. At Trelleborg in Zealand, the best known of the three, there is a circular earthwork with an inner diameter of 136 metres, 17 metres thick. It is divided into quarters by two straight roads, crossing at right angles at the centre, and passing under the earthwork by four gates. Each quarter contains an open square formed of four long-houses each 29·5 metres in length. An outer earthwork encloses a further fifteen similar houses each built with its long axis pointing to the centre of the inner earthwork. The unit of measurement used is the Roman foot; the inner diameter for instance is 468 Roman feet. Presumably both earthworks would have been stockaded along the top.

It is scarcely surprising that, with a body of troops like these in the field, the English were swiftly brought to their knees. That they were mercenaries is implicit in this type of organization and is confirmed by runic inscriptions in Sweden. One, for instance, commemorates a certain Úlfr who received geld three times in England; the first paid by Tósti, the second by Thorkill the Tall, and the third by Cnut himself. When Cnut dismissed a large part of his army of conquest in 1018, England paid it 82,500 pounds of silver.

Although this was the greatest conquest of the Vikings it was by no means their last fling. The Norman conquest of 1066 was after all achieved by the descendants of Norse settlers, and the invasion of Harald Hardrada in the same year, aimed at regaining the throne of Cnut, was a very serious threat. Scotland was not free of Viking raiders until after the great battle of Largs in 1263.

Viking Armour and Arms

Very little is known about their armour since very few illustrations of Vikings survive. Grave finds have included mail, among them the greater part of a mail shirt found at Jarlshaug, Trøndelag, Norway. The shields found in the Gokstad ship of the late ninth or early tenth century have central bosses of iron and round wooden discs similar to those shown on the Gotland stones. The boss of a Viking shield usually has a more or less hemispherical dome, sometimes with a slight waist just above the flange by which it is nailed to the wood. The Norsemen living in Ireland often used bosses with a conical point, perhaps derived from native Irish shields. Giraldus Cambrensis describes the round red shields bound round about with iron, carried by the Norsemen at Dublin in 1172. He also describes them as wearing long hauberks and body armour apparently of lames or strips of iron, but this, of course, is a good deal later than the classic Viking age.

A mid tenth-century cross from Middleton, Yorkshire, shows a Viking with conical helm, round shield with central boss, sword, spear, and axe. The winged helm of tradition seems to be imaginary, but one of the textiles found in the ninth-century Oseberg ship showed a man wearing a pointed helm or cap with upcurved horns mounted on the sides. Similar horns, but with birds' heads on the points, are shown on a seventh-century matrix for making decorative plates from Torslunda, Öland, Sweden, and on the Sutton Hoo helmet. Viking graves very often contain the remains of horses or horse furniture, including simple snaffle bits, stirrups, sometimes inlaid with silver or brass, and short pointed spurs similarly decorated. The raiders soon learnt to rustle horses to increase their mobility, and by 993 the contingent sent to the French army by the Norsemen settled in Normandy was serving as cavalry.

The great two-handed axe was the characteristic weapon of the Vikings in the tenth and eleventh centuries. It developed from a fairly light axe with an upper and lower edge more or less straight, diverging only slightly towards a relatively

Figure 2 Danish axe of the tenth century found at Mammen in Jutland. The iron is inlaid with silver wire. (Nationalmuseet, Copenhagen)

short cutting edge. This type is found as early as about 900, as at Harbuck in County Durham; while one found at Mammen in Jutland is decorated with silver wire inlay of interlacing animals and scrolls in tenth-century style (Figure 2). Some of them were exported from Norway or Sweden. Twelve heads found near Grenaa in Jutland were strung together on a stave of spruce wood passing through all the sockets. The spruce was not native to Denmark at that time,

Plate 4 Crescentic axe of the type used by the Vikings in the eleventh century. Found in the Thames opposite the Tower of London and now in the London Museum. (Reproduced by permission of the Trustees)

and this must represent a trader's stock from southern Norway or Sweden where bog iron was worked and where the spruce grew.

Another popular form of axe-head in Scandinavia in the eighth and ninth centuries developed under the influence of the late francisca, with the longer lower point of the cutting edge much longer than the upper. This type, which had the lower point cut off square, is now called the 'bearded' axe. The upper and lower edges usually have a slight, pointed projection in line with the socket. The head slowly increased in size and developed a more or less symmetrical trumpet-shaped head with a convex cutting edge, some nine inches in length and acutely pointed above and below. This is the characteristic Viking war axe in the eleventh century (Plate 4). Seven axe-heads of this type, found lying together near the north end of Old London Bridge, are now in the London Museum. With them was a woodman's axe, six spear-heads, a pair of tongs, and a four-pronged grappling iron. It is thought that these may represent part of the equipment of a Viking warship sunk during one of the eleventh-century attacks on London, possibly the attack on the bridge in 1014 by Olaf Tryggvason. Two of these axes have decorated metal sheathing covering the haft where it passes through the socket. The length of the original haft can be gauged from the Bayeux Tapestry where they appear to be about four feet long. The metal of the head is fairly thin but thickens suddenly to join the stout, but exceedingly sharp, cutting edge. Transitional axes between this type and the earlier 'bearded' axe have a slight point mid-way along their lower edge, the legacy of the squared off lower end of the cutting edge. These date from between about 850 and about 950.

The typical spear used by the Vikings, such as those found with the axes near Old London Bridge, has a narrow conical

socket, in some cases decorated with silver inlay, and a long
narrow blade spreading out sharply from the socket and then
tapering gradually, with almost straight edges, to the point.
The shaft was of ash, and the weapon was used either in both
hands for close combat or for casting at a distance.

The swords used by the early Vikings had blades similar
to those described under the Franks and, indeed, they were
probably imported from the Rhineland. The characteristic
early hilt has a short thick cross-guard of iron and a pommel
consisting of a similar but shorter cross-bar, on the outside
of which was fitted a triangular cap in the same way as the
'cocked-hat' of Migration period hilts. In some cases the cross-
bar and cap are made in one, sometimes with the position of
the division still indicated by a groove. Examples of this
type of hilt have been found over an area bounded by Russia
and Ireland, Switzerland and Iceland. Their decoration
usually consists of plating with a combination of metals, tin,
gold, silver, or copper, arranged to form simple patterns of
squares and lines in contrasting colours. This plating was
fixed to the iron of the hilt by hammering it into innumerable
thin, parallel-sided grooves cut into the surface of the iron.
In Norway, many of these hilts are found mounted on single-
edged, straight blades, having the point in line with the back
edge, which are uncommon outside the area of Norse
influence. A very few of these single-edged blades are curved.
An alternative form of hilt, common in early times, has a
rather longer cross-bar in front of the hand, and a similar
but shorter one behind it; these are again common in Norway,
often on single-edged blades. Both these hilts belong to the
period before 950. Contemporary in origin to these are hilts
in which the triangular cap is replaced by one made up of
three or, less often, five graduated lobes, arranged along the
pommel-bar with the largest one in the centre. In some cases

the lobes are very marked, as on a tenth-century sword found at Sigridsholm, Uppland, Sweden, now in the Statens Historiska Museum, Stockholm; and as on the sword held by King Cnut in the *Register of Hyde Abbey* of 1020–30 (British Museum, Stowe Ms. 944). Pommels of this type are still occasionally found in the thirteenth century, as on the effigy of Robert Duke of Normandy of about 1280 in Gloucester Cathedral. Many examples of these very lobated pommels have curved pommel-bars and cross-guards curved to match, like a sword now in the London Museum found in the Thames at Wandsworth Reach. Late examples usually have longer cross-guards. In others, the outline of the pommel is more flowing and the lobes only indicated by lines or thin ribs on its side, as on several swords from the Viking cemetery at Kilmainham, Dublin. Occasionally, the end lobes are shaped to resemble the animal heads sometimes found on ends of the pommel cap of the Migration period from which these pommels descend. In the first group the decoration usually consists of simple plating in metals of contrasting colour. Occasionally, as on the Sigridsholm sword, the decoration, in this case consisting of interlace, is picked out with niello. This is a black compound let into grooves in the metal, and is formed by fusing a mixture of powdered silver, copper, lead, and sulphur, which is then burnished. In the second group the decoration is sometimes very much more lavish than those already described. The metal is chiselled with a repeating pattern of crosses and circles and occasionally zoomorphic motifs, and parts of the design are plated with silver or gold, sometimes worked decoratively. In some cases, the grip is covered in metal decorated to match the rest of the hilt. Swords with hilts of walrus ivory and gold are described in the Sagas, like Legbiter the sword of Magnus Barefoot. The hilt of the sword, called that of St Stephen, in Prague

Cathedral, has pommel and cross-guard of ivory engraved with entwined monsters (see Figure 3).

A number of swords, apparently of English origin, have been found in Scandinavia. A magnificent silver hilt discovered at Dybeck, Schonen, Sweden, is decorated in English style with vigorous entwined monsters and zoomorphic strapwork in high relief (Statens Historiska Museum, Stockholm).

The later Viking swords, those thought to date from about 900 or later, have a new type of blade, no longer made of pattern-welded iron, but of a flexible, fine-quality steel. They are now tapered towards the point, thus making the sword less point-heavy and more wieldy. While better balanced for cutting, this type can be recovered more quickly and can also be used for thrusting. Many of these blades are inlaid in the central groove with large Roman capitals forming the names ULFBERHT and INGELRII. Although originally

Figure 3 A reconstruction of a Danish sword of about AD 900

personal names, these were probably applied by a factory, since they continued to be used for a very long period. On the other face of the blade, instead of the name, there is usually an inlaid trellis-like pattern. These inscriptions were apparently made by cutting the name in the blade, and hammering into the grooves sections of thin iron rod while the blade was white hot. The inlay was further secured by more hammering at welding heat. It has been suggested that these blades were made in the Rhineland; they have been found almost all over northern Europe. A sword of this type with blade signed

INGELRII, found in the Thames, is in the British Museum, and one signed by ULFBERHT, also found in the Thames at Shifford, is in the Reading Museum.

The Sagas, when describing the sword in use, made it clear that sword play was a question of swapping blows. No attempt seems to have been made to catch these on the sword; parries were made with the shield which was soon cut to pieces. *Kormáks Saga* describes a formal duel, called the *hólmganga,* in which the use of three shields in turn was allowed. When Bjarni and Thorstein fought together, on a less formal occasion, once they had hacked each other's shield to pieces, Thorstein went into his house and got two replacements, while his opponent was doing up his shoe. Once these shields were smashed they decided to call it a day. Blows were given with enormous force, hewing off heads and limbs. If the striker hesitated for an instant in disengaging his sword from his opponent's shield, he might lose his hand. Occasionally someone is described as grasping his sword in both hands if his shield has gone, or if in desperation he has slung it on his back in order to swing his weapon more freely. The use of the point is only rarely mentioned, although, in *Beowulf,* Sigemund pierces the dragon and strikes the wall behind it.

When getting ready to fight, as in a duel, or when bear-hunting for instance, the unsheathed sword could be kept hanging on a cord around the right wrist. This is mentioned in *Egils Saga,* but no illustration of it seems to exist before about 1220 when a figure in the *Eneide* manuscript at Tübingen University is shown carrying his sword in this way. Although maces were frequently supplied with wrist-cords they are not normally found on swords before the sixteenth century. Apparently, the Vikings tied their swords into their scabbards by means of 'peace bands', and these had to be undone before the weapon could be drawn.

As in Saxon times, famous swords were passed on from one owner to another as presents or bequests. They were given names, like *Kvernbítr* (Quern-biter) the gift of King Athelstan to King Hakon of Norway, and a named sword is sometimes mentioned in more than one Saga, as it passes from hand to hand gaining fame as it accumulates victories. The sword Skofnung was taken from the burial mound of King Hrolf of Denmark by one of the first Icelandic settlers, Skeggi of Midfirth. Many generations later, and after many voyages, it found its way back to Roskilde in Denmark near Hrolf's burial place.

There are several references in the Sagas to swords of Francia which confirm the suggested source of the blades. Such blades were said never to fail.

The bow was used as a weapon throughout Scandinavia but, judging by the Chronicles, probably as a weapon of war only among the lower social orders. A yew bow found in a crannog at Ballinderry in Ireland, together with a sword of Viking type, was 185 cm long. The bow-stave was of D-shaped cross-section; the flat side forming the back of the bow, the side facing the target when the bow was bent. When strung, this bow would have taken up a more or less even arc of a circle. It differs only in very minor details from the only surviving English medieval longbows. Early medieval Scandinavian laws include the bow among the weapons of freemen.

Viking Ships

One of the most interesting products of the Viking age was its ships. Rather surprisingly a number of these have survived, including two nearly complete vessels in the nature of princely yachts, used in this case as burial ships. These were rather smaller than sea-going warships and certainly much smaller than the great ships of about AD 1000; like the *Long Serpent* built by Thorbergr Skafhogg for King Olaf Tryggvason, which was probably about 48·8 metres overall with 34 pairs of oars.

An almost complete 32-oar ship excavated at Gokstad, in Norway, now in Oslo, is 23·33 metres long and 5·25 metres in the beam. Its height amidships from the bottom of the keel to the top of the gunnel is 195 cm. It draws 85 cm, leaving a freeboard of 110 cm. An exact copy made in 1893 had a tonnage of 31·78 registered tons. It is thought that this ship was built in the second half of the ninth century or early in the tenth century.

This ship is built of oak throughout. Special pieces of suitable shape were kept supple by being buried in bogs until they were required. The keel is formed from a single tree hewn to form a longitudinal fin below the planking, and drawing nearly a foot more water at the centre, which allows this type of ship to sail much closer to the wind than earlier models. To this is attached at each end a short curved transitional piece to which are nailed by stout wooden pins the curved bow- and stern-posts. The hull is constructed of sixteen strakes (planks) on each side, each over-lapping the one below. They are held together by round-headed iron rivets with square iron clinch-plates (washers) fitted inside, except near the very ends where the hull is too narrow for a hammer to be wielded inside, and the clinch-plates are therefore fitted outside. The hull must have been nailed together with the aid of some form of mould, since some of the clinch-plates are under the ribs which therefore must have been fitted after the hull was formed. Where it has been necessary to join strakes vertically, the ends are bevelled to give an overlap away from the bow to help prevent the sea getting in. There are 19 one-piece ribs at intervals of a bare metre, formed of naturally curved pieces of oak. Except for the topmost one, all the nine bottom strakes on each side are not nailed to the ribs but lashed to them by means of withies or fine spruce roots attached through cleats carved out of the solid strake. The tie passes through a hole pierced in a ridge carved out along the underside of the rib: the ninth strake from the keel on both sides is fixed to the end of each rib by a wooden nail. The keel itself, and the strake on each side of it, are not attached to the ribs in any way. This method was probably adopted in order to allow the hull the greatest possible flexibility, allowing it to twist with the waves which might otherwise break it. The captain of the copy of 1893 reported that the gunnel of his ship would twist up to six inches out of line in a heavy sea. The end ribs actually fill the hull from side to side forming bulkheads. Each of the others supports a cross-beam on which the loose pine deck planking was laid. Since the upper strakes receive the buffeting of the waves, this part of the hull is constructed entirely differently from the lower part. The seven upper strakes are nailed to knees fitted on the ends of the cross-beams, and to top-ribs, one for every second cross-beam, which gives them much greater strength. In the third strake from the top are 16 pairs of ports for oars, 12 cm in diameter, one for each space between the ribs, except the end spaces where the ship was too narrow for oars to be used. These ports could be closed by round pivoted shutters on the inside.

The rear rib forms a support for the huge paddle-shaped steering-oar mounted on the starboard side. This was pivoted on a great wooden 'wart' nailed to the ship's side. The pivot itself was formed of a withy, knotted at the outer end. The inner end passed through the oar just below the neck, the wart, and the ship's side, and was fixed firmly by being twisted through a series of three holes bored in the rib. When lowered, the rudder reached about 50 cm deeper than the keel. The upper part of the steering-oar was supported by means of a strap through the gunnel, passed round the oar and back through the gunnel again. It was manoeuvered by means of a tiller fitted to the narrow top end of the oar. It could be raised out of the water by means of a rope attached to its heel. One of the boats carved on the Gotland stones shows a platform built in the stern above the level of the side, presumably for the steersman to stand on.

The top of the pine-wood mast no longer survived since it had been in the stepped position when the ship was buried. It was 30 cm thick and probably originally about 13 metres tall and would have had a yard of 9·5 to 10·5 metres long. The foot of the mast was supported in a socket cut in a great oak block 3·75 metres long resting on the keel and on the eighth to eleventh ribs counting from the stern. The block was steadied by knees from the ribs. At deck level the mast passed through a five metre beam, called the mast-partner, lying fore and aft on top of the cross-beams and mortised to them. In this is a long narrow hole through which the mast passes, the back of which was plugged with a wedge to support the mast when it was stepped.

There are no signs of any stays for the mast and these may not have been necessary on such a short mast. The few illustrations we have of early Scandinavian ships, which are on carved stones in Gotland, show that they were square rigged with a single yard and a complicated system of ropes from the bottom edge of the sail, presumably for reefing. Some show stays for the mast. It appears that when sailing close to the wind, in order to keep the forward edge of the sail stretched, a device called a *beitass* (sprit) was used. This consisted of a pole, one end of which fitted into the leading edge of the sail while the other end fitted into a depression in a block of wood fixed against the opposite side of the ship, a little astern of the mast. The pole was long enough to keep the sail fully stretched forward. The yard would be adjusted by means of braces attached at each end. The place of the beitass was later taken by bowlines.

The Gokstad ship had 32 shields on each side, painted alternately yellow and black, hung on a special rack along the gunnel. The Sagas make it clear that these were only used for dressing the ship in harbour and were not used at sea.

The seams of the hull were caulked with tarred rope made of animal hair in special caulking grooves cut in each plank. Finally, the ship would be tarred all over to close the seams. The Icelandic *King's Mirror,* of the mid-thirteenth century, describes the annual retarring of boats and implies that they sometimes overwintered in boat-sheds.

There are no rowing seats in the Gokstad ship, and presumably the oarsmen sat on their sea-chests which are mentioned in the Sagas. The narrow bladed, pine wood oars vary in length from 530 cm to 585 cm; the longer ones being for use near the ends where the gunnel rises higher above the water. The ship contained a small iron anchor, too small actually to hold this ship, but sufficient to hold it off-shore when it was tied up at night. The ship was in fact tied up to a large rock when it was buried. There was also a gang plank, but no bailer, although this has been found in other ships. One of the three boats found in the ship when it was excavated represents the ship's-boat, the others were too large and should be considered as grave-goods.

The Gokstad boat was rather a plain and simple object. Just how magnificent a ship of the age could be is shown by another earlier vessel excavated at Oseberg, the burial ship of a young princess. The bow and stern are decorated with rich and complicated carvings and the upper end of the bow-post is carved as a spiral serpent. The stone carvings in Gotland show ships with dragon's head prows and curled dragon's tails at the stern. The Ulfljot's laws, an early Icelandic code, lay down that the dragon's head must be removed when approaching Iceland so as not to frighten away the guardian spirits of the island. It is very important when sailing close to the wind to have a wind-direction indicator, and a number of wind-vanes from Scandinavian churches are thought originally to have been mast-head vanes from ships. One, decorated in English style, which may have come from a ship of Canute's fleet, was formerly in Söderala church, Hälsingland, Sweden (Statens Historiska Museet, Stockholm).

A normal day's sailing in the Sagas is 100 miles at 4 knots. The copy of the Gokstad ship crossed the Atlantic in 27 days and was capable of 11 knots. It is thought to have been a little smaller than the average Viking ship which probably had 20 to 25 pairs of oars and would have been about 24 to 29 metres long, with a crew of 80 to 120 men.[1]

---

[1] A brief description of the construction of two later Viking warships, originally sunk as block-ships in the approaches to Roskilde, Denmark, is published by Dr Ole Crumlin-Pedersen in *Aspects of the history of wooden shipbuilding*, National Maritime Museum, Maritime Monographs and Reports, No. 1, Greenwich 1970, pp. 7–23.

4

The Saxons

The colonization of England and the lowlands of Scotland by peoples of Teutonic origin probably took place in much the same way as the colonization of France. Apparently the invaders first came as *foederati,* mercenaries granted land in return for their protection against their kinsmen and against the Picts.

Gildas, a Briton, probably writing before AD 548, records that three war-ships of Saxons had come to Britain at the invitation of an un-named king, and were granted land in the eastern part of the island on condition that they protected the country. Later, they were joined by more ship-loads of warriors who were also given grants of land. When the colonists became more numerous they rebelled against their paymasters and began to spread across the country. They were defeated by the Britons under Ambrosius Aurelianus and, after more fighting culminating in the British victory at *Mons Badonicus*, there was a period of peace during which Gildas was actually writing. The Venerable Bede, writing before AD 731, only adds to this account the names of the British king, Vortigern, and the leaders of the invaders, Hengest and Horsa, and the fact that Horsa was believed to be buried in Kent. He places the date of the first landing shortly after AD 449.

That at least part of Gildas's story is based on fact is confirmed by finds of Germanic pottery of the fourth or early fifth century date and military metalwork on Roman sites, both in Yorkshire and East Anglia. This suggests that Saxons were settled there as *foederati,* probably even before the final abandonment of the island by the Romans and before the appeal by Vortigern. However, once the early revolt had proved successful, other chiefs clearly came without invitation. The settlement of Wessex by the West Saxons seems to have been by invasion, although here there is the difficulty of the possibly Celtic origin of the name Cerdic, the first of the West Saxon line of kings.

The departure of the Romans does not seem to have left the Britons quite as helpless as tradition would have us believe. There appears to have been a revival of Celtic tribalism, and, at least in the northern part of the province, the barbarians were held for a time, while in the south the Saxons seem to have met with a stiff resistance. The invaders did not finally reach the Bristol Channel until the battle of Deorham (Dyrham) in AD 577, nor the Irish Sea until the battle of Chester in AD 613; and, of course, both Wales and Cornwall survived as Celtic areas.

The evidence of archaeology and the study of place names, and the evidence of the *Anglo-Saxon Chronicle,* are often contradictory and their interpretation open to discussion. Early Saxon cemeteries in areas where early Saxon place names are apparently not found or are rare, as in the Cambridge and Oxford areas, may suggest a period of re-conquest by the Britons, who would not of course use Saxon place names. The *Chronicle* records the capture by the Saxons of Limbury in Bedfordshire, Aylesbury in Buckinghamshire, and Benson and Eynsham in Oxfordshire in AD 571. It is extremely unlikely that an area so far to the east was not in Saxon hands at an early date. If this date is correct, which has been doubted, it suggests that the Britons had recaptured the area possibly after Mons Badonicus. A series of earth-works of post-Roman date built across the Icknield Way have been seen as Saxon defences built to hold back Britons advancing to the North East from the Upper Thames valley, an area certainly in Saxon hands by about the year 500. There is some evidence that at this time the invaders began to leave these shores and settle among the Franks. It is possible that this period coincides with the era of peace in which Gildas was writing. We are unlikely ever to know for certain the precise chronology of the conquest.

The invaders, although divided by Bede into Angles, Saxons, and Jutes, were a mongrel race, judging by the mixed origin and character of the earliest grave-goods. In general, however, the Jutes, who had connections with the Rhineland Franks, settled in Kent, the Isle of Wight and possibly southern Hampshire; while the Essex, Wessex, Middlesex and Sussex areas, as their names imply, were settled by people of Saxon stock stemming from Old Saxony in north Germany and Holland. East Anglia, the Midlands and the north of England were settled by Angles from the area to the south of Denmark, called to this day Angeln. A number of graves containing Frankish goods of fifth-century date suggest that Frankish war-bands and their women were among the first wave. The warriors who carried out the invasion followed aristo-cratic war leaders in the Teutonic tradition. The earlier evidence of Tacitus is here reinforced by the great epic poem *Beowulf,* written down in Christian times but containing much traditional feeling and descriptions of the relation-ship between a lord and the members of his war-band.

The difficulty of the conquest no doubt caused the coalescence of the smaller war-bands into larger groups, and these formed the many small kingdoms of the earliest period.

There were probably about twelve in AD 600 and three on the eve of the Danish invasions. Occasionally, one ruler managed to make himself supreme over all the others but this suzerainty rarely crossed the Humber, the great dividing line between the Northumbrians and the Southern English. By the seventh century the meaning of the word *Bretwalda,* the title given to this overlord, began to change from a leader of a confederacy of warrior kingdoms united against a common foe, into the ruler of them all, whose safe-conduct ran from one end of the land to the other and whose under-kings required his consent to their decisions. By the eighth century, the relationship between Offa of Mercia as Bretwalda and the subject kings was that of lord and man. However, no Bretwalda passed on his power to his successor and no single royal line reached pre-eminence, until the complete dis-appearance of all except the West Saxon house during the Danish invasions of the ninth century.

This was a heroic age; fighting was a pleasure; the comradeship and loyalty of the war-band were the theme of much of the poetry declaimed in the hall. The warrior fought on behalf of his chosen lord to win him greater glory, and the treasure and arms he won belonged to his lord. In return, he expected his lord to protect him, or to avenge him with the blood of his slayer, or the exaction of the wergild of his rank from the slayer or his kin. The *Anglo-Saxon Chronicle* makes it quite clear that the terrible years of the reign of Æthelred the Unready were looked on as the result of the failure to avenge the murder of his brother and predecessor. The warrior expected rich gifts, gold rings, horses, and armour in particular, and feasting in his lord's hall; and, most important of all, he hoped to win renown. Beowulf says to Hrothgar, 'Let him who can, achieve glory before he die; that will be best for the noble warrior when life is over.' The lord was also responsible in law for his men's actions, and must produce them to answer in court or pay their fines for them.

In old age, Beowulf looks back to the deeds he performed for Hygelac, king of the Geats, his lord: 'With gleaming sword I repaid in war ... the treasures he bestowed on me. He gave me land, domain, an ancestral seat. Ever I wished to be before him on foot, alone in the van, ...' The rewards given to him by Hrothgar for killing the monster Grendel and his mother, Beowulf accepts on behalf of Hygelac and passes on to him banner, helm, byrnie, sword, and four matched horses. Hygelac, in return, gives him a sword that had belonged to his father, Beowulf's maternal grandfather: 'there was not at that time with the Geats a better treasure among swords.' Kings and great leaders are normally described poetically as 'giver of treasure', 'giver of rings', 'refuge of the warriors'. The poem *The Wanderer* describes the deep sense of emptiness and loneliness of the man who has lost his lord. He remembers the happy days in the mead hall, the giving of treasure, the companionship.

Beowulf himself in his last battle was badly served by his followers, and his young kinsman, Wiglaf, bitterly reproached his companions for their cowardice. 'He who wishes to tell the truth can say that the lord who gave you treasure, the war gear wherein you stand there, when he often gave to men sitting in the hall on the ale bench, as a prince, to his thegns, helm and byrnie, the most excellent he could find anywhere far or near, that without doubt he cast away miserably the garments of war when battle beset him.' He goes on to describe the dishonour that will befall them.

The *Anglo-Saxon Chronicle* tells of a fight in 786 when the thegns of King Cynewulf of Wessex discovered that the king had been killed in a surprise attack while they slept.

Although offered quarter by his murderers, they preferred to fight on until all were dead except one Welsh hostage and he was grievously wounded. In the same way, those of Cynewulf's murderers offered quarter by their kinsmen in his main host indignantly refused. Loyalty was the lynch pin of the war-band. The warrior who fled would be called *nithing*, coward, and live out his life dishonoured.

When Penda of Mercia went to war he was followed by thirty *duces regii* or ealdormen. These clearly represent the princes or sub-kings of once independent peoples. A charter of Offa of Mercia in 777 includes the phrase 'my under-king, ealdorman, that is, of his own people of the Hwicce'. The earliest references to the ruler of this people had called him king *(rex)*. The ealdorman of later Saxon times became the king's representative in the shire, leading the local forces and administering justice in the shire-court. It was, however, an office and was held by one of the king's thegns chosen for his ability. Byrhtnoth, Ealdorman of East Anglia, was also described in the poem *Maldon* as 'the noble thegn of Æthelred' In 860 Osric and Æthelwulf, the Ealdormen of Hampshire and of Berkshire respectively, led the forces of their shires against the Danes and defeated them. The Wessex shires appear to represent the areas settled by originally independent peoples. In the remainder of the country the shires had to be remade after the Danish conquest and are more a matter of administrative convenience. They generally centre round the town that gives them their name. In the Danelaw they each represent the settlement of a Danish army of the Alfredian period. Payment of the ealdorman was by a proportion of the fines and revenues from the burghs in his territory and possibly by grants of land. He appears to have had a higher wergild than an ordinary thegn; in the North by as much as four times.

The companion of the war-band of the age of conquest becomes the thegn of the age of settlement and consolidation. By the eighth century he could normally expect to receive in due course a grant of land suitable to this rank. This was usually held free from all dues and services except the military service, bridge repair, and work on fortifications – known as *trimoda necessitas* – which every freeman was obliged to do. In some cases, however, a specific service, such as escort duty, was also required of the thegn. The greater thegns were served by their own thegns. The church also had thegns of its own settled on its estates. The younger of a king's thegns accompanied him everywhere, acting as his bodyguard, upper servants, and officials. His older thegns, the experienced men, some of whom acted as chamberlains and seneschals, were his advisers and did not spend all their time at the court. Alfred organized his thegns so that they served one month in three, thus giving them time to oversee their estates. They had a wergild of 1200 shillings as opposed to the 200 due for a ceorl, an ordinary freeman. In Alfred's time, a thegn paid 120 shillings for neglect of military service but a ceorl only 30 shillings. Latterly, once thegndom had become hereditary, the qualification seems to have been the holding of at least five hides. A hide was originally almost certainly the land required to support one household; it therefore varied in acreage according to the quality of the land on which it was situated. A ceorl who throve, so that he held five hides on which he paid the royal dues, was to be paid for with a thegn's wergild if he was slain. The rank did not become hereditary until the land had been held for three generations. A ceorl who throve remained a ceorl, however, if he did not have five hides, even if he had a gold-plated sword, a byrnie, and a helm.

A later writer states that a merchant who had voyaged

overseas three times in his own ship was worthy of the rank of thegn. Although we do not know what it was, some form of ceremony must have accompanied the making of a man into a thegn, since it would be necessary to make his promotion public knowledge. In the same way, the ceremony of freeing a slave included the placing in his hands of the weapons of a ceorl as a symbol of his new rank. The *Laws of Henry I* stipulate that a serf should be liberated by placing in his hands the arms suitable to a freeman, and that the ceremony should take place in some public place – the church, or the market-place, or the county- or hundred-court – in front of witnesses.

Domesday distinguishes between thegns holding land which they cannot alienate without the leave of their lord, and those who can do with it what they will. It is probable that the distinction is that the first class are those whose land is a gift from their lord, while the second class are those who have placed themselves under the lord's protection by commendation.

Many thegns held large estates scattered over many shires. *Domesday* indicates that at the other end of the scale many thegns held less than the five hides one would expect of them, presumably due to the division of land between his sons on a thegn's death. The manor of Salden in Buckinghamshire, assessed in *Domesday* at a little over three hides, was held by four thegns each owing allegiance to a different lord.

Arms and Armour of the Saxons

The arming of the Anglo Saxons at the earliest period can be reconstructed both from the very large number of grave-finds and from references in poetry. Much the most common weapon was the spear, the traditional weapon of Woden. Usually only the head survives with, occasionally, the ferule

Figure 4 Spear head found in the Thames at Wandsworth and now in the London Museum. It is a type found in most areas of northern and western Europe. Probably ninth to tenth century

from the lower end and a few fragments of the wooden shaft (Figure 4). This was normally of ash wood, as is shown by the use of *aesc* as a synonym for the spear in Saxon poetry. The warrior himself could be described as *aesc-berend,* the spear-bearer. Grave-finds indicate a length of a little over two metres between point and ferule, but later manuscript illuminations show much taller spears. The *heriot* of a certain Wulfsige included a spear twined with gold.[1] Some surviving spear heads have their sockets inlaid with silver, copper, or bronze. Lengths vary from a few cms to sixty. In a few cases, the blade is pattern welded. Barbed heads are rarely found but occur frequently in manuscript illustrations. The spear was used either in the hand as a thrusting weapon, or hurled like a dart. At Maldon, the poet says, 'Then let the spears, hard as files go; let the darts, ground sharp, fly.' Later manuscript illustrations sometimes show warriors holding a group of two or three barbed spears, one of which they are throwing. This probably indicates the use of one or two lighter casting spears, together with a heavier spear for hand-to-hand fighting. Three barbed, angon-like heads were among the eight spears in the Sutton Hoo Ship, while true angons of Frankish type have been found in Kentish graves and in a few early burials in other parts of southern England.

---

[1] On the death of a man, unless in battle, his lord's gifts to him of arms were returned symbolically by the due called *heriot,* literally 'war gear'.

Very much less common in graves than the spear is the sword, probably partly because of its much greater rarity and because of its magical and historical importance. One of the commonest poetic synonyms for the sword is 'the ancient heirloom'. They are frequently mentioned in wills. Among the eleven swords left by the young prince Athelstan in 1015 was one 'which King Offa owned', presumably the great Mercian king (died 796). A certain Ælfgar left to his lord about AD 958 a sword valued at 120 mancuses of gold, which King Edmund had given him. This would have been worth 120 oxen or fifteen male slaves. In poetry some swords have names like 'Hrunting' which Unferth lent Beowulf for his fight in Grendelsmere, or 'Naegling' which was the hero's sword in old age, which we are told was 'an ancient heirloom, exceeding keen of edge' and had a blade which gleamed with patterns. Such swords were considered particularly valuable since they were thought to possess some of the 'luck', courage, and prowess of their former owner. Swords were sometimes said to have been the ancient work of giants, like the sword Beowulf found in Grendelsmere, or of the mythical smith Weland, like the sword 'Mimming' in the poem *Waldere*, or they are found in the burial mounds of heroes, like 'Skofnung' the famous Icelandic sword.

A number of swords with hilts similar in construction to those described in the section dealing with the Lombards have been found in England (Figure 5). The guard and pommel bar rarely survive but their form is shown by the plates riveted above and below them. A wooden bar survives on a hilt found at Crundale Down, now so heavily varnished as to have been mistaken for iron; and a horn guard survives on a sword from Lakenheath Fen (both now in the British Museum). A comparable hilt found at Valsgärde in Sweden has both the pommel bar and guard of metal decorated to match the

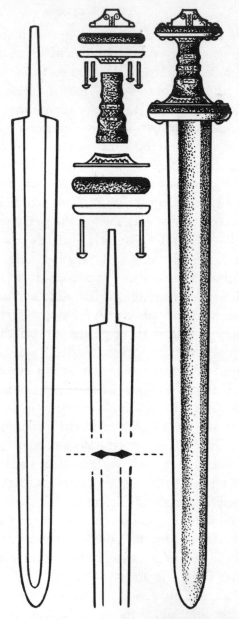

Figure 5 An early Saxon sword, with diagrams showing the construction

plate riveted above and below them. Some late fifth-century swords found at Petersfinger in Wiltshire and Abingdon in Berkshire are probably from the same factory as swords found in the German lands; the area of Namur has been suggested as the place of manufacture. Several hilts found in Kent have a small ring attached to them by means of a loop riveted to one end of the pommel. The reason for this is not clear, but it is known that oaths were often taken either on a sword hilt or on a ring, and these ring-hilts may have been designed with oath-taking in mind. Alternatively it has been suggested that, since they are not found on royal swords but have been attached to some old swords and are missing from others which have had them, they may be a symbol of comradeship given by kings to their most important thegns. The ring would then have to have been removed when the sword passed to a new owner. Certainly it is unlikely to have had any practical purpose, since the majority of those found on the Continent are of the coalesced type, in which ring and loop are of one single piece without any opening, and could not be used for attaching a sword-knot or a charm.

The hilt found in the memorial ship-burial of an East-Anglian king of the mid-seventh century at Sutton Hoo in Suffolk, is of the same general construction, but was decorated with cut and polished garnets in a pattern of steps and quatrefoils. Also in the ship was a fixed ring made in one with its mount which, in this case, had apparently not been attached to the sword. This kind of ring, which is presumably a development of the loose ring, and therefore later, has also been found on swords in Scandinavia and the Frankish lands. A complete hilt found in Cumberland, and now in the British Museum, probably of seventh-century date, is made entirely of horn – pommel, grip, and cross-guard – and is decorated with inlaid plates of gold filigree work. The grip is indented

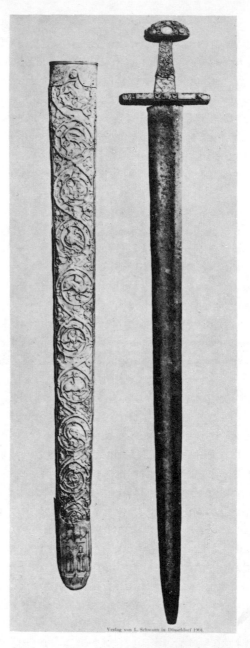

Verlag von L. Schwann in Düsseldorf 1904.

Plate 5 Two-edged sword, probably German early eleventh century, preserved in the Treasury of Essen Cathedral. The hilt is covered with gold filagree set with enamels and cabochon stones. The scabbard is of embossed gold sheet. (Reproduced by permission of the authorities of the Cathedral)

for the fingers. The cross-guard is straight and the pommel shaped like a broad boat.

Blades, which scarcely differ from those described under the Franks, were probably frequently imported. Hilts, however, could be added in England and may have been changed from time to time as fashion demanded. The frequent association in Saxon literature of poison with sword blades is probably not to be taken literally. The reference may either be to the acid used in etching the pattern welding of the blade, or to the symbolic comparison of swords with serpents – both because of their ability to strike swiftly and because of the serpentine patterning of their blades.

As a child, King Athelstan was invested by his grandfather, Alfred, with 'a Saxon sword with a golden sheath', but the normal sheath was of two strips of wood, one on each side of the blade, covered with leather, and bound around the edge and tip with metal. Fleece-lined scabbards have been found in England. A silver mount for the mouth of a scabbard, found at Chessel Down, Isle of Wight, is decorated by piercing on the front and has an inscription in runes engraved on the back; possibly the weapon's name. A u-shaped chape, the mount for the scabbard tip, found at Brighthampton, is of silver decorated with gilt running animals.

The axe does not seem to have been common as a weapon in early Saxon times, but the francisca is found in graves in Kent and Wiltshire, where it probably indicates the presence of Frankish settlers. Among the weapons in the Sutton Hoo ship, however, was a narrow axe with a hammer head on the back of the head and with an iron haft about two feet long.

Many graves contain a single-edged knife, sometimes almost long enough to be classed as a short sword. The blades of late examples are often inlaid with copper or bronze wire. A knife from Sittingbourne is inscribed with the names of both its owner and maker in Anglo-Saxon, and another found in the Thames has the complete runic alphabet on it. Two letters written from Northumbrian monasteries refer to presents of small knives being sent to the Rhineland, which suggests that they must have been of exceptional quality, since the Rhineland was already well-known for its weapons and tools. These knives are probably to be identified with the *handseax* or *hip seax*. The scabbards of this type of knife were in general similar to those found on the Continent, judging by the fragmentary mounts that have survived.

After the spear, the shield is the commonest military object found in graves. All that usually survives is the iron boss and the handle with its bars extending almost to the shield rim. Occasionally traces of a metal rim are found, and at Caenby in Lincolnshire a shield was found decorated with a number of interlace-ornamented, gilt-bronze plaques. The wooden disc that formed the shield was apparently about 2·5 cm thick, judging by the length of surviving rivets, and flat. It is now in the British Museum. Saxon poetry shows again and again that the chosen wood of the shield was lime – Wiglaf 'seized his shield, the yellow linden-wood.' A law of Athelstan forbids the covering of shields with sheepskin, presumably because it is thin and easily pierced compared with bull's hide. The Sutton Hoo shield is quite exceptional in its richness. The grip, which is slightly off-set behind the boss to allow more room for the palm of the hand than for the fingers, is extended at each end by an ornamented bar stretching across the inside of the shield: there are two studs to hold a leather strap or brase across the forearm to make the metre in diameter disc more wieldy: there are attachments for a strap by which the shield could be hung up in the hall or slung on the back. The surface has applied to it a monster and a bird

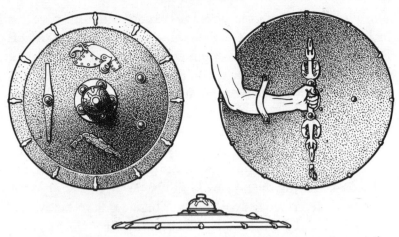

Figure 6 A tentative reconstruction of the shield found in the Sutton Hoo ship; now in the British Museum. This reconstruction is at present under review

as decoration and an ornamental representation of a reinforcing bar to the right of the boss; the disc was apparently convex. Like other objects in this monument, the shield has connections with the Vendel people of Sweden and was old and repaired when buried (Figure 6).[1]

The remaining fragments of wood from a shield discovered at Petersfinger appear to have been of at least two thicknesses of wood with the grain of one board laid at right angles to the next, as in plywood.

The absence of body armour in Saxon graves is as noticeable as it is in the Frankish lands. Pieces of mail, now lost, were found in a grave at Benty Grange in Derbyshire. The mail found at Sutton Hoo was made of butted rings; that is, the ends were not riveted together, and so was therefore probably votive rather than defensive. No doubt, as later

[1] The reconstruction described here is at present under review by Mr R.L.S. Bruce-Mitford, Keeper of the Department of British and Medieval Antiquities at the British Museum.

illuminations show, the average Saxon warrior wore his ordinary clothes and was armed only with a spear and shield. Poetry however makes it quite clear that the Hero wears a byrnie; that is, a shirt of mail. The poetic synonyms 'ring-woven corslets', 'the woven breast net', 'the war-byrnie hard hand-locked', 'the war-byrnie twisted with hands' makes it clear that no other type of armour can be intended. The Franks Casket in the British Museum, which was probably carved in Northumbria about 700, shows two of the warriors attacking the house of Egil the Archer wearing what have been described as mail shirts. These come to below the waist level and have sleeves. Their surface is covered with contiguous studs but, unfortunately, the carving is so schematic that it is quite impossible to be sure what material the artist intended to represent. A manuscript of about AD 1000, the *Psychomachia* of Prudentius, in the British Museum, shows byrnies with short sleeves and reaching only to just below the waist. (Cotton Ms. Cleopatra C. VIII). The edges are van dyked to represent the small triangles of mail which are found along the edges of later surviving mail shirts. No example of a helm shaped like the 'Phrygian' caps worn by the warriors in this and other manuscripts has been found, and it has been suggested that they were made of leather.

The barbaric version of an Imperial Roman general's equipment in the Sutton Hoo ship cannot be considered as true armour. Presumably King Æthelhere, if it is he who is commemorated, was wearing his real battle gear when he met his death at Winwaed (655) in Yorkshire. Bede's statement that many were drowned in this battle is a possible explanation of the absence of human remains in the ship, the king's body having been lost in the floods. It has been suggested alternatively that the memorial was to Redwald, the Bretwalda who died in 624 or 625 and who was a lapsed

Christian convert. The gold-plated helm in the ship belongs to the Swedish Vendel culture and was old when buried. It has a face-guard recalling the 'masking helms' of *Beowulf*. The only portions of the body armour to survive are the great hinged clasps of gold set with garnets, mosaic glass, and filigree, which are thought to have held together the halves of a leather cuirass on the shoulders, as on the statue of the Emperor Augustus in the Vatican. The pivot pins of the hinges can be pulled out to release the two halves. Small chains attach these pins to the clasps so that they do not get lost. A sash could have held the back and front of the cuirass together at the waist, or they could have been laced together under the arms.

A single Saxon fighting helm has survived, found in the grave at Benty Grange, mentioned above, and now in the Sheffield Museum (Figure 7). It consists of an iron brow-band supporting four iron arches crossing on top of the head. The

Figure 7 The Saxon helm excavated from a grave at Benty Grange, Derbyshire, and now in the Sheffield Museum. The spaces between the bars were originally filled with sheets of cowhorn

interspaces were once filled with horn plates, traces of which remain, held on by silver rivets. There is a straight bar forming a nose-guard or nasal. The mail found in this grave may have formed a neck-guard for this helm as on Frankish ones. One of the most interesting features of this helm is its decoration. On the very top stands a bronze wild boar, the emblem of the ancient Teutonic god Frey, which the warrior believed would protect him. The silver on its flanks is cut from an old Roman vessel. Its eyes are garnets and it was probably once enamelled all over. Helms guarded by boars are mentioned in *Beowulf,* wrought by the weapon-smiths of old so that no blade could pierce them. In this case, the powers of the ancient gods have been reinforced by the symbol of the new 'Prince of Victory, Refuge of the Warriors', for on the nose-guard is the cross of Christ in silver. A helm with a highly stylised beast standing on its top is illustrated in a page of an eighth-century manuscript, probably from Northumbria, in Leningrad Public Library. (Ms. Lat. Q. v. xiv. N. 1). The Franks Casket of about AD 700 illustrates a nasal helm which encloses the whole head and neck except the face. This presumably represents a helm with a flexible neck guard, perhaps lacing together across the throat.

Alfred's Reforms

In the ninth century the West Saxons found themselves facing a number of well-armed and well-led armies of professional soldiers, living off the land and highly mobile as they rode across the country on stolen horses. The Danes were able to strike by sea or by land and be far away before the local *fyrd* could be gathered to deal with them.[1]

---

[1] The term *fyrd,* meaning army, is used by modern historians to identify the part of the Saxon army owing personal or territorial military service but excluding the mercenary element.

Although the Saxon obligation to military service was probably originally unlimited in time, the demands of agriculture and local administration would make this impractical. On the land the seasons wait for no man; a harvest or sowing lost by the absence of the ceorls on campaign meant starvation for everyone. According to the *Anglo-Saxon Chronicle*, Alfred overcame this difficulty by organizing the fyrd so that only half would be serving at one time, while the other half remained at home to cultivate the land and administer justice. In this way, he could plan and fight long campaigns knowing that a second army would be ready to replace the first when that had completed its set period of service and consumed its provisions. The Danish armies had no such relief and could be worn down by keeping them constantly on the move. They were forced at times to withdraw into Wales, or into the Danelaw to recruit. Alfred had probably profited by the long peace after the battle of Edington (878), since the first reference to this reorganization is in 893 when a new Danish invasion struck the country. The system seems certainly to have been in use as late as AD 920. Alfred is said to have used a sixth part of his income for the support of the soldiers and thegns who served at his court. He reorganized his thegns so that they served in rotation, one month in three, at least in peace time.

Although a few earlier charters mention fortifications 'against the pagans', it is only under Alfred and his children, Edward the Elder and Æthelflæd, the Lady of the Mercians, that systematic fortification of strong points began. Probably following the example of the fortified base camps used by the Danes so successfully in the campaigns of 875–7, the Saxons built a series of fortified towns, called *burghs,* both to house garrisons able to sally out and take the offensive independently, and to act as rallying points for the local forces.

One of the three invariable services owed by freemen to the king, the *trimoda necessitas,* was the building of fortifications; presumably it was by this means that Offa's Dyke had been built to mark the border of Mercia and Wales. The defences of the second half of the sixth century recently excavated beside the Saxon royal hall at Old Yeavering, Northumberland, consisted of an outer palisade with a double inner palisade perhaps supporting a fighting platform. Asser, Alfred's biographer, records how slowly and unwillingly the work went forward. The charter of Worcester states quite clearly that the purpose of the burgh was to protect the bishop and churches, 'and to shelter all the folk.'

Between the death of Æthelred of Mercia in 911 and that of Edward the Elder in 924, no fewer than twenty-seven burghs were built. Those that can be identified are almost all strategically placed on important waterways like Oxford, or on a Roman road. Eddisbury in Cheshire, an Iron Age fort, refortified by Æthelflæd in 915, is still identifiable at the junction of Watling Street with the road to Kinderton. Its enclosure is approximately oval and is surrounded by a ditch with a high outer bank and traces of an inner rampart. In some cases it was only necessary to repair the Roman walls, as at London, which Alfred restored in 886. Chester was similarly restored and presumably garrisoned in 908, since it was apparently deserted in 893 when seized by the remains of the Danish army. The burgh of Towcester was provided with stone walls in 920. At Wareham in Dorset, the earthen ramparts were faced with stone in place of the original timber revetment. Rochester and Exeter both successfully stood siege in 885 and 893 respectively. In fact, the failure of the great army brought over by Haesten after his defeat by King Arnulf in 891, may be a measure of the success of Alfred's scheme of fortification. Apparently, no burgh was taken and the *Anglo-Saxon Chronicle* mentions many success-ful sallies by the *burghware,* the town garrison.

As the reconquest of the Danelaw proceeded under Edward the Elder, the Danish towns were captured one by one and, as at Nottingham, refortified and garrisoned with Danes and English. A document of Edward's reign, called the *Burghal Hidage,* records the districts assigned to each burgh under West Saxon rule, while another slightly later document adds to this 'For the maintenance and defence of an acre's breadth of wall 16 hides are required. If every hide is represented by one man, then every pole of wall can be manned by 4 men.' As late as the Domesday Survey the reeve of Chester is recorded as having the right to summon one man from every hide of the shire for the repair of the city wall and the bridge. If any man failed to appear his lord must pay the king and earl a fine of 40 shillings. Some entries in *Domes-day* seem to suggest that settlers were attracted to the new towns by the offer of favourable conditions of tenure.

The building of fortified towns on the Continent began at much the same time. Charles the Bald of France ordered the constructions of fortresses in 862 and the fortification of all towns between the Seine and the Loire in 869. Henry the Fowler, in Germany, who had married his eldest son to Edith, daughter of Edward the Elder, faced with Danes and Mag-yars, also successfully used the foundation of fortified frontier towns to subdue the raiders. The chronicler Widukind records that he ordered that every ninth man of the peasants should live in the new towns and build houses for his fellows, and that a third of the produce of the other eight was to be stored in the towns in case they were forced to take cover there. All markets, meetings, and feasts were to take place in these towns.

In order to meet the Danes at sea and limit their mobility

along the coast, Alfred had special ships built in 896 'almost twice as long as the others. Some had 60 oars, some more. They were both swifter and steadier and also higher than the others.' According to the *Anglo-Saxon Chronicle* they were built neither after the Frisian nor the Danish fashion, but as it seemed to the King that they would be most useful. It is not known how the building of these ships was financed nor how they were manned, but ship-service is occasionally mentioned in *Domesday*. In 1008 King Æthelred ordered a ship to be built by every 300, or possibly 310, hides, and there is other evidence in some counties of groupings of three hundreds, called a *ship-soke,* to provide a ship. In 1003 or 1004 Archbishop Ælfric left in his will three ships, one to the king, one to the people of Kent, and one to the people of Wiltshire. This clearly implies not only that inland counties were liable to provide ships but that 1008 was not the first year in which ships were ordered.

In a number of cases, it is clear from documents that fyrd service was applicable equally to naval or military campaigns and that ships were therefore manned by ordinary soldiers of the fyrd. Occasionally, the obligations differed; Warwick, for instance, sent ten men for a land campaign, but four boat-swains or four pounds if the king led a naval expedition.

The south-coast towns, later known as the Cinque Ports, and a few other ports, had to provide a fixed quota of ships, much in excess of the assessment one would expect, in return for certain special municipal privileges. Æthelred the Un-ready took one of the *Jómsviking* chiefs, Thorkill the Tall, into his service in 1012 together with 45 Danish ships. A mercenary royal navy certainly survived until 1051 when, according to the *Anglo-Saxon Chronicle,* Edward the Con-fessor dismissed the last five of his fourteen ships. There are, however, references to mercenary amphibious warriors, called *lithsmen,* in royal pay manning ships against Earl Godwin in the following year, so possibly the disbandment was only very temporary. The payment of these mercenaries came from the tax called Dane-geld or *Heregeld* (army tax) originally raised to buy off raiders and continued as a permanent tax. No doubt other ships would be provided by the thegns and bishops, since both these classes bequeath warships in their wills.

For a period at least, during the reign of Edgar the Peaceable (959–75), the navy was mustered annually after Easter and manoeuvres took place.

The English Army on the Eve of the Conquest

The spearhead of any Saxon army had always been the personal following of the leaders, whether king or ealdorman, the ancient Germanic war-band. In spite of the mystic bond uniting them, these men were basically mercenaries, serving for reward if not actually for pay. During the reign of Æthelred the Unready (978–1016), the mercenary in its modern sense became much more important. Olaf Tryggavson, later King of Norway, is said to have served him as the leader of a Norwegian war-band in royal pay, and Thorkell the Tall certainly came into his pay. After the Danish conquest by Swein Forkbeard and his son Cnut in 1016, a new element appeared in the mercenary forces. This was the bodyguard of housecarls, probably raised by Cnut in 1018. It was probably modelled on the closely organized Viking fraternity centred at Jómsborg at the mouth of the Oder, reputedly founded by Swein. This consisted of professional warriors of proven valour who had dedicated their lives to warfare and were governed by strict rules of conduct. The housecarls formed a guild or fraternity living at court and receiving the king's pay. They seem to have had their own court to decide, with the king, offences against their code. Their pay came largely from the Dane-geld, and from special taxes paid by certain towns, from payments made in lieu of military service or as fines for failure to come to the army. At least two of Cnut's housecarls received grants of land from him. The housecarls formed a small, but efficient, disciplined, and heavily-armed standing army, and were retained by Edward the Confessor and Harold. The system seems to have been copied in the households of the Earls; Earl Tostig's English and Danish retainers are called housecarls in one version of the *Anglo-Saxon Chronicle,* but here the word may be used in a general sense. There are numerous other references at this time to mercenary troops in the pay of the king or the earls who are clearly not housecarls.

The second part of the English army consisted of those who owed military service because they were land holders. However, presumably in order to improve the quality of the warrior, a system of selective service, parallel to that set up by Charlemagne, has been introduced at some unknown date. A passage in the *Domesday Book* referring to Berkshire, states that 'If the king sent an army anywhere, only one soldier went from five hides, and four shillings were given him from each hide as subsistence and wages for two months. This money, indeed, was not sent to the king but was given to the soldiers.' There is considerable evidence that the basic unit for military assessment in Saxon England consisted of five hides, as with all Saxon fiscal arrangements regardless of the size of the hide which varied greatly from shire to shire. Many towns are assessed for service as estates of five hides or of multiples of five hides. For instance, Malmesbury was assessed at five hides and owed the king either 20 s. to maintain his mercenaries, or one man to serve in the army by land or sea. Colchester, Cambridge, and Shrewsbury, on the other hand, were each assessed at one hundred hides, while Barn-staple, Totnes, and Lidford were grouped together to form a single unit. The normal holding of a thegn in *Domesday* is an estate of five hides, while the ceorl who throve so that he had five hides became worthy of a thegn's wergild. This five hide holding of a thegn seems to go back to early Saxon times. Although, latterly, many thegns had smaller estates than this, they were presumably members of old but declining families, since the rank had become hereditary.

Although many five-hide units were held by thegns who would serve in person, others would be held by two or more poorer thegns or ceorls who would combine to send one of their number to the fyrd. Normally, the man chosen to represent the unit was apparently the same one on each occasion, thus ensuring that he was an experienced warrior who, in his own interest, would equip himself to the best of his ability. If he were unable to go for any reason, then one of the others went in his place.

Where the unit formed one of several on the estate of a wealthy thegn or an abbey, it might be represented in the normal way by one of its ceorls, or by a retainer of the thegn or abbey, or in some cases by a man granted a small holding in return for this service.

The *Rectitudines Singularum Personarum* states specifically that the thegn contributes three things, military service, the repairing of fortresses, and work on bridges, 'in respect of his land', thus showing that the military service of thegns was territorial and not personal as has sometimes been claimed. This is borne out by a case of two brothers, both thegns, who held a single unit for which only one served, and by a document which states that the warrior representative of the five-hide unit 'served as a thegn.'

A similar select service apparently operated in the Dane-law, but was probably based on a fixed number (possibly six) of *curucates,* the area taking the place of the hide in the Saxon area.

Although the period of continuous service was only two months, there is no evidence that the fyrd could not be called out more than once a year in case of necessity. In fact, in 1016, it was summoned five times. Unlike the latter feudal levy, however, it could only be called out 'whenever the need arises' and not for training.

The select fyrd system survived certainly down to 1094 when William Rufus summoned it for service overseas only to confiscate the 10 s. carried by each man, after which he sent them home. Presumably this was the man's subsistence money, and another 10 s., representing the wages mentioned in the *Domesday* passage, would normally have been paid at the end of the campaign. The 20 s. paid by Malmesbury for mercenaries if the one man it owed was not sent to the army seems therefore to represent the normal wage and subsistence of a member of the fyrd. This is the beginning of the commutation of military service for a money payment, later known as *scutage,* which spread over the whole of Europe and finally replaced feudal military service.

It was these two parts of the English army, the housecarls and the representatives of five hides, who rode to battle and which are very occasionally referred to as actually fighting on horseback. Although the *Anglo-Saxon Chronicle* frequently describes the fyrd as pursuing the Danes on horseback (as in 877, 'King Alfred rode after the mounted army with the English army as far as Exeter'), probably the English normally dismounted to fight. At Maldon, for instance, Earl Byrhtnoth rode to the place of battle and marshalled his troops from horseback, but when action was about to begin he sent his horse away, and took his place on foot among his men. His horse cannot have been far away, however, since the poet describes one of his companions escaping from the slaughter on it. The *Chronicle* describes the West Saxons pursuing the Scots 'with mounted companies' after Brunanburh in 937.

The remaining part of the army consisted of the entire body of freemen, all of whom were liable to military service. In a writ of Edward the Confessor to Ramsay Abbey the freemen are defined as 'foldworthy, mootworthy, and fyrdworthy', that is liable to fyrd service. All the burghers of Swansea and Pembroke were obliged to serve at their own expense, but only in their own neighbourhood and only for one day. For longer service the king had to pay them. The service of the general fyrd was local and principally defensive; they rarely served beyond the further boundary of the neighbouring shires. A special form of general fyrd service is traceable on the borders of Wales and Scotland, where the local fyrd was obliged to form the vanguard of the royal army advancing on a frontier campaign and to guard the rear when it was retiring. Doubtless the king valued their experience and local knowledge. This part of the army was not mounted and was presumably lightly armed. The unarmoured English clubmen and archers shown in the Bayeux Tapestry fighting beside their armoured fellows, are probably the general fyrd of Sussex and Kent.

The forces of each shire still fought as separate units. When the fyrds of East Anglia and Cambridgeshire fought against the Danes in 1010, the East Anglians gave way while the Cambridge men stood firm. The king usually led the army himself in early times and desertion was a more serious offence when the king was present: death or a fine equal to the man's wergild, as opposed to 120 shillings if the king was absent. In his absence, an ealdorman or even a bishop might lead the whole army. In 1010 both fyrds were led by Ulfkytel, the ealdorman of East Anglia. From this time the title *eorl,* originally only applied to Scandinavians, began to replace ealdorman. Byrhtnoth, the Saxon leader at Maldon in 991, is called 'ealdorman' by the *Anglo-Saxon Chronicle,* but 'eorl' in the poem *Maldon.* The laws of Edgar (962) state that every shire is to have its ealdorman, but a little later the title became more important and the ealdorman or eorl governs several shires. In 1048 Odda was made Earl of Devon, Somerset, Dorset and Cornwall. Whereas Alfred had had an ealdorman in every West Saxon shire, and two in Kent and four in Mercia, Edward the Confessor's much larger kingdom was divided into only six or seven earldoms. The king's officer in the individual shire was now the shire-reeve *(scir gerefa)* who led the fyrd and held the shire-moot. It is not clear when the office of ealdorman or earl became hereditary. Athelstan Half-king was succeeded about 956 in East Anglia by his son Æthelwold, and the latter by Æthelwine, another son, but a few such instances do not prove that this was a general rule.

Of the service of smaller units within the army, we know very little. From *Domesday* we know that the responsibility of producing the men due from his estates lay with its lord. At the time of the Conquest a certain Eadric is recorded as being steersman of the bishop of Worcester's ship and commander of his troops, and it seems that these served as a distinct unit.

Later Saxon Arms and Armour

The absence of grave-goods in the Christian era means that not a great deal is known about the armour of the later Saxons. The stipulation in the *Law of Wergilds* that a ceorl who prospers so that he possesses a helm, byrnie, and a sword ornamented with gold, but does not have five hides of land on which he pays the king's dues, is still a ceorl, may suggest that a thegn would be expected to have these arms. That eight hides should produce a helm and a byrnie is mentioned in the *Anglo-Saxon Chronicle* under the year 1008, but this seems to be a special requirement for the navy on a single occasion. The spear and the shield remained the principal weapons of all freemen and, judging by manuscript illustrations, the majority of warriors wore neither byrnie nor helm.

The British Museum manuscript of Ælfric's *Paraphrase of the Pentateuch* of about 1050 shows a king wearing a knee-length byrnie split up the front, presumably for ease on horseback (Cotton Ms. Claudius B. iv). It still has short sleeves. He has no helmet and none of his companions wear any armour. On their heads are 'Phrygian' caps with an inverted comb at the back. Goliath, in the *Canterbury Psalter* of about 1000, wears a similar byrnie but has a one-piece conical helm, with a broad nasal and no neck-guard (British Museum, Ms. Harl. 603). A mid-eleventh-century Psalter in the British Museum (Cotton Ms. Tiberius C. vi) twice shows Goliath wearing a conical helm, apparently made up of several segments mounted on a browband. He has no byrnie, but carries a large convex and apparently circular shield with a central boss. The short byrnies of the *Psychomachia* have already been mentioned, and some of the pointed caps in this manuscript could represent conical helms.

The Bayeux Tapestry shows many of the Saxons carrying the same long kite-shaped shield as the Normans (Plate 6). Its use in Saxon England is confirmed by some of the pages of the British Museum's copy of the *Utrecht Psalter* of about AD 1000, which shows kite-shaped shields in place of the round ones of the original (Ms. Harl. 603). The illustrations of Ælfric's *Paraphrase* show the round shield gripped by the centre boss only and held at arm's length, while Cotton Tiberius C. VI. shows what is probably the type of grip on the Sutton Hoo shield, with the fore-arm through a brase.

The main change in the arming of the Saxon warrior was the widespread adoption of the Danish axe. The housecarls fighting around Harold in the Bayeux Tapestry are shown wielding it, and in fact it is used almost as a distinguishing mark of the Saxons in the Tapestry. The only Norman shown holding one of these long fighting axes is Count Guy who had just captured Harold and may well be holding his prisoner's axe: the shaft must be about 1·25 metres long; the great trumpet-shaped head has a crescentic cutting edge, the honed edge shown in a different colour. Earl Godwin's bribe to Hardecanute was a fine ship with eighty warriors with gold helms, spears, and Danish axes. Wace, the chronicler, describing the battle of Hastings, says that when wielding the axe in both hands it was impossible to cover the

Plate 6 A section of the Bayeux Tapestry showing the final attack by the Norman cavalry on the English position at Hastings. A Saxon round shield lies on the ground. Probably English work before 1077. (Reproduced by permission of the Municipality of Bayeux.)

body. Doubtless, the shield would be slung on the back at that time.

The ninth-century Saxon sword has a hilt of different form from earlier ones. The iron guard in front of the hand is much longer and almost always curves towards the blade (Figure 8). The shorter iron bar behind the hand curves away from the blade and is made in one with the three lobed projection which derived from the earlier independent 'cocked hat.' A few are five lobed. Many of these hilts have been found in England and others with characteristic English decoration have found their way to Scandinavia, presumably as trophies of war. The decoration usually consists of applied silver plates chiselled with strapwork, foliage, animals, or chequers. A few hilts with English decoration have the straight bar with several graduated knobs along it like late Frankish pommels. A silver example found in Fetter Lane, London, now in the British Museum, has seven knobs, the central one being much

Figure 8 A reconstruction of a late Saxon sword, based on one in the Ashmolean Museum, Oxford, found at Bog Mill, Abingdon. Probably about 875–900

bigger than the others, and retains half the metal covering to the grip which is deeply engraved with a spiral design of snakes.

In the ninth or tenth century two new pommels appeared, shaped respectively like a tea-cosy, and a brazil nut in its shell. In some cases, the tea-cosy pommel is still marked off as if made of a bar with several lobes on it. Cotton Ms. Tiberius C. VI, of about 1050, shows a number of swords with brazil-nut pommel and long cross-guards curved towards the blade, while Ælfric's *Paraphrase* still shows three-lobed pommels, as well as a circular one. The last probably represents a disc pommel, a few of which have been found in eleventh-century Viking graves in Finland. In these, the end of the tang passes through the pommel as a diameter.

Blades of late Saxon swords are generally similar to those described under the Vikings. No scabbards have survived from the period but a carving in Ebberston Church, near Scarborough, apparently shows a u-shaped chape and a d-shaped locket at the mouth. Manuscript illustrations show the sword hung either on a waist-belt or on a belt slung over the right shoulder.

Duke William is said to have criticised the Saxons for their poor archery, but the use of the bow was certainly not unknown to the English. Traces of bows have been found in graves at Bifrons and Chessel Down together with arrow heads. Archers are frequently illustrated in manuscripts, for instance in Ælfric's *Paraphrase*. The Saxon *Ridle of the Bow* refers to a weapon of war rather than of the chase. Beowulf himself shoots one of the water monsters in Grendelsmere, and at Maldon in 991 the poet mentions the use of the bow. Most of the early bows found in Danish bogs and in German graves are of yew-wood.

The arrows were carried, point downward, in a cylindrical quiver hung on the left hip by a strap over the right shoulder.

Part II

Feudalism and Chivalry

5

Feudalism

The 'Feudal System' in England, as it is taught
in schools, seems fairly simple and consistent, the
result of the imposition by a small conquering minority of a system already developed beyond these shores, and
modified even as it was imposed. But even in England it was
extremely complex, developing fairly rapidly from the hour
of its introduction, modified by the adoption of Saxon law
and custom and by changing conditions within the kingdom,
and even now still open to re-interpretation in many of its
features. On the Continent, however, it differed greatly from
country to country depending on the circumstances under
which it developed. In those areas which have been studied,
custom and feudal law varied widely and it would be quite
impractical to try to cover the whole of Europe except in the
most general terms. Outside northern France and those lands
where feudalism was deliberately imported, England, Sicily
and the Latin Kingdom of Jerusalem, many variations are
found. Almost everywhere else, even in France south of the
Loire, some allodial land remained, that is land held free of
any overlord, and the frequency and complexities of vassalage
varied from place to place. For instance, in parts of the south
of France vassalage was established by a simple oath of fealty,
a promise not to harm the lord or his interests in any way,
without any question of homage; that is, without the cere-

mony of clasping hands and the statement of willingness by the vassal and acceptance by the lord. In northern Italy homage disappeared by the twelfth century and vassalage was established by an oath of fealty only. The special class of unfree knights, called *ministeriales,* found in Germany and the Low Countries, did not perform homage since they were already regarded as the property of their lord.

In Russia, Scandinavia, Castile and León, a few feudal customs were found but the system never developed fully in these lands. Even feudal terminology was not uniform all over Europe. For instance, the word *vavassor* refers in France to a sub-vassal of lowly rank, sometimes serving with incomplete armour; in northern Italy a sub-vassal of the crown; while in England it could imply a freeman owing military service, not necessarily a vassal at all. In northern Italy, the power and organization of the great mercantile cities and the tradition of urban life going back to Roman times always outshone feudalism which is an institution based essentially on land and rural communities. The wealth of the cities overshadowed that of the feudatories. The Italian nobility, many of whom were heavily engaged in trade, tended to live in the towns, sometimes in fortified houses like those of many-towered San Gimignano. Similarly in Germany, relatively free from the devastation of the Norsemen, and with a series of strong kings able to assert themselves and to prevent the chaos which rent France during the disintegration of the Carolingian Empire, a rather different social system developed.

In general, the essence of the system, as we have seen, was protection in exchange for service. Even as late as the fourteenth century the exchange of services between knight and peasant, inherent in the earliest stages of feudalism, was still recognized. The peasant in *Piers Plowman* says that he will

work and sweat for the knight who in turn will protect him
and Holy Church from evildoers, and protect the land from
vermin large and small. In France, the cradle of feudalism,
one can add to this the phrase 'no land without a lord, no lord
without a fief.'

All land was regarded as belonging to the king under God.
The greater nobles, the tenants-in-chief, held their land,
now beginning to be called a *fief* rather than a benefice, in
return for *auxilium* and *consilium;* the duty of serving the
king with a stipulated number of knights *(servicium debitum),*
and the duty of assisting the king with their advice in all
matters on which the king required it. The tenants-in-chief
in turn granted part of their fief to sub-tenants who helped
to make up the quota of knights owed by them to the king, by
personal military service and, if their tenement was large, by
providing an additional fixed number of knights. The lord
in return must protect his vassal, which on the Continent
might mean going to war on his behalf, and defend him in
the courts of law, even in the royal courts. He must also advise
him and maintain him, which usually entailed the granting
of a fief. Many vassals are recorded in France holding very
small fiefs and owing military service less than knight's service,
that is, not fully armed. The vassal without a fief still existed
in the twelfth century and was maintained in his lord's household but was becoming increasingly rare. The centrifugal
force of feudalism was so great in France under the very weak
kings that the dukes and counts managed to force many
originally royal vassals to do homage to them instead. By
the eleventh century the dukes of Burgundy were able to
prevent the building of castles on allods within their sphere
of influence, and the allod had to be converted into a fief held
of the duke before permission was granted.

The land remained the possession of the overlord, to whom

the payment of a 'relief' was due before the heir could take possession. If the tenant died without heirs or failed in his feudal duty, the fief returned to the grantor who could either retain it or grant it to another vassal. The overlord had the right of 'wardship', that is, the right to administer the fief and enjoy its profits during the minority of the heir or heiress, and the right to dispose of him or her in marriage. Similarly, he could dispose of the widow of a tenant in marriage. Two clauses in *Magna Carta* (1215) seek to prevent the abuse of the estates of minors, while another prevents a widow from being forced to remarry against her will. In the Latin Kingdom of Jerusalem, the heiress of a great feudatory was allowed to choose from three suitable candidates for her hand selected by the king. In parts of France wardship was replaced by a system in which a close kinsman of the heir was appointed baillie and did homage and was invested with the fief during the minority. In Germany very high reliefs, fixed arbitrarily, were normal for important fiefs, but for smaller ones relief often consisted of a horse and arms, a practice going back to the return of the gifts made by his lord in the man's lifetime, during the era of the war-bands of early times. By the late twelfth century, relief was fixed in France at one year's revenue of the fief. In England, *Magna Carta* fixed relief for an earl at 100 l. and for a knight at 100 s., and less for those who held less land.

Originally, the lord had the right to an arbitrary tax from his vassals whenever he wished, but this was gradually reduced to the three customary 'aids' which could be demanded at the knighting of the lord's eldest son, the wedding of his eldest daughter for the first time, and to pay his own ransom if he was captured in war. Even these aids were not universal in Italy and the German lands. A similar tax from the unfree was called tallage.

The tenants and sub-tenants had a duty to the peasants on their land to administer justice in the local courts, and to defend them from raiders, robbers, and enemies human and animal, in return for agricultural labour on the lord's own demesne lands, carriage of his goods, and payments of food and produce. The right to administer justice developed from the power of a man to judge his own slaves, from the need to keep order among a lord's dependants, and from simple usurpation of royal rights as the Carolingian Empire broke up. Medieval justice, resting largely upon fines, was profitable to those who administered it. To those judged, justice of any sort is better than no justice at all.

Many offices, such as those of duke, count, and in Germany of some bishops, were held as fiefs, but alongside these were many very minor offices and even duties which were held in this way; for instance the mayor of a town, the constable of a castle, or the right to tolls of a certain bridge or ferry.

The money fief or *fief-rente* was a device by which homage was rendered and stipulated military service was supplied in exchange, not for a fief, but for an annual fixed payment, sometimes secured on a particular tax or custom due. The best known example is the agreement with the Count of Flanders to supply troops to the Norman kings which lasted, with interruptions, until the death of Henry I or even later. This type of vassalage in return for an annuity was much more common later and was found particularly useful by Edward III and his Low Country allies.

Feudalism in Germany

In Germany feudalism was established later than in France. The Norsemen only attacked the area of the lower Rhine, and the period of their raids was relatively short. The greater danger came from the Magyars and Slavs along the eastern borders. Although their raids influenced the development of serfdom and the growth of feudalism even before the reforms of Henry the Fowler (919–36), it was not until the civil wars of the reign of Henry IV (1056–1106), the baronial revolts of the twelfth century, and the weakening of the crown by the Investiture Contest that the power of the nobility was greatly strengthened and many of the freemen peasantry were depressed into servility. The traditional German war leader, the duke *(Herzog),* had survived from tribal times, and his power, together with that of the great church magnates, prevented complete chaos from breaking out, even under weak kings like Ludwig the Child (899–911) and Conrad I (911–18). Although Charlemagne had suppressed the original tribal dukes and replaced them by his own Frankish officials, by the time of Henry the Fowler they had once more become identified with the racial origins of their dukedoms, Franconia, Swabia, Bavaria, and Saxony. The tribal origin of the great dukedoms prevented feudalism becoming as rigid as it did, for instance, in France. The dukes recognized that they held their offices of the king but did not admit to holding their lands from him. Within their dukedoms they coined money, called assemblies, administered justice, and controlled the church, as in Merovingian times.

The nobility always included many who regarded their lands as being allods which they might divide up into fiefs as they liked, without asking leave of the king. These were at first called 'sun fiefs' *(Sonnenlehen)* since they were held free of any earthly overlord, and later 'banner fiefs' *(Fahnlehen)* because investiture was by the gift of a banner. At first only the duchies were of this rank, later margravates, and finally all princely fiefs were conferred in this way. Investiture by means of a banner is illustrated in the manuscript of the *Sachsenspiegel* of about 1360, as well as investiture by means of a glove, also referred to in the *Chanson de Roland*. The *Sachsenspiegel* also illustrates the act of doing homage both singly and in groups, and the subsequent oath on saintly relics (Sächsische Landesbibliothek, Dresden, M. 32).

French-style feudalism, the union of benefice or fief with vassalage and the adoption of the principle of commendation and homage, came later and was always more common in the lands nearest to France. The growth of feudalism was everywhere checked by the existence of the royal officials, dukes, counts, and hundred-men. Otto the Great (936–73) had incorporated into the military hierarchy the bishops and the abbots appointed by the Crown. The Concordat of Worms of 1122 confirmed this by making the princes of the Church princes of Germany with the Pope's approval. The Church magnates were expected to serve in the army in person, and their forces were one of the mainstays of the king. The feudatories, as opposed to the dukes, were forbidden to wage private wars, and were not allowed to coin money. They had only simple jurisdiction within their lands. Under Otto I even the dukes were not immune from the king's justice. The feudal anarchy prevailing in France was considered to be a scandal and the attempt of Henry II to introduce the 'Peace of God' was thought to be an unjust reflection on public law.

Fiefs did not become hereditary until the eleventh century, and although counties had become hereditary by the time of Henry II (1002–24) even the greatest duchies were not absolutely hereditary until the reign of Henry IV. Knights and knighthood were apparently unknown until the twelfth century. The first recorded instance of knighthood being conferred in the German lands is the knighting of the Hungarian king by Conrad III in 1146, possibly in imitation of French practice seen on the Second Crusade.

Very many freemen survived in Germany without dependance on any lord, vassals without fiefs were common until the eleventh century, and the *Heerban,* the levy of all freemen to defend the realm, survived as a fighting force much later than elsewhere. At Bouvines (1214) there were many Saxon freemen fighting on foot. These freemen *(Frîgebur)* who were particularly common in Saxony and Bavaria and rather less so in Swabia and Franconia, had the same wergild as a knight *(Ritter),* acted as jurors as in England, and formed the Heerban.

The main feature distinguishing German feudalism from that of other lands is the *ministerialis,* the unfree knight. Although in England and France vassals could be sold, given away, or bequeathed by the will of their overlords, they remained free in law, and noble; the *ministeriales* did not. They appear to have derived from a superior class of serf who rendered service rather than labour, and in Carolingian times they are found as managers and stewards of estates. Originally their service was essentially non-military, and in 789 Charlemagne ruled that a *ministerialis* who rendered genuine military service was by the very fact made free. As time went on they developed into court officials at both royal and noble courts, because their employment meant that land was not lost by enfeofment, and because of the unreliability of vassals. A serf had the habit of obedience, a free vassal had not. By the twelfth century when the class was fully formed, they are found regularly performing military duties, and their status had become hereditary in fact, if not in law. The Italian expeditions greatly increased the military use of *ministeriales* since the German feudatories were reluctant to serve so far from home. Among south German contingents sent on these campaigns the proportion of vassals decreased from 71 per cent in the period 1096–1146 to 3 per cent in 1191–1240. The balance were *ministeriales*. They made up the majority of the army of Conrad III on the Second Crusade. Their term of service is unknown but it may have been longer than that of knights, which was six weeks without pay with a further period of service on demand after an interval of six weeks.

Under Henry IV (1056–1106) almost all the court officials were *ministeriales*. They were cordially detested for their coarse manners, pride, and petty tyranny. In the twelfth century they began to receive knighthood and to assume titles like nobles from the lands granted to them, and by the end of the century the two classes, the free and unfree nobility, were virtually indistinguishable. In Italy they sometimes held great administrative offices, like Markward of Anweiler who was regent of Sicily and, at the time of his enfranchisement in 1197, was made Duke of Ravenna and Marquis of Ancona.

Society took much longer to stratify in Germany than it did, for instance, in France, partly because of the position of *ministeriales* bridging all ranks, and partly because of the large number of freemen peasants which prevented the growth of the contempt for the peasantry typical of France. Few of the smaller barons had any vassals, their place being taken by *ministeriales,* and those that did had rarely enfeofed them. The barons lived on their estates in unfortified manor houses made possible by the peaceful condition of the country-side. Castles were usually only held by royal officials and were often provisioned and garrisoned at the expense of the king. During the reign of Henry IV, on the other hand, many unlicensed castles were built by rebellious barons or self-seeking *ministeriales*. The long minority of this king and his subsequent quarrel with the Pope over investiture of bishops weakened the royal power, encouraged the centrifugal force of feudalism, and lost him the support of the church so laboriously built up, as a counterweight to the baronage, by Conrad II (1024–39). This king had done what he could to undermine the growing power of the great barons by recognizing the hereditary nature of fiefs held by sub-vassals in Germany and legalising it in Italy. This gained him the sympathy and support of the sub-vassals and weakened the grip on them of the tenants-in-chief, but at the same time encouraged the fragmentation of Germany.

In the late eleventh century Benzo of Alba suggested that Henry IV should replace feudal military service by a tax similar to scutage, and employ a mercenary army. The same suggestion was made after the battle of Bouvines in 1214 but mercenaries never seem to have played a major part in German armies until late in the Middle Ages. Instead, kings like Henry V (1106–25) and Frederick I of Hohenstaufen (1152–90) relied on their great personal wealth and family connections to provide themselves with vassals and allies. The fall of Henry the Lion, Duke of Saxony, in 1181, weakened the traditional power of the ancient dukedoms and allowed the emergence of many small feudal states. The fall of the Hohenstaufen family in the thirteenth century prevented a strong kingship from growing up, as in France and England. The centrifugal forces of feudalism took over. Vassals became independent of their overlords, and the condition of Germany began to resemble that of France under the later Carolingians.

Feudalism in England

The Norman conquest of England introduced feudalism to these islands with several modifications, some apparently intended to improve on the system operating in Normandy,

others as the result of the adoption of existing Saxon instruments of government. Of the 5,000 or so knights who formed
the expeditionary force, only about half were Normans and
the remainder were Frenchmen, Bretons, Aquitanians, and
Flemings serving as mercenaries or seeking their fortunes.
William's own tenants refused to follow him as such, since
feudal service was not obligatory outside the realm, and only
the promise of conquered lands induced them to set out. As
no prior feudal obligation to his own men existed, and as
eventually all the important English landowners were dis-
possessed, William was able to make a fresh start and introduce a more or less uniform system over the whole country,
and to modify such Continental customs as he found dangerous. Since the loyalty of his men was at first assured because
their future depended on his holding his new kingdom successfully, he could impose on them any conditions he thought
necessary. Private wars between his barons, limited in
Normandy, were forbidden in England, and quarrels between
them had to be brought to his courts. Private warfare was
not successfully suppressed in France until the reign of St
Louis (1226–70). William partitioned out the land to something under 200 great lords, many of them his tenants-in-
chief in Normandy, in return for the services of a stipulated
number of knights, often apparently in fives or multiples
of five. The Church was granted land in return for the service
of some 780 knights, allocated to abbeys, cathedrals, monasteries, and churches, exactly as if they were lay land-holders.
The quotas were larger than the equivalent ones in Normandy
and were entirely at the disposal of the king, unlike the custom
of the Duchy, where only a fraction of the knights enfeofed
on an estate was due to the duke and even fewer to the overlord, the king of France. The Bayeux Inquest of 1133 shows
that of the knights owing military service to the Bishop of

Bayeux only one-sixth owed service to the duke and only one-twelfth to the king of France. Varying periods of service by half-armed knights, common in Normandy and elsewhere, were apparently unknown in England. The King himself kept the largest single group of estates in his own hands, and he placed his most trusted lieutenants in the key positions; his half-brother Bishop Odo of Bayeux, for example, at Dover, the main Channel port, and William fitz-Osbern at Hereford to guard the Welsh Marches.

The tenants-in-chief each received many manors scattered up and down the land. There seem to have been three reasons for this; firstly, because the country was only conquered piecemeal; secondly, because the only estates confiscated at first were those of Saxons who had fought at Hastings or been slow to submit, and it was only after the great revolt of 1069 that wholesale confiscation of Saxon lands took place; thirdly, because in some cases one Norman might be given the lands held by a single Saxon before the Conquest, and these might not necessarily have been all in one shire. Geoffrey Alselin held the entire lands of the thegn Toki, son of Outi, scattered all over the Danelaw. These lands were held by Geoffrey for the same dues paid by Toki to King Edward, as well as for military service. In a very few cases Saxon landholders were allowed to buy back their land, in others they became sub-tenants under a Norman lord. In the case of some of the most important baronial castles the bulk of the estates of its lord were grouped round it to form a *castellaria* for its support, although other estates belonging to its lord might be scattered all over England. An example of this is the 'honour' of Henry de Ferrars for the maintenance of Tutbury Castle on the border of Derbyshire and Staffordshire, with 114 estates in Derbyshire and eight in Staffordshire, and lands more scattered and less numerous in twelve other shires. The fiefs of great continental barons were also scattered, though in this case by the accidents of their acquisition over a very long period rather than by any plan imposed by their sovereigns. The estate of a Norman was usually called his 'fee', that is, the land with which he was enfeofed, and if an important one held by a tenant-in-chief it was called his 'honour.' Although normally referred to as 'Normans' many of the new settlers of all ranks were French, Flemish, or Breton.

Apparently no system was laid down as to how the tenants-in-chief were to produce their *servicium debitum*. Some hired knights, when the king required them, from the many landless younger sons seeking their fortunes and hoping to win a knight's fee of their own in return for services. Others kept knights permanently in their households to escort them from manor to manor in their travels between England and Normandy and to guard their castles. As the land settled down and the danger of an English rising receded, the necessity for keeping large numbers of household knights grew less, and the great majority of lords granted parts of their estates to lesser barons or to individual knights in return for their military service. Even as late as 1166, the *Cartae Baronum* shows some honours with insufficient enfeofed knights to complete their quotas, indicating that household knights or pure mercenaries must have been employed to make up the required numbers. Church magnates must have found it particularly irksome to have rough knights permanently quartered in their halls, but equally they were unwilling to lose control of land by enfeofment. Originally these grants of land were apparently not hereditary; the earliest three charters confirming enfeofment of this sort, all of the reign of William I, stipulate that the grant is for one life only, although one is to the son of the previous holder and this particular holding is known to have become hereditary in this family at a later date. By the reign of Henry I the knight's fee normally descended to the heir without question.

The sub-vassal holding several knight's fees in the honour of a great tenant-in-chief stood in a similar relation to his lord as the lord did to the king. He helped to administer the honour, filling the baron's subordinate offices as steward, marshal, butler, or constable, as the great barons did at the royal court, advising in the honour-court, and leading his own *servicium debitum* to join that of his lord when summoned to do so. It was probably from this class, as well as from minor tenants-in-chief, that the officer known in the fourteenth century as the 'banneret' was originally drawn.

The annual period of military service for knights in France, Normandy, and northern Italy, recorded in many documents, was 40 days in peace or war. In England, however, only one document mentions the length of service for knights, and this is a grant made about 1140 by none other than the King's Marshal, John fitz-Gilbert, of a fief in return for knight's service for two months in time of war and 40 days in time of peace, and the wording suggests that this was customary. Since it is not normally stated, the period of service may have been so well known as not to need stating and this particular grant may therefore refer to an exceptional period. However, the period served by the pre-Conquest fyrd was certainly also two months, and if this was continued after the Conquest the period of service by knights could very well have been made to conform with it. Castle guard, another knightly service, at Richmond Castle, Yorkshire, is also recorded as being for two months. Later in the twelfth century the period was probably reduced to the 40 days customary elsewhere, as sergeants and infantry of the shire are both recorded as serving for this period by the end of the

century. In France, but apparently not in England, the tenant
of a fraction of a knight's fee sometimes served for the same
fraction of 40 days; the holder of half a fee would serve for
20 days.

In 1086, late in his reign, William I ordered an oath of
personal fealty to himself to be taken at Salisbury, by, or on
behalf of, all landholders of any account, regardless of who
their overlord might be. He realised that the normal oath of
fealty of a sub-vassal to his lord, which excluded his duty to
the king, was insufficient to prevent the sub-vassal from
following his lord if the latter revolted. It is unlikely that a
knight of that period, still a fairly insignificant person socially,
would have been considered of sufficient importance to be
called to the oath taking, and probably only the larger sub-
vassals were summoned.

This personal oath to the king was repeated on a number of
later occasions, most important of which was the oath of 1166
when Henry II ordered a survey to be made of the state of
the knighthood of the kingdom, so that all those knights who
had not yet done homage to him might do so before a certain
date. He asked his tenants-in-chief how many knights each
had enfeofed on his estates at the time of the death of Henry I,
how many were enfeofed at the time of writing, and how
many more had to be provided to fulfil their *servicium
debitum*. The answers to this survey were recorded in the
Cartae Baronum. One result of this was an increased assessment
of the quotas in 1168. In fact, in many cases many more
knights had been enfeofed than were due. As early as 1135
the Bishop of Durham had enfeofed 64 knights although his
servicium debitum was only ten; however, this may have
been because of the need to defend the frontier from
Scottish raids.

Alongside knight's tenure was also tenure by sergeanty *(in sergentaria)*: tenure by some specified service less than knight's service and very often rendered personally to the lord. It might be a purely civilian service such as keeping a hawk or hound for the king, providing the table-cloths for a specific animal feast, or providing the king with a meal of roast pork when he hunted in Wychwood; on the other hand it might be military service such as carrying the king's banner on campaign in Wales, or leading the forces of the hundred in which the man lived. Some tenants in sergeanty did actually owe the service of a knight to the army but this was exceptional. The characteristic of the service is that it differs from sergeant to sergeant and, therefore, unlike knight's service, must be fully described in any grant. Where the service was military it was normally for 40 days at the expense of the sergeant, although shorter periods are also recorded. One sergeant was to provide an infantryman for service in Wales supplied with a side of bacon; when this was eaten he was free to go home. Some sergeants had to provide horsemen, others footmen, and the supplying of bowmen and crossbowmen is also recorded. In 1213 John's summons of the army to Dover included the *servientes* and implied that they were to serve mounted, but the sergeants of the French demesne recorded in the *Prisia Servientum* of 1202–3 were infantry. Sergeants from fairly early times were able to serve by proxy and by the thirteenth century they had very often commuted their service for a money payment.

The medieval chronicler frequently described the lower ranks of the army as sergeants *(servientes)* but this includes many more than the tenants in sergeanty. These would be present in the army without doubt; the military sergeants fulfilling their tenurial obligations, the others serving because of the personal obligation of all freemen to do so. The towns and ecclesiastical tenants of the Latin Kingdom of Jerusalem are described by John of Ibelin as owing the service of 5,025 sergeants in time of great need and within the realm. In some cases these may have been lightly armed horsemen and horse-bowmen. William of Tyre, writing about 1170–80. refers to lightly armed horse.

As far as mounted sergeants are concerned, it is normally assumed that they were less well armed than the knights, and it is true that they are occasionally encountered on campaign carrying out reconnaissances, a traditional light cavalry role, and in later documents the service of two sergeants is frequently equated with that of one knight. Fees in sergeanty were occasionally changed to half a knight's fee, and knight's fees were sometimes commuted for the service of two ser-geants. For instance, the muster rolls for the campaign in Wales in 1245 show that the services of two sergeants might be accepted in place of those of a knight. Nevertheless, chroniclers describe sergeants as taking part with the knights in cavalry actions, and they must therefore have been similarly equipped.

The *servientes armorum* (sergeants-at-arms) were raised, apparently by Philip Augustus, to act as a body-guard against the Assassins on the Third Crusade. They were later copied by most European kings and can normally be identified in medieval paintings by the maces they carry. Although originally a guard, their constant presence around the king meant that he inevitably used them as messengers to deliver his orders, and also to carry them out. At a time when few people could read, the royal arms on their mace was their means of identification and thus the weapon itself became the sign of their royal authority. By the fourteenth century the French royal sergeants' maces were silver mounted and had the royal arms enamelled on them.

As well as these Norman innovations, William I also used

Saxon institutions of government which were more highly developed than those on the Continent; the writ – the king's formal letter of instructions – the shire- and hundred-courts, and the excellent Saxon coinage, as well as the annual tax, the Danegeld. Norman barons were given office as sheriffs, and until the revolt of 1069 many Englishmen were employed in high office; like Earl Morcar of Northumbria. The most important English institution William used was the pre-feudal military organization, comprising the right to call upon the service of every freeman in time of war, the selective service by which those who stayed at home equipped and paid the man who served on their behalf, and the summons of the force by a writ to the sheriff. This force, later known as the shire levy, together with similar levies from the towns, augmented the feudal army and could be used against over-powerful tenants-in-chief even if they had called out their sub-vassals against the king.

Although William had forbidden his barons to fight each other, they were violent men unused to such restraint, and his own reign and those of his sons were disturbed by numerous baronial wars and revolts. Saxon thegns and freemen fought for the king alongside his loyal feudatories in the baronial revolts, such as that of Eustace of Boulogne in 1067 and of the Earls of Hereford and East Anglia in 1075. As early as 1068 Englishmen were fighting against the forces of Harold's sons, and the commander of the forces of Somerset on that occasion was Eadnoth, who had been one of King Edward's household officers. In the following year the men of London, Salisbury, and Winchester were employed in putting down a revolt in Somerset and Dorset. The chronicler Ordericus Vitalis again and again describes Englishmen fighting for the king against rebels. The continuation of pre-Conquest military institutions is shown for instance by the *Domesday*

Book, which in several places refers to military service owed by ordinary sub-tenants at the time of King Edward's death and still owed at the time of the survey. There are a number of references to the duty of serving by land and sea which suggests a survival of the Saxon ship-fyrd obligation. The right to collect *fyrdwite,* the fine for failure to serve in the fyrd, is mentioned in post-Conquest documents. A number of small land-holders holding by sergeanty are recorded as doing so in return for leading the local forces or carrying the banner of their hundred. The large numbers of Englishmen summoned for service in 1094 were infantry and were almost certainly representatives of the select fyrd, since they each had 10 s. which the king took from them and which, it has been suggested, was their subsistence money mentioned in the Berkshire passage in *Domesday.* Englishmen, as distinct from Anglo-Normans, certainly served in France in the campaign of 1078 against Fulk of Anjou, when Ordericus speaks of '*Normannos et Anglos*' and also records the name of one, Toki, son of Wigot of Wallingford, present at the siege of Gerberoi. The presence of men of the fyrd in France is explained by the early twelfth-century *Leis Willelmi* which lay down that freemen are obliged to serve beyond the seas. The disappearance of select service is unrecorded but the basis of fyrd service, the obligation of all freemen to serve the king in time of war, remained to be incorporated in the Assize of Arms of 1186. The development of the Anglo-Norman feudal army of later periods was greatly influenced by the incorporation of the Saxon military system.

Although a somewhat similar organization existed on the Continent, the *arrière-ban,* which could be summoned in time of war, William cannot have failed to have been impressed by the quality of the Saxon select fyrd at Hastings. In France the *arrière-ban* seems to have been called out only very occasionally, and, untrained and probably poorly armed, seems to have been of little use against cavalry. The king of France was forced to rely on the men of his own demesne lands and such vassals as remained loyal when a revolt broke out.

What evidence there is shows that the English continued to fight as infantrymen and, in fact, their methods influenced the Normans, since at Tinchebrai (1106) the Normans dismounted to fight, and at the Standard (1138) the north countrymen and the Norman knights stood shoulder to shoulder on foot, almost like Harold's army at Hastings.

6

Organization

Homage

By the middle of the eleventh century men were holding fiefs from more than one lord, and to overcome the difficulty of doing homage to several people the concept of liege homage developed. Liege homage was done to a principal lord, in some areas to the first lord to make a grant, in others to the one who granted the largest fief; homage to other lords was done excepting the allegiance to the liege lord. Since personal service to each lord was impossible, the commuting of the service for money became inevitable. By the reign of Henry I every contract of vassalage in England reserved the allegiance to the king, so that eventually liege homage there became entirely royal, as it did in France generally by the thirteenth century. In Germany, Frederick Barbarossa (1152–90) tried unsuccessfully to introduce liege homage, but sub-infeudation without it continued and eventually was one of the reasons for the fragmentation of Germany.

Although allods were normally divisible between heirs, important fiefs usually passed complete to the nearest male heir, or, in some areas, to a member of the family appointed by the overlord. In Normandy and France a system called *parage* existed; the fief was divided between the heirs but was held of the overlord by the senior heir on behalf of his co-heirs, who aided him in supplying his *servicium debitum* but did not do homage themselves. In the German lands all the heirs were enfeofed and invested together. Both systems broke down because of the enormous complexity of tenures which developed after a few generations. Minute fractions, such as one-ninetieth of an estate, are known, and sub-vassalage through as many as nine overlords. In England, the Justiciar, Rannulf de Glanville, laid down that lands held by military service passed to the eldest son complete. The statute *quia Emptores* of 1290 was intended to stop sub-infeudation; land alienated by a freeman was to be held by the new tenant directly from the last tenant's overlord.

Service

Several different forms of service by knights are found on the Continent. For instance, while the Count of Hainault as vassal of the Bishop of Liège had to serve with all his men, both horse and foot, in France and Normandy, on the other hand, the *servicium debitum* was rather small in proportion to the size of the estates. In both countries tenants are found owing small quotas to the sovereign for service with the army *(in exercitu* or *service d'host)* for a period of 40 days, and rather larger quotas for a similar period to their immediate overlord, both these quotas being very much less than the full number of knights they had enfeofed. The Inquest of Bayeux of 1133 records that these reduced quotas served at the expense of the full body of enfeofed knights, and therefore not at the expense of their lord or over-lord. This is a parallel development to the select-fyrd support system in England, although it is also recorded there, since the four knights who served for Reading Abbey were supported by all the other tenants. The full number of knights enfeofed by the Bishop of Bayeux only served on a summons to war *(pro bello nominato* or *nomine belli)*, that is when the *arrière-ban*, the full levy of freemen, was called out in a national emergency, and they then served as freemen rather than as feudatories.

In theory at least, the tenant-in-chief could only summon all his enfeofed knights for a more limited form of service *(service de chevauchée)* unless he had a royal summons; and, according to the Inquest of Bayeux, the tenants of the Bishop, who were said to be liable to this service whenever the Bishop required it, claimed that they then served at his expense. Since private wars were forbidden in England, this type of service, when it occurs there, must have been confined to escort and guard duty about a baron's person or family; but no doubt it would be used illegally in time of revolt. The English marcher lords apparently also had the right of calling out their tenants *in exercitu*, since they might be called upon to repel raiders at any time.

The Bayeux Inquest also refers to the service of tenants holding 50 or 60 acres or more, serving in time of national emergency, mounted and with lance, shield, and sword. These were tenants holding less than a knight's fee and there-fore not considered capable of producing a hauberk, and no armour was therefore mentioned for them. Whenever arms and armour were stipulated in a medieval ordinance the minimum permitted requirement was given. Probably many of these tenants would try to supply themselves with at least a hauberk. These men would probably have been referred to by Chroniclers as mounted sergeants *(servientes)*, the word loosely used for those of the cavalry below the rank of knight and very often for the ordinary infantryman as well.

Although in the fourteenth century there are an increasing number of references to uniformly dressed bodies of troops, it is probable that some baronial contingents were dressed

in the livery of their lord at a much earlier date. There is a
reference in 1218 to a robber chief buying 100 marks of cloth
to clothe his men as if he were a baron or earl.

Castle-guard

Apart from the duty of serving in the field, knights were
also obliged to serve as garrisons for particular royal and
baronial castles. Originally, these obligations were probably quite separate. A castle needed its garrison most at the
very moment that the field army had to be called out.
Obviously a knight could not be expected to do both duties
at once. Certainly in Germany, in some areas of France, and
in Normandy, the duty of castle-guard fell on the social
group below that of knights. In England too, townspeople
are recorded as owing castle-guard, as at Portchester, and
tenants in sergeanty also very often owed it. Of course, in
most cases it would not be necessary to garrison all castles.
For a campaign in Wales, only the border fortresses needed
to be manned, and the knights due to other castles far from the
seat of war could serve with the field army. In moments of
danger, many more knights and sergeants could be sent to
reinforce a garrison made up of men owing castle-guard.
The need to strip castles of their garrisons to produce a large
enough army to resist invasions was particularly marked in
the Latin Kingdom. When Balian of Ibelin arrived at the
Castle of La Fève during a Saracen raid on the area, he could
find only two men (both sick) in the building. After the disaster at the Horns of Hattin (1187) Balian, called upon to
organize the defence of Jerusalem, found only two knights
left in the city.

The evidence is very incomplete, but there are a number
of certain cases in England where the duty of both serving

in the host and doing castle-guard are stipulated. The knights of the Abbey of Bury St Edmunds garrisoned Norwich Castle and, at a later date, Bury Castle, as well as owing host-duty. Elsewhere, castle-guard excluded any other military service unless it was paid for, as, for instance, the Count of Eu's 60 knights who formed the garrison of Hastings Castle but did no service outside the county, unless taken into the Count's pay. Sometimes, an honour might owe a large quota of knights to guard a particular castle and a smaller quota for host-services, but sometimes the reverse was true. For instance, the Earl of Salisbury owed 40 knights for host-duty but only 20 for garrison-duty at Salisbury Castle. Some of these variations may be due to unrecorded service at the baron's own castle, in addition to the recorded service at the royal castle. Probably there was a good deal of resistance to having to do both services and in *Magna Carta* it is stated that 'A knight taken or sent on military service shall be excused castle-guard for the period of this service.'

The duration of the service differed from castle to castle. In a few early cases on the Continent, service seems to have been perpetual, but in England it varied from the three months served in rotation by the knights of Bury St Edmunds and of the Count of Eu, to the 15 days owed by the knights serving at Dover, although some of these short periods were served more than once a year. Elsewhere, duty was for 40 days, and sometimes it was stated that it was due only in time of war. The rotation of service ensured that a fraction of the knights were always on duty; for instance, the 40 Bury knights served in Norwich Castle 10 at a time for a quarter of the year. Some 200 knights in all were due to this castle.

Commuted castle-guard is recorded as early as the reign of Henry 1 and became general by the end of the twelfth century, although *Magna Carta* lays down that a knight willing to serve must not be forced to commute. The evidence that the payment for commuting the service was actually the sum necessary to hire a substitute is rather stronger for castle-guard than it is for host-duty. Fees owing 15 days duty each year at Dover commuted at the rate of 10 s., while those owing two 15 day periods commuted at 20 s. These sums are sufficient to pay a replacement for the correct period at 8 d. a day, which is in fact known to be the pay of knights serving in Dover Castle in 1165. Unfortunately, those figures that survive for other castles do not bear out this theory, and elsewhere it may be that the payments were fixed by agreement between lord and vassal made at different periods.

It is difficult to discover the size of wartime garrisons. The peacetime garrison of Norwich seems to have been some 50 knights, but in 1075 it was 300 knights and sergeants with some additional archers, while in 1193 it was some 75 knights and sergeants. Both were times of revolt, but in 1075 Norwich Castle had only just been recaptured by the royal forces. When Framlingham surrendered in 1216, the garrison included 26 knights, 20 sergeants, and seven crossbowmen. At Richmond in Yorkshire, the list of fees owing castle-guard shows that the garrison was made up of 186 knights divided into six groups, varying from 26 to 42 in number, each of which served for two months. The smaller groups served in the winter when raids were unlikely, the larger ones in the summer during the raiding season. The garrison at Hastings Castle in peacetime was 15 knights. The Castle of Odiham in Hampshire was held against the French invaders in 1216 by three knights and ten sergeants.

Scutage

As soon as the knight's fee became hereditary it might pass

to someone too young to serve, or to a woman, or be divided between heirs; and, in any case, the knight might become too old to serve. It therefore became customary to pay a sum of money, called *scutage* (i.e. shield money), in place of personal military service so that the king could hire mercenary soldiers. A grant of a third part of a knight's fee in Warwickshire on payment of 20 s. annually, is recorded about 1125. This payment was quite distinct from the fines for failure to serve in the *arrière-ban* or fyrd which were charged of all freemen and not only of knights. By the end of the Confessor's reign a few towns like Malmesbury were already commuting their military service for a money payment. Commutation of military service is recorded in Germany in the eleventh century, and of *arrière-ban* service from townsmen in France in the twelfth century. Scutage was certainly being paid in England in the reign of Henry I and is mentioned in a charter to the monastery of Lewes in 1100, while a charter of 1130 implies that scutage was already being paid in the reign of William Rufus. By the late twelfth century it was absolutely normal in Normandy and England, and demanded whenever a campaign was in preparation. In John's reign, tenants by sergeanty in England were also commuting their services. By the end of the thirteenth century scutage was also general in France. It was not an annual tax like the Danegeld but was apparently demanded by the king only when he required troops for a campaign. Compulsory peace-time service by knights seems to have disappeared by the second half of the twelfth century, apparently without commutation. Scutage was demanded by the king from his tenants-in-chief who collected it from their vassals, not only those of knightly class but from those holding minute portions of fees. In the reign of Stephen there is a reference to a man who was obliged to pay 24 d. when scutage was 20 s. on the fee. If scutage was

demanded at a different rate his contribution altered proportionately. This sort of payment of scutage by people not
liable to feudal military service became increasingly common
as scutage became a normal tax rather than a military one.
Scutage was demanded and paid not only on the knights of
the *servicium debitum* but also on any additional enfeofed
knights, but this seems to have been successfully resisted over
a period of time.

   Richard fitz-Nigel, the Treasurer, writing during the
reign of Henry II, specifically states that scutage was levied
to provide payment for soldiers, but it is not certain whether
this can be taken to mean that it was precisely the sum required
to pay a substitute. Although this is certainly true of the scutage
assessments fixed by Philip III of France in 1274, the evidence
for England a century earlier is not clear, since the wages of
a knight increased from 6d. to 1s. a day during the century,
and scutage was demanded at different rates on different
occasions, varying between 2 marks (26/8d.) and 1 mark
during the reign of Henry II. Furthermore, the time of wartime service due from English knights in the twelfth century
is not known for certain. Towards the end of the century
scutage was normally demanded at a lower sum than earlier,
although prices were rising all the time, and by that date it
cannot possibly have hired a replacement.

Mercenaries

Mercenary troops *(stipendiarii* or *solidarii),* men serving for
pay without any feudal link, with or without a tribal or
national link with their employer, formed an important part
of most Anglo-Norman armies. The Normans themselves
had entered Apulia as mercenaries of whichever side was
prepared to pay the better. After the Conquest many Saxons

made their way to Byzantium to take service under the Eastern Emperor. The army led by Duke William in 1066 included large numbers of mercenaries, many of whom were not disbanded until 1070 when the first wave of English revolts was over, and the Duke was reported to have paid them off liberally. On this occasion, as on many others, it was necessary to employ them because feudal service outside the realm was not obligatory. The time limit set on *servicium debitum* made mercenaries essential for prolonged campaigns, since the only limit set on their employment was the depth of their employer's purse. Almost certainly the enfeofed knight-hood decreased in efficiency as time went on and as the knights became involved in civil administration, and professional soldiers were presumably more satisfactory on campaign.

In England, where resistance to overseas service was very strong, and where, in order to cross the Channel, the concentration of ships had to be synchronised with the concentration of the army, the use of mercenaries for Continental campaigns was very common. The continued use of the Danegeld, an annual tax unique in western Europe, levied at a rate of 2s. on the hide, gave the kings of England the ability to hire mercenaries in very large numbers. In time of revolt, kings like Henry I and John relied heavily on their mercenaries, since they were uncertain of the loyalty of even those vassals who rallied to them. Their use by John was one of the barons' complaints against him, and *Magna Carta* stipulated that all mercenaries should be removed from the kingdom. Danegeld died out during Stephen's reign, and was only briefly revived by Henry II.

Mercenaries can be divided into three types. Firstly, there were the household knights of kings and barons, particularly of barons with under-enfeofed estates. The Bishop of Worcester, for instance, preferred to keep a large number of household knights, probably because of the risk of losing control of land by enfeofing it. The household knights of the English kings developed in the fourteenth century, not only into a small body of household cavalry augmented by sergeants of the royal household, but also into a head-quarter staff for the organizing of campaigns, and a cadre of officers from which field commanders could be drawn. Secondly, there were professional soldiers domestic and foreign, hired for the duration of a campaign. In northern Europe the Low Country infantry, particularly those from Brabant, were among the most sought after. The men of this province are said to have acquitted themselves particularly well at Bouvines in 1214. During the twelfth century Wales became an important recruiting ground for Anglo-Norman armies. Mercenaries were also hired by barons, either for use against the king or for independent overseas expeditions, like those of Strongbow into Ireland when he was accompanied by many Welsh infantry archers. In some cases mercenaries of this kind might be enfeofed at the end of the campaign, like those of the Abbey of Peterborough, originally hired to put down Hereward the Wake. As time went on, all knights began to receive pay if they were required to serve longer than the stipulated period of their feudal service. By the late twelfth century, knights in parts of Normandy and France began to be paid even for their 40 days service. By 1208 a grant of land in Peebleshire was given in return for 12d. at Martinmas, and mounted service in the royal army, but the grantor was to find food for man and beast on campaign and replace the horse if it was killed. Thirdly, there were the armies of subsidized allies, which may or may not have had a feudal link. The money-fief granted to the Count of Flanders in return for knight's service is an example of this where a feudal link is certain. In 1100 the agreement was for the service of 1,000 knights for a fief of 500 l. per annum. The crucial cavalry charge at Tinchebrai (1106) was made by squadrons from Maine and Brittany led by their own counts. The Count of Brittany was a vassal of Henry I, but the Count of Maine does not seem to have been one.

Mercenary troops, together with the Military Orders, formed the backbone of the forces of the Latin Kingdom once it was fully established, since there were never enough feudatories to defend the land. Inter-marriage causing the amalgamation of fiefs, a high rate of infant mortality, and constant devastation of fiefs by raiders, all combined to prevent the growth of a strong feudal force. John of Ibelin, Count of Jaffa, gives the total number of knights in the kingdom in the time of Baldwin IV (1174–85) as 577, excluding the knights of the Military Orders. The native population, with the exception of the Armenians, were not particularly good soldiers. Mercenaries therefore, always formed a considerable part of the Latin armies. The greater part of the army lost at Hattin (1187) had been hired with the money sent out by Henry II of England.

The pay of soldiers varied from time to time, and according to the quality of the troops, and how they were equipped. The pay of knights at the beginning of the twelfth century in England was probably 6d. a day. During the period 1162–8 they were certainly paid at a rate of 8d. a day, while by 1173 this had risen to 1s. By 1205 it was 2s. a day, although Richard I claimed in 1198 that mercenary knights would cost him 3s. a day. In 1136 mounted sergeants were being paid 3d. a day, at a time when knights were probably paid 6d; and since they are frequently equated with half a knight one would expect their wages to be half those of a knight during the century. Richard I paid his Welsh infantry on campaign in France 2d. or 3d. a day, and Welsh light horse 4d. or 6d. a day.

Military Command

The great military officers of the Crown – the Seneschal, Constable, and Marshal – all derive from household officers of early kings. The Seneschal, originally meaning 'old servant', later rendered into Latin as *dapifer* (one who bears things at a feast) and into English as steward, became in course of time an hereditary officer holding the chief command in the royal household, and acting as the king's agent, and deputising for him in the royal courts. In the eleventh century the Seneschal was commander-in-chief of the forces of the French crown, but the abuse of the office by the Garlande family led to their suppression in 1127 by Louis VI. Thereafter, the appointment was made for life only and generally given to a great feudatory closely connected to the king by blood. After the death of Thibaut de Blois in 1191, the office was allowed to remain vacant except for special appointments made for coronation ceremonies. Some of the great feudatories in France had seneschals of their own, and in a few cases the office survived the reabsorption of the fief by the Crown, as it did for instance in Poitou.

The Constable derives from the count of the stable *(comes stabuli)*, a name borrowed by the Franks from Byzantium. In the eleventh century this officer was found commanding troops under the Seneschal, and when the latter disappeared the Constable took over much of his work. By the thirteenth century the Constable of France led the van of the royal army and in the following century became commander-in-chief. The post was never hereditary in France but sometimes was in the case of constables of vassals; the Crespin family, for instance, were hereditary Constables of Normandy. The office was introduced to England by the Anglo-Norman kings but, unlike the French Constable, it was not superior to that of the Marshal. Although Constables are occasionally recorded as commanding troops in English armies, they were not at first military officers, and in these cases were commanding because they were also barons. Their official task, as it still is in Scotland, was the maintenance of order in the neighbourhood of the court and the protection of the king's person and household. Their later military functions apparently developed from their carrying out these duties in the royal camp. When Edward III set up the Court of Chivalry, the Lord High Constable and the Earl Marshal presided in cases of crimes committed by knights, and of other military affairs, such as the organization of trials by combat and tournaments. The Earl Marshal sat alone, as he still does, in cases relating to heraldry.

The Marshal, originally meaning only 'horse servant', referred in Merovingian times to the Master of the Horse, an officer below the Constable in rank. Later it became associated with military command probably, like the Constable, because of the duty of keeping order in the camp. By the twelfth century the Marshal had apparently taken over the Constable's command in the field, at least in English armies when the office became hereditary in the Marshal family. In France the office never became hereditary. The official title in England was changed to Earl Marshal by a grant of 1386. Officers called *marescalci campi*, subordinate to the Marshal, preceded the army on the march to choose a suitable site for the camp and to allocate to the various nobles places to pitch their pavilions.

In general, as far as can be discovered, the army at this time was normally divided up in the field into the quotas of the great tenants-in-chiefs and commanded by them in person or by a deputy, one of their sub-barons. Early crusading armies were normally divided into groups consisting of the men of one nation, which is only an extension of the tenant-in-chief idea. The native infantry in England were apparently sometimes commanded by tenants of the crown holding their lands by performing this service. A constable was sometimes appointed to organize and lead the contingent of a churchman unless, like Odo of Bayeux and Adhemar of le Puy, he was also a warrior. In spite of the ruling of the Synod of Westminster of 1175 that the clergy should not bear arms or wear armour, a number of abbots led their *servicium debitum* in person at the siege of Windsor in 1193, and chroniclers continued to be scandalised by fighting clerics for many years. In 1369 Edward III summoned all the men of his kingdom, whether clerics or laymen, to take up arms against a French invasion. Even as late as 1513 the young Archbishop of St Andrews was among the dead at Flodden.

The title of constable was in fact used very loosely for the commanders of troops, castles, and even ships, but by the end of the twelfth century the word constabulary seems to have been applied to a definite field force. Fines are recorded for knights absent from their constabulary. In 1196 William Marisco is mentioned as constable of 500 Welsh infantry and this seems to have been a uniform size of unit about that time. Cavalry constabularies of unknown size are also recorded. The 40 knights of Bury St Edmunds owing castle-guard at Norwich Castle were divided into four groups of ten, each under one of their number as constable, each group serving for a quarter of the year. This does not prove the existence of 10-knight constabularies, since, had the number of the Abbey's knights been greater, the constabulary would have been proportionately increased. Constables of burghs and hundreds were ordered to organize the *jurati ad arma* in their area in 1205 in England, under the orders of the constable of the shire.

In England the summons to the army was apparently sent by a writ to the tenants-in-chief, both clerical and lay, and to the sheriffs who would summon the minor tenants and those bound only by allegiance, i.e. the fyrd.

The Rule of the Knights Templar describes the knight in battle accompanied by two squires, one of whom stood in front of him and held his lance while the other stood behind him and held his spare horses. Before the action commenced the remounts were led to the rear where the horse-holder fell in under the command of an officer called the *gonfanonier*. Neither of these squires took any part in the fighting. Wace, writing about 1170, describes spare horses for the Conqueror each led by a man carrying a spare spear. In early times the squire apparently was actually forbidden to wear hauberk and helm and was only allowed to use a light lance. Of the two earliest clear representations of people holding knight's horses in England, small figures on the foot of tombs, one in Exeter Cathedral, of about 1320, is unarmoured, and the other, in Minster, Isle of Sheppey, of about 1330, is wearing a thick quilted gambeson, not a hauberk.

Ordinances of War

In order to control discipline within the army, particularly in camp, regulations were apparently drawn up at the outset of a campaign, and proclaimed throughout the army. The earliest published code of this type is that of Frederick Barbarossa, promulgated in 1158 when he was campaigning in Italy. In 1155 he had forbidden the carrying of swords in the camp. Anyone wounding his fellow in violation of this rule was to lose his hand or even his head. Three years later he had his entire force sworn to keep the peace in the army. If quarrels broke out no one was to call out the rallying call of the camp, nor were they to join in except to part the contestants with staves. The punishment for wounding a comrade was mutilation and for killing him it was death. In either case two witnesses not related to the victim were required. If no witnesses were available the accused could clear himself by a duel. A soldier who had robbed a merchant was to repay him two-fold, and to swear that he had not known he was a merchant. If the offender was a varlet he was to be shorn and branded in the cheek, unless his lord restored the plunder on his behalf. A regulation stating that anyone seeing a comrade robbing a church or a market was to prevent him if possible, but without strife, or should denounce him to the authorities, is typical of this code which aimed at preventing crime with the minimum of loss of blood.

The Development of Military Forces in England

Inflation during the twelfth century made horses, weapons and armour increasingly expensive and at the same time decreased the value of the sum paid as scutage, although as time went on, the crown seems to have tried to demand a larger payment. Enfeofment gave the knightly class an interest in the land, and as they became involved in estate management and increasingly in the civil administration of the honour and shire, they became less willing to undertake military service. For instance, on a great many juries only knights were eligible to serve, and this might mean that, as well as his other shire business, a knight might have to serve on five or six juries during a single assize. As money became more readily available – as early as the reign of Henry I the food rents of the royal demesne were commuted for a money payment – it became simpler to pay scutage than to go to the expense of both equipment and training, and of undergoing the ceremony of knighthood with its attendant celebrations. As a result fewer people took up knighthood.

The long period of internal peace under Henry I meant that the general levy was only rarely called out and its value as a fighting force declined. It seems to have taken little part in the civil war of Stephen's reign, although the hardy country-men of the north proved their fighting ability against the Scots at the Battle of the Standard (1138), and the levies of some towns, like London and Dunwich, are recorded as fighting well in the early years of the next reign.

Henry II, one of England's greatest administrators, saw that the time was ripe for a complete re-organization of the military system. By the Inquest of 1166 he demanded from all his tenants-in-chief a return of all the knights they had enfeofed on their estates, and how many were still to be provided to complete their quotas to the royal army. He also asked for the names of all their knights, so that all those who had not yet done so could do him homage before a certain date. In 1169 the knights, freemen, tenants and all those over fifteen years of age were bound to him personally by an oath. The simple assessment on the size of tenement was now entirely out of date and for some time taxes had been assessed instead on the income of the land and on a man's movable possessions. The great Assize of Arms of 1181 recognized this system for military assessment also. In order to get round the shortage of knights, every holder of a knight's fee, regardless of whether he was actually a knight, was to have a hauberk, a helm, a shield, and a spear; that is, the arms of a knight. Every tenant-in-chief who had not enfeofed sufficient knights to fulfil his *servicium debitum* must possess the necessary armour and arms to equip all the knights he owed. Every freeman with goods or rent to the value of sixteen marks was to be equipped in the same way as the holder of a knight's fee. Freemen with goods or rents to the value of ten marks were to have a haubergeon (a diminutive form of the hauberk), a light iron head-piece called a *capelet*, and a spear. All burgesses and the whole community of freemen were to serve in gambeson and iron *capelet,* and with a spear. The regulations about freemen constitute the re-organization of the fyrd, while the Assize as a whole brings the feudal and pre-feudal elements into a single system. None was to be admitted to take the oath to arms except freemen, a stipulation absent from the slightly earlier regulations issued for Anjou. The first mention of villeins (i.e. unfreemen) being sworn to arms in England is in a writ for the collection of a tax in 1225. From early in the thirteenth century summonses to arms sent to sheriffs certainly included not only feudatories, but also the *jurati ad arma,* that is those sworn to arms under the Assize of 1181. In the emergency of 1205 all those over the age of twelve were sworn to arms and were organized under constables of borough, vill, or hundred, as the case might be, and the constable of the shire was ordered to muster them for the defence of the realm. Those who failed to turn out were to forfeit their land or, if landless, pay a fine of 4d. The shire constable lasted down to 1230, when his job was once again taken over by the sheriff.

By 1224 the shortage of actual knights was so great that all holders of knight's fees were ordered to be knighted before Easter of 1225. This would almost certainly entail them being actually equipped as a knight, as did a similar order of 1234. This order was repeated at intervals throughout this century, very often immediately before an important campaign, usually on pain of distraint upon their property. This was not merely a method of raising money, as is shown by the fact that in 1242 it was specifically stated that the fine was to be repaid to anyone who actually served in the army. By the end of Henry's reign, apparently about four-fifths of those liable to do so had become knights.

During the second half of the twelfth century there are instances of the king asking his tenants-in-chief to serve with a reduced quota of knights, particularly for service beyond the borders of the realm in France or Wales. For instance, Henry II summoned one third of the *servicium debitum* for the Welsh campaign of 1157 in order, it is said, not to bear too heavily on the ordinary knighthood, burgesses, and free-men. In 1177 Henry asked his tenants-in-chief to serve abroad for one year with as many knights as they could bring with-out hardship to themselves. It would appear that although scutage was customarily payable on such a request, service was not obligatory and perhaps not even due at all. For instance, in 1197 the knights of Bury St Edmunds specifically denied that they owed service in France. There are a number of records of fines for not crossing into Normandy, and these were greater than the sum of the scutage owed. In 1197, when scutage was 20s. per fee, the Abbot of St Augustine's Abbey at Canterbury was fined 40l. on a *servicium debitum* of fifteen knights. Possibly the additional sum represented the expense of equipping and sending his knights to France which the Abbot might have been expected to face. Many of the great tenants-in-chief held lands on both sides of the Channel, so that the presence of an important English baron in the army in France does not prove that he was serving with the *servicium debitum* from his English estates.

Similar reductions in the number of knights summoned continued during the reigns of Henry's sons. Richard, when he required troops for a long campaign in France in 1196, wrote to Hubert Walter, Archbishop of Canterbury, asking that the English tenants-in-chief should come to Normandy with only seven knights apiece at the most, but should serve for a prolonged period. Those of the ecclesiastical tenants who owed military service were asked to supply such help 'as would please the king.' The Norman tenants were to serve with their full quotas. Two years later he wrote again asking that the tenants-in-chief should either supply him with a total of 300 knights for one year or money to hire them at 3s. a day. In 1205 John summoned his tenants-in-chief to produce one knight out of every ten owed, to serve for 80 days at least. Each was to be paid 2s. a day provided by the other nine.

The outcome of the struggle over *Magna Carta* greatly weakened the king and encouraged the barons to try to increase their privileges at the expense of the rights of the Crown. Summonses for feudal service in the first half of the thirteenth century show that reduced quotas had become customary, and these had now begun to be looked on as a fixed right.

7

Chivalry and Knighting

In origin the knight is no more than a mounted warrior, and the Saxons, by applying to him the word *cniht,* meaning a serving youth or household retainer, indicated his status as it appeared to the conquered race. We know nothing of the forbears of the first knights enfeofed in England but, no doubt, as soon as their fees became hereditary a certain pride of ancestry must have appeared. The *Domesday Book* occasionally used the word *miles,* usually translated as 'knight', for tenants of some very small holdings, which suggests that they can have lived little better than the peasants. In fact, there are early Continental references to villeins actually being knighted. The Assize of Arms of 1181 appears to equate the knight with a freeman having sixteen marks in rents or movable goods. By the thirteenth century the knight's fee seems to have been generally reckoned to be worth 20l. a year, since on many occasions men holding land of this value were ordered to take up knighthood.

The change of status of a knight from a mere cavalryman into a member of a hereditary caste is very well illustrated by the Rules of the Knights Templar. Although the knights and sergeants of the rules published in 1130 are distinguished by the colour of their dress – white for the knights, brown for the sergeants – nothing definite is said about the social background of the knights. In 1250, however, the rules state that a knight must have received knighthood before entering the Order and must be the son of a knight or at least the descendant of a knight on his father's side. No knight might serve as a sergeant of the Order, even out of humility, and if he did so by stealth was to be punished.

Matthew Paris records the knighting in 1250 of a man 'although not descended from noble or knightly ancestors', but it was clearly unusual, and demonstrates the background expected of a knight by that date. As early as 1140, Roger II of Sicily ordained that only the descendants of knights should receive knighthood, and many other rulers followed suit during the next century and a half. An ordinance of Frederick Barbarossa forbade peasants to use the knightly weapons of lance and sword, but this certainly did not apply in the rest of Europe. In France there was no actual ordinance but under St Louis (1226–70) the royal courts laid down a similar ruling to that of Barbarossa. In fact, as always happens, wealthy burgers who bought country estates in France were slowly accepted over several generations as being 'noble'. By the end of the thirteenth century it had become customary for rich townsmen in Provence to be knighted. However, the idea of hereditary nobility became so ingrained that, as Léon Gautier pointed out, if in a romance a villein shows any signs at all of noble characteristics he is sure to turn out to be the long lost son of a king or baron.

As far as England was concerned no rule was ever made. In order, apparently, to encourage reluctant vassals to take up knighthood, the kings, starting with Henry III, seem to have made a determined effort to make the rank more desirable by the introduction of elaborate pageantry into the actual knighting ceremony. Many knights were made on occasions of particular importance, like the group knighted at the same time as the king's brother, Richard of Cornwall, in 1225. Whatever the motives for this were, it certainly resulted in the elevation of the knight well above the sergeants of the cavalry.

Knighthood never became hereditary, except for the sons of very important princes at a very late period. Baronets, instituted by James I of Great Britain in 1611, although styled Sir like a knight, are in fact not knights, although they used to have the right to ask to be knighted. A few Irish titles, like the Knight of Kerry and the White Knight, are hereditary nicknames of considerable antiquity, but the holders are not knights.

The knight of the eleventh century was trained from childhood in the arts of war, the use of weapons – sword, lance, axe, mace, and bow–the management of his shield, wrestling, and above all horsemanship and horse-mastery. The horse must be schooled to obey his rider's command instantly and precisely, to stand still in the press and uproar of battle, to turn, to move forward or backward, to halt without the use of the rein, and to charge a wall of humans or other horses without turning aside. Almost certainly this standard was not achieved in the earliest times and may, in fact, not have been reached until the sixteenth century when it was first described in books. The chronicler Monstrelet, writing of the year 1410, describes the surprise of the knights of Northern France, Flanders, and Brabant, at the ability of the Lombard and Gascon troops to turn their horses at full gallop, a manoeuvre of which they themselves were incapable. Nevertheless, the horse and its training were so indispensable a part of knighthood that the French word for horse-mastery – *chevalerie* – became the name applied to the whole concept of knighthood, while in all other lands except Britain the word for knight–*caballero, chevalier, Ritter*–means horseman.

Chivalry derives from the Germanic concept of a youth

entering man's estate with the ceremonial gift of arms from his father, a kinsman, or his tribal chief. This was later blessed by the Church and modified by its ideals, and finally given some of its finest polish and its romance by contact with the Saracens both in Spain and the Holy Land. The Germanic concept of loyalty runs through it; to Roland it would be unthinkable dishonour to desert the post entrusted to him by the Emperor. It was not even considered knightly to make use of the treachery of an enemy; William Marshal reproved Philip Augustus for taking advantage of the treachery of John's castle commanders in Normandy. This is paralleled by the fear of showing cowardice – 'Better to be dead than called a coward' – and by the admiration for noble feats of arms. Over and over again we read of battles lost because a rash attack was made against the advice of the most experienced knights, which had been refuted by a taunt against them of treachery or cowardice by some more reckless knight. In 1187 Gerard of Ridfort, Grand-Master of the Temple, taunted his own Marshal and the Master of the Hospital into a wildly hopeless attack when they had advised caution. The Marshal was one of the last to fall, but Gerard fled with the only two knights to escape from an original force of about 130. Although the impulsive action, whether sudden generosity or a wild charge in battle, was highly praised, the need for discipline was clearly realised in practice. The rules of the Order of the Temple were very strict about keeping to the ranks, and anyone leaving the ranks in the face of the enemy might be expelled from the Order.

The Church modified these primitive ideals by teaching the Christian virtues, adding charity to the poor to the liberality of the Teutonic tradition. Godfrey de Boulogne was praised for feeding and giving aid to the poor, suffering soldiers of his army; while liberality, the giving of rich presents, is one of the main virtues praised in their heroes by chroniclers and poets alike. Hugh de Méry in *Le tornoiment de l'Antechrist* wrote 'If *Largesse* die, we shall all perish of poverty and misery', and no doubt such pleas by wandering minstrels were not entirely disinterested. The Church laid on the knight the duty of defending the weak, the widow and the orphan, and instructed him that women of noble birth should be especially under his care. However near death he was himself, St Louis tried to share the suffering of the poorest of his soldiers. The idea of the knight having special Christian obligations because of his knighthood was first apparently propounded by John of Salisbury in his *Policraticus* completed by 1159. He implies that knights should, and sometimes did, take a religious oath at their investiture and that their arms were laid on the altar before the ceremony of knighthood. This concept was embroidered by Stephen of Fougères who, in his *Livre des manières* of about 1170, first refers to knighthood as an Order and to the possibility of demoting a dishonoured knight. Ideally it could be said of the knight that he never betrayed a trust, nor deserted a good man, nor a starving widow or a little child.

This whole concept is most movingly illustrated by Jean de Joinville (1224/5–1319) in his *Vie de St Louis*. He was writing of the time when, as a captive in Egyptian hands, he had been offered the chance of being repatriated. He refused, ostensibly because he had no money, but in reality because of something said to him by his cousin, the Lord of Boulaincourt, as he was on the point of setting out: 'You are going oversea, but take care how you come back; for no knight, whether rich or poor, can return without dishonour if he leaves our Lord's humbler servants in whose company he set out, at the mercy of the Saracens.'

Probably the strain of idealized love of fair and noble

women so typical of late chivalry was encouraged by the emergence of the cult of the Virgin Mary in the eleventh century, particularly in Normandy. This aspect of chivalry was certainly fostered by the *trouvères* at the court of Eleanor of Aquitaine and of her daughter Marie, wife of one of France's richest and most powerful princes, Henry, Count of Champagne and Brie. Marie's own *trouvère*, Chrétien de Troyes, wrote on her instructions *Le Chevalier à la charrette*, the story of the perfect knightly lover, Lancelot of the Lake, and Queen Guinevere.

The Church commanded the knight to defend it and to turn his sword against the infidel ceaselessly and without mercy. He fought in certainty of a heavenly reward to which he would be borne by the angels, as was sometimes represented on his tomb. The perfect knight was like St Louis who attended mass every day. The knight was exhorted to avoid all base actions and to love truth above everything, to defend the right and avenge injustice, and to be courteous to all and humble in all things. To the mythical heroes like Roland and Ogier the Dane, the Church added its own heroes, St George and St Michael, as examples of military virtue; and men like Godfrey de Boulogne, who refused to wear an earthly crown in the city where his Lord had worn one of thorns, and who was added to the legendary Nine Heroes of romance.

The Church also strengthened the feudal bond and the bond of loyalty by the sanctity of the oath. The romances often refer to the loyalty of knights to their chosen companion – Roland and Oliver – or to the lord in whose household they were trained.

Needless to say these very high ideals were very rarely, if ever, attained. As early as about 1100 Guibert of Nogent inveighs against the knighthood for failing in everything they were supposed to be, and he is followed by moralists throughout the Middle Ages. St Bernard of Clairvaux in his *De Laude novae militae* berated the secular knights and pointed out how far below their ideals they fell, with their vanity, greed, and lust. Nevertheless these ideals were at least something to aim for, probably as high as any offered to a society not entirely ecclesiastical. They were an ideal code of behaviour which certainly modified the brutish and callous manners of the early Middle Ages.

Contact with the Saracens had two opposite effects on the Christians. In Spain and the Holy Land the Christians found themselves living beside a cultured people with a very much higher standard of life than their own. Saracen writers frequently express horror at the barbarism of the Christians. While accepting the luxuries of Saracen life, comfortable houses, native dress suitable for the climate, highly trained doctors and native servants, they also imbibed some of their learning, and with understanding came tolerance. Some of the fire went out of the battle against the infidel, and was replaced in part by a love of soft living and a growing interest in the profits of trade. In 1236 Pope Gregory IX had to issue a Bull to prevent the Hospitallers and Templars making an alliance with the Assassins. In war they found the Saracens worthy and magnanimous foes. The mercy shown to the inhabitants by the Saracens when they captured Jerusalem was very different from the terrible massacre perpetrated by the Crusaders when it fell to them. Equally, the noble gesture of Saladin's brother in freeing poor captives taken when Jerusalem fell, compares very favourably with the behaviour of the Patriarch on that occasion, who paid his own ransom and went off with all the wealth of his church, leaving many hundreds of his flock to go into life-long slavery. Saladin's own behaviour was always magnanimous. He returned his captive King Guy in 1181 at the request of his Queen, and

Humphrey of Toron at the request of his mother, although his castles had not yet surrendered. He sent presents to the Christian princes besieging Acre and later to Richard 1 when he was sick. While besieging Kerak in 1183 he refrained from aiming his siege-engines at the tower in which the newly-married owner and his bride were sleeping. No knight would wish to be less noble than Saladin, the arch-enemy. These ideas were carried to Europe by returning Crusaders. No hero in a romance would attack an unarmed man, and on many occasions the fallen foe was spared.

Chivalry was an order transcending national boundaries. In 1389 the English knights in the Portuguese camp, sick with dysentery and weakened by famine, were able to convalesce under safe conduct in the camp of their opponents, the French, and later return restored to the fight. In contrast to this, when a town fell to an assault or after a siege it was, by the laws of war, sacked, sometimes after a pause of several days while the victor made a triumphal entry, and only too frequently the common soldiers and town people were butchered. Froissart refers in several places to knights patrolling the streets during orgies of this type to protect well-born ladies, but Enguerrand de Monstrelet, the Chronicler, relates an occasion, admittedly with horror, when some French knights joined in the rape with the sergeants. This illustrates one of the worst aspects of chivalry, that while ostensibly teaching service to the poor and weak without looking for a reward, it bred a complete contempt of those outside the caste. This sort of contrast between the theory and the practice seems to be typical of many aspects of medieval life. A king could carry on his work in his seat in church during the celebration of the Mass and a bishop would not hesitate to interrupt him to discuss urgent business. The later rulers of the Latin kingdom used Saracen allies to strengthen their armies.

Knighting

Although from the earliest times some ceremony always accompanied the entry of a young man into the warrior group in the German lands, it is not clear how early the ceremony of knighting first appeared. In 791 Charlemagne formally girded the arms of manhood on his thirteen-year-old son Louis. German custom included the ceremonial gift of arms, and the ceremony of knighting invariably included the girding on of the sword by the knight's sponsor or by his lord, and the buckling on of the knightly spurs, the second most important of the attributes of chivalry. John of Salisbury, writing before 1159, describes a new custom that had grown up; the young man about to be knighted went to church, laid his sword on the altar and solemnly offered himself to God. As time went on symbolism increased; the knight was cleansed and purified by a ceremonial bath, and reclothed in new robes. In 1204 King John spent 33l. on three scarlet robes, three green ones, two baldaquins (canopies), a mattress, and other things for making an un-named knight. The drawing by Matthew Paris in the *Lifes of the Two Offas* (British Museum, Cotton Ms. Nero D.1.) illustrates the knighting of the young Offa. In one scene, while two people buckle on his spurs, King Warmund girds the young knight with his sword. In the following scene Offa is shown receiving his armour and arms. As he puts on his hauberk an attendant stands by with his shield and his banner, both bearing the golden saltire of his coat of arms. Since the ceremony of knighting was so expensive, the knighting of a lord's eldest son was one of the occasions when he could ask his vassals for payment of an aid. The ceremony itself varied from place to place, and from time to time. For instance, the vigil in the church seems to have been unknown in Germany. One of the great holidays of the Church, Christmas, Easter, Whit Sunday, and so on, was usually chosen as a suitable occasion for making knights, or an important family event like a marriage – as in the case of Alexander III of Scotland in 1252. At first, any knight could confer knighthood and, again in the German tradition, the knight might prefer to receive it from his father or from his paternal uncle. In the *Chansons* many aspirants choose to be knighted by some great lord, or by their king in a great ceremony shared with many others, receiving horses, arms. robes, and sometimes even fiefs. When Alexander III was knighted by his father-in-law, Henry III of England, he was accompanied by twenty other aspirants for the honour. As time went on, kings tried to prevent knighthood being conferred on their subjects by anyone other than themselves but, at least until the sixteenth century, cases still occurred of knighthood being conferred by Royal Lieutenants in the field, or by particularly famous knights; like Bayard, who knighted Francis I.

What is now looked on as the actual moment of knighthood came after the robing and the girding, and consisted of a touch on the shoulder with the flat of a sword, or a hearty buffet with the fist, accompanied by some such phrase as 'Be a good knight', to which the new knight might reply 'So shall I, with God's help.' Nothing like this appears to have occurred during the knighting of Geoffrey of Anjou in 1127 as described by Jean de Tours writing a generation later, but the buffet is certainly described in the ceremony of knighting Arnoul II, Count of Ardres, at Guines on Whit Sunday 1181. After this, the knight would be embraced by the person who had given him the honour. In many cases the new knight would then mount his horse and display his skill at arms at the quintain, a dummy opponent, or in a full-blown tournament.

Although the church played its part in the Vigil and the

blessing of the arms, the arms were conferred by a layman not by a cleric. Later, however, the church devised a ceremony by which it actually conferred knighthood. Clerics of all ranks, from the Pope downward, are found making knights.

The Tournament

The young man in training to be a knight would have had to practise constantly both with his weapons and with his horse. The *De re militari* of Vegetius, one of the most popular of Roman books during the Middle Ages, describes how the Roman recruit practised the various sword cuts on a stout post planted in the earth of the exercise ground, all the time keeping himself carefully covered with his shield. The marginal drawings of the fourteenth-century manuscript of the *Romance of Alexander* in the Bodleian Library, Oxford (Ms. Bodley 264), illustrate youths practising the use of the spear on foot, aiming at a shield held by a companion, or mounted on a wooden horse on wheels propelled by their comrades at a square target on a pole. One boy is running on foot at a quintain. This was a horizontal arm pivoted on an upright post. It had a shield fixed to one end as a target and a weight hung from the other. When the target was struck the other end of the arm whirled round and, unless the novice was able to duck quickly enough, he received a severe buffet, and, if on horseback, he could even be unhorsed. Finally, the young squire would wrestle and fight with various weapons against his companions and against more experienced men. This type of training was aimed not only at teaching skill in arms and horsemanship, but also at hardening the young man to acute physical pain and the strain of battle. The chronicler Roger of Hoveden wrote, 'a youth must have seen his blood flow and felt his teeth crack under the blow of his adversary and have been thrown on the ground twenty times – thus will he be able to face real war with the hope of victory.' Richard I of England seems to have considered tournaments valuable as training, and their absence in England hitherto the reason for the English being less violent than the French, who were accustomed to take part in them.

Various dates have been suggested for the invention of the tournament and various names have been put forward as its instigator; however, practise combats between two groups for training purposes must be almost as old as war itself, and the tournament probably developed from these. In the German lands they often took place at the beginning and end of campaigns, and possibly hark back to barbarian times. Nithart, the chronicler, describes friendly contests held at the meeting of Lewis of Bavaria and Charles the Bald in 842. They may perhaps have been encouraged by the classical precedent of the *Ludus Trojae,* described by Virgil in the *Aeneid,* Lib. V, 553–87. Throughout the whole Middle Ages there were friendly combats between groups of cavalry, the 'tournament' proper; between individual horsemen, known as 'jousts'; and between dismounted men in 'the barriers', the arena in which the fight took place. Foot combats were usually fought by two people at a time, less often between small teams of two or three, very occasionally between quite large groups. The precise meaning of the various names used by contemporary writers for different combats is still far from clear. During the eleventh and twelfth centuries, tournaments were extremely dangerous since ordinary weapons of war were used, and the loss of life was considerable. Pope Innocent II issued a ban on tournaments at the Synod of Clermont in 1130, because of the loss of life which

ensued, and this was repeated in 1139 and 1179. The Church
frowned on tournaments because knights who might otherwise have gone on a crusade wasted their time and treasure
on them. In 1148 Eugene III issued a decree forbidding them
and calling on the knights to join the Crusade, and this was
repeated for later expeditions. Innocent III, in 1206, allowed
a relaxation of the ban, at the discretion of each bishop, in
return for a payment towards the Crusade, and a letter to the
Bishop of Tours in the same year indicates how successful
this was in raising money. Apart from the excitement, the
tournament was a fairly easy way to win glory under the very
eyes of the admiring ladies (once they began to attend towards
the end of the twelfth century), without the discomfort and
expense of a long campaign in an area where ladies might be
few and far between. Some knights, like William Marshal,
Earl of Pembroke (died 1219) found it a road to wealth, gained
from the ransoms of captured knights and the sale of their
forfeited horses and armour. Pembroke is said to have captured
some 500 knights during a lifetime of tournaments. Death
in the lists meant that Christian burial would be withheld
and in many cases this rule was definitely upheld, even for
those of the highest rank. However, the growth of education
slowly weakened the force of the threat and reduced the fear
of spending eternity riding endlessly and without hope of
rest. Later writers like the Master of the Dominicans, Humbert
de Romans, stressed the sinfulness involved; tournaments
were at the same time the result and cause of pride, and they
encouraged greed, gambling, and fornication. The preval-
ence of the last is amply confirmed by the chroniclers of the
day.

The very weak early kings were unable to enforce the ban
on the tournament in France, but between 1200 and 1348
there were some one hundred and forty royal edicts against

tournaments in England alone. Knights attending tournaments were ordered to be arrested, and the lands and goods
of those going overseas to take part in them were to be confiscated. To kings, they were not only wasteful of manpower
but an opportunity for discontented barons to meet and plot.
Furthermore, a quarrel begun on the tournament field might
end up as a civil war. According to Matthew Paris, the tournament at which Gilbert, Earl of Essex, among many others,
was killed, began in fun and ended in deadly earnest. Richard
I, desperately in need of money, sold licences to hold tournaments at five named sites, under the careful supervision of
royal officers. There was a sliding scale of charges according
to rank. Richard was, in any case, virtually a Frenchman and
looked on tournaments as a normal and desirable part of life.
All those taking part had to sign a document stating that they
agreed to keep the peace while riding to the ground. The
combat was to be overseen by the Justiciar and two of his
knights, with two of his clerks to record the names of the
contestants. In 1260 St Louis of France forbade the holding
of tournaments in his realm because of the Crusade, and on
several occasions later kings of France repeated the
prohibition.

According to Matthew Paris, by the middle of the thirteenth
century it was customary for the lance to be blunted for some
types of combat; while the *Book of Hours of Joffrey d'Aspremont*
of about 1290 shows the head of the lance divided into three
points so as to reduce the chance of penetration (Nat. Gallery,
Melbourne). This type of lance head was called a 'coronel'
because of its resemblance to a crown. *Lances enrochies,* that is
with coronels, are mentioned in the poem *Les Tournois de
Chauvenci* of 1284. Towards the end of the century, the
tournament proper was beginning to be regulated by rules
stipulating the type of armour to be worn and the weapons

to be used. A set of these rules, issued in England not later than 1295, stipulates that the swords to be used should have no points. These rules include one of the earliest references to the knights being accompanied by lightly armed esquires to carry their banners. Those who came to watch the tournament were forbidden to bear any arms whatsoever, or even carry a stone, on pain of seven years' imprisonment.

Although tournaments began as private exercises, they soon developed into public spectacles held on such occasions as weddings and knightings, and, as a result, led to those taking part going to a great deal of expense over their own equipment and magnificent costumes and over that of their attendants. The lavish generosity demanded of the perfect knight meant that he must give without stint to the minstrels who would sing of his noble deeds and freehanded bounty, he must remit ransoms to captured knights, and either return to them their forfeited arms and horses or give them better ones in exchange, while handing over the captured ones to his esquires. Thus his absolute scorn of worldly gain was clear for all to see, not least for his lady who, far from being the unattainable vision of purity of courtly love lyrics, was in fact the prize, as the poets and, occasionally, illustrators make absolutely clear. The knight would wear his lady's favour, her sleeve or scarf, and, after the fight was over, this might be returned for her to wear, bloody and torn. Since marriage was a question of lands and far too important to be settled by the chances of the tournament, and anyway the knight was probably already married, it can be seen that this particular aspect of chivalry was becoming part of an elaborate game quite divorced from reality.

The tournament described in the poem *Moriz von Craûn*, of about 1200, is a typical example. It was held by a French knight, Maurice de Craon, in honour of his neighbour's wife, the vicomtesse de Beaumont. The combat and the expense of holding it were to be the proof of his devotion to her: none but the brave and extravagant deserve the fair. He arrived at the field in a great wheeled ship, and, after performing prodigies of valour, he demonstrated his generosity by sending away a captive knight free from ransom and with the gift of his own hauberk. There was no question of a competition for the favours of the vicomtesse; these were to be Maurice's reward.

Armour designed specifically for use in the tournament had apparently begun to be developed by the middle of the thirteenth century. Joinville describes how, as he lay on the deck of his ship, racked by fever, his men protected him from the attacking Egyptians by covering him with a *'haubert à tournoier.'* A list of armour purchased for a tournament held in Windsor Park in 1278, included leather helms *(galée de cor)* at 16d. each, some of which were silvered and others, for those of higher rank, gilded. Leather cuirasses *(quiretis)* at 3s. each, leather ailettes, and leather shaffrons were provided by Milo le Cuireur. Wooden shields were bought from Stephen the Joiner at 5d. each, and were then painted with the wearer's arms as were his gown and his horse's couverture. Peter the Fourbisseur provided swords of parchment and whalebone at 7d. each, which were then silvered and their hilts and pommels gilded. Since no other weapons were provided, this tournament probably took the form of a simple *mêlée* with these relatively harmless whalebone swords.

8

The Military Orders

The driving force of the Crusades was the combination of the military with the religious side of medieval life, and it was in the Holy Land that the logical conclusion of this appeared in the fraternities of knight-monks of the great Military Orders.

What was thought to be the site of the Latin Hospice founded in Jerusalem by Charlemagne was bought in 1070 by a group of merchants from Amalfi, and a hospital for Christian pilgrims built there, under the Benedictine rule. After the capture of the city in 1099, Godfrey de Boulogne and many other nobles endowed the Hospital with land in the Holy Land and also in Europe. At that time the Hospital was under the leadership of one Gerard, who is referred to in a later Papal Bull as institutor of the Order. In 1113 the Hospitallers were granted Papal protection by Pope Paschal II. They were gradually granted complete independence from the jurisdiction of the local clergy and became answerable only to the Pope. Their earliest rules, which were similar to those of the Augustinian Canons, bound the members of the Order by a vow of poverty (the possessions of the Order were held in common), chastity (marriage was forbidden) and obedience (to the rules of the community and of the superior officers). In the earliest known rules of the Order of the Hospital of St John of Jerusalem no mention is made of military duties, nor of the division into knights and sergeants. However, the rule that arms were only to be carried in defence of the realm, or in the attack of a Saracen city, was described in a Bull of Pope Alexander III (1178–80) as being 'according to the custom of Raymond'; that is, Raymond de Le Puy who was the first Grand Master of the Order after Gerard, and died about 1160. They were certainly organized as a military order by about 1135 when they were granted the castle of Bethgibelin on the road from Ascalon to Hebron, and thereafter they took part in every campaign of the Latin Kingdom and were granted more and more of the key castles. They were granted Le Krak des Chevaliers in 1142, and it was held until 1271. The European organization was by Provinces (later called *Langues*) consisting of groups of Priories, themselves divided up into Commanderies of a few knights and sergeants.

The example of the Knights Templar probably led to the change of aim of the Hospitallers. They did not, in fact, ever completely lose sight of their original aims, and nursing and the maintenance of hospitals remain one of the principal activities of the Order down to the present time. Women were first affiliated to this Order from the time of the re-capture of Jerusalem but, of course, lived in separate com-munities. Over a period of time the patron saint of the original foundation, St John the Almsgiver, was gradually replaced by the better known and more important St John the Evange-list. The dress of the knights was originally black with a white cross with divided ends to the arms, of the type now known as a 'Maltese cross' because, for the greater part of their exile from the Holy Land, the headquarters of the Knights of the Hospital was in Malta. In 1259 the colour of the military gown of the knights was changed to red, still with a white cross on it.

Together with the Knights Templar, the Order of the Hospital formed the shield of the Latin Kingdom, garrisoning many of the greatest fortresses and providing a large body of well disciplined, skilful and experienced knights for royal campaigns. Each generation of knights came direct from the recruiting grounds of Europe and had not grown up in the unhealthy climate of the East, nor among the enervating customs of the native Franks. As feudatories became more difficult to find to man vacant fiefs, these were granted to the Orders. After the loss of the last fortress in the Holy Land, the Hospitallers withdrew to Cyprus, and in 1310 to Rhodes. The appointment of an Admiral of the Galleys for the first time, in 1299, shows that they had found their new role and thereafter they patrolled the waters of the Eastern Mediterranean, keeping down piracy and escorting pilgrims, while their consuls in Saracen cities looked after the interests of pilgrims.

The Order of the Knights of the Temple was a purely military one founded as such in 1118 by Hughes de Payens, a simple knight from Champagne, and a Fleming, Godeffroi de St Omer, to patrol the road to Jerusalem and to protect pilgrims from robbers and raiders. The name was taken from the quarters granted them by Baldwin I in part of the royal palace then believed to be the Temple of Solomon. The rules of the Order were drawn up by St Bernard himself and approved by Pope Honorius II in 1128 at the Council of Troyes. Like the Hospitallers, they were granted complete immunity from outside control, and, like them, became answerable only to the Pope. They were granted the right to wear a white mantle with a red cross by Pope Eugenius III in 1145, but this was confined to the knights, and sergeants and others wore black or brown, also with the red cross. Their banner, the upper half black and the lower half white, 'they

call Beauséant, because they are fair and friendly to the friends
of Christ, to his enemies stern and black.' Married knights
were permitted to enter this Order for life or for a term of
years but had to promise to leave the Order half their
property; they were not, however, granted the white mantle.
There was a carefully graded hierarchy within the Order;
the Grand Master and the great officers, the Seneschal, the
Marshal with Provincial marshals, the Commander of the
Land and Realm of Jerusalem with, under him, the fleet
commander at Acre. This hierarchy spread out over all
Europe where the estates given to the Order were grouped
under Commanders of Provinces and were administered by
the Priors of great estates and the Preceptors of individual
houses. This organization channelled wealth and a constant
supply of new recruits to the Holy Land. Many lords who
could not go on Crusades in person instead gave land to the
Knights, and by astute management the Order grew increasingly rich: even as early as William of Tyre they were sus-
pected of greed for worldly wealth. In the mid-thirteenth
century, Matthew Paris claimed that they held 9,000 manors.
After the loss of the Holy Land, unlike the Hospitallers, they
failed to find a new role for themselves. They became inter-
national bankers and money lenders, and it was in the Temple,
their headquarters in London, that Hubert de Burgh, for
instance, stored his treasure. Their great wealth and their
virtual independence of all authority within a kingdom
inevitably excited the greed of their contemporaries. Their
secretiveness about their ritual and organization led to gossip
about unspeakable rites taking place. Eventually, Philip IV of
France, in his efforts to increase the power of the crown,
wishing to refill his own treasury and at the same time regain
control over the lands of the Order in France, managed to
find an informer, one Esquiu de Floyran, a renegade Knight.

With the connivance of a pro-French Pope, Clement v, the king had the Templars charged with blasphemy, idolatory, murder, betrayal of the Holy Land, and sodomy. Under terrible tortures many knights confessed and implicated their colleagues. In 1310, after nearly two years of investigation by the Inquisition, the first fifty-four Knights were burnt to death in Paris, at the Porte de Saint Antoine. The Order was totally suppressed in 1312 and its lands handed over, at least theoretically, to the Hospitallers. Whatever truth there may have been in the original charges, confessions exacted under torture cannot be regarded as reliable evidence.

Although these two great Orders dominated the Crusading era, there were a number of others, even in the Holy Land. The Teutonic Knights stem from a hospital set up in a ship hauled up on the shore by some German merchants during the siege of Acre (1189). Unlike the other two Orders which had priories or commanderies in every country, the Teutonic Knights were exclusively German. Their dress was white with a black cross. The Emperor Frederick ii later granted them the black Imperial Eagle as an augmentation to their arms. In 1191 they received a Bull of confirmation from Clement iii as a military order like the Hospitallers. Their great change of fortune came in 1226 when Konrad of Masovia, a Polish Duke, offered to grant them the province of Kulm on the Vistula, south of modern Gdańsk (Danzig), if the Order would defend it against the heathen Slavs of Prussia. The Grand Master of the day, Hermann von Salza, a friend of the Emperor Frederick ii, persuaded the latter to grant Kulm to the Order with any further conquests in Prussia that they might make. The first Knights arrived in Prussia in 1231 and rapidly expanded, building castles to hold down their conquests as they advanced. Later, they also introduced German settlers into their lands. In 1237 they were formally combined with the smaller Order of the Sword, which had been founded in 1200 by the Bishop of Riga to convert the people of Livonia (southern Estonia and northern Lithuania). In 1309 the headquarters and residence of the Grand Master was finally moved to Marienburg, and the entire attention of the Order was given up to expansion into the Baltic States, at first in the name of the Church but later in the name of the German Emperor. In Portugal, the extinction of the Order of the Temple led in 1318 to the formation of the Order of Christ by King Diniz acting in conjunction with the Pope. Both king and Pope could nominate Knights to this order.

Three separate military orders existed in Spain in the twelfth century, dedicated to the crusade in their homeland. The Knights of Calatrava and the Knights of St Julian del Pereyro were both Cistercian Orders. The former were founded by Sancho III of Castile in 1158 to hold the city of Calatrava, captured from the Moors by Alfonso VII in 1146 and granted by him to the Cistercian Order. They received their confirmation as a military order in 1164. The Knights of St Julian were founded about 1156 by two brothers of the de Barrientos family. They received confirmation from Pope Alexander III in 1177. In 1213 they were entrusted with the defence of Alcantara and thenceforward became known as the Order of Alcantara. Both these Orders wore a cross with fleur-de-lys on the end of the arms, Calatrava in green, Alcantara in red.

The third order, the Knights of St James (Santiago) of Compostela, were traditionally founded by Ramiro II of León (931–50), but the date of their confirmation by Pope Alexander III is 1175. The badge was the red sword of St James with fleur-de-lys pommel and ends to the cross-guard.

9

The Crusades

The Seldjuks were one of many tribes of Islamic Turkish nomads wandering across Asia in the tenth and eleventh centuries, seeking new lands to conquer. They were a loose confederation of tribal groups held together by the desire for plunder and power, and by the common ancestry claimed by their chiefs from a prince named Seldjuk. The decline of the Abbasid Caliphate at Baghdad led them, with many other tribes, into the Near East both to serve as mercenaries and to carve out semi-independent states for themselves. In 1050, Tughril Bey, the chief prince of the family, siezed Ispahan and united Iran and Khorassan into a single state. In 1055, he marched on Baghdad at the invitation of the Orthodox Caliph to deliver him from the power of the Bowide Emirs. In return, Tughril was made Sultan of the East and West with temporal dominion over all the Caliph's spiritual followers. As the power of the Seldjuks increased they began to raid into the Christian lands of Armenia, Georgia, and the Empire, with growing ferocity and success. Under Alp Arslan, Tughril's successor and nephew, Ani, the old capital of Armenia, was sacked in 1064, and by 1068 the whole country was over-run. By 1070 a major raid reached the Imperial city of Chonae almost on the Aegean coast. At that time the Empire was almost defenceless. The highly organized regular regiments – particularly the heavy

163

cavalry with their well trained aristocratic officers – and the supporting militia of the *themes* (provinces) described by the Emperor Leo in his *Tactica,* no longer existed. The bribes and the pay for Imperial officials had frequently taken the form of grants of land which the new owner had then often turned into sheep-farms at the expense of the small, independent land-owners who had once farmed the backbone of the militia for the defence of the theme. Where they survived at all, they owed allegiance to the new proprietor, and in faction-torn Byzantium that very often meant that they were entirely lost to the Emperor. The Empire had been weakened by its struggle with the Normans in Italy, and lack of money had led Constantine X Ducas to disband many of the irreplaceable regular regiments. Those that survived were under-strength, poorly equipped, and apparently badly trained. As a result, neither the well-proven tactics described by Leo, nor the carefully thought-out strategy for frontier warfare, described in a military treatise written about 980, could be put into practice.

In 1071 the new Emperor, Romanus Diogenes, realizing the importance of recapturing the Armenian fortresses, set out with the largest army he could raise; possibly nearly 100,000 men. To make up this number he had to rely heavily on foreign mercenaries, among them Cuman Turks, Franks and Normans. The Emperor seems to have been rash by nature, and, because of his rise to power by marriage with the Empress Mother, was surrounded by personal enemies, not least of whom was one of his commanders, Andronicus Ducas, the late Emperor's nephew. He marched rapidly towards Lake Van near the eastern frontier of modern Turkey, and here at Manzikert he was surprised by the approach of Alp Arslan, while many of his mercenaries were absent. The Cuman Turks in any case deserted to the enemy, and Roussel of Bailleul, the Norman commander of the Frankish mercenaries, never joined the battle.

Some idea of the lack of training or discipline, or both, of the Imperial troops can be gauged by the disaster which overtook Basilakes, the commander of the theme of Theodosiopolis. Charging a body of Turkish cavalry scouts he allowed himself to be lured out of sight of the camp and into an ambush. The *Tactica* expressly describes the danger of such an action. His force was wiped out.

Romanus drew up his army in front of his camp according to the precepts of Leo for a force consisting only of cavalry. His flanks were protected by two wings of cavalry, probably slightly advanced in order to outflank the enemy's line. He placed a strong reserve commanded by Andronicus Ducas as a second line behind his main body. In fact, a cavalry force was not considered ideal for action against lightly armed cavalry bowmen like the Turks, and should have been supported by infantry archers who could outshoot horsed archers. According to the *Tactica,* if his horse was killed under him the Turk was almost helpless on foot. In the absence of infantry archers scattered bands of Turks would ride along their opponent's front pouring in clouds of arrows, and only charging home with sword and mace if they saw the ranks waver or break. In this case, the proper tactics were apparently to close with them at once since they could not face heavy cavalry, but the flanks and rear of the army had to be protected by a natural feature like a river or marsh to prevent encirclement.

In the event, the Turks attacked in their normal way and the Byzantine skirmishers, also horsed archers, replied; but since they were outnumbered, it was with little effect and with considerable losses to themselves. The Imperial Army began to lose horses and, later in the day, Romanus was forced to advance; this was done in excellent order. The Turks, however, withdrawing slowly, refused to make a stand. Towards evening the Byzantines passed over the site of the Turkish camp and halted, exhausted and thirsty. Romanus then ordered the army to face about and to return to camp. Apparently the order was not immediately understood throughout all units, and, as the withdrawal commenced, gaps began to appear on the flanks which the Turks were quick to exploit. Eventually Romanus ordered a halt and faced about to beat off his attackers. Most contemporary writers agree that the failure of the reserve line, now leading the withdrawal, to halt, was due to the treachery of its commander, Andronicus. Although the remaining troops put up a gallant defence, fighting back to back against the encircling foe, and parts of the wings managed to break out, the Emperor himself was captured and the whole centre of his army destroyed.

The Empire, and particularly its army, never recovered from this disaster, from the subsequent civil war at home, and from the complete devastation of the themes of Asia Minor, for long its most fruitful recruiting ground. When the Crusaders later crossed this once fertile area they found it virtually a desert. The Turks rode almost unimpeded over these lands as the Byzantines quarrelled over the succession, and by 1078 the holy city of Nicaea, within a hundred miles of Constantinople itself, was the capital of the Turkish Sultanate of Rum (Anatolia). Control of Asia Minor was secured by the Seldjuks in 1084 when the great city of Antioch fell to them by the treachery of its commander, Philaretus. The economy of the Empire had also been disastrously affected; in the years following Manzikert the proportion of precious metal in the coinage was reduced to half its previous level. The remnants of the Empire, attacked in the north by Slavs and Turks, and in the west by Normans from southern Italy, were saved only by the brilliant diplomatic intrigues of the Emperor Alexius Comnenus, and by the quarrels, some of which he fomented, between various groups of Seldjuks. The death of the most powerful of the Turkish rulers, Malik Shah, in 1092, and the subsequent civil war between his sons, coming at a time when Alexius had refilled his Treasury, reconstructed his fleet and settled himself firmly on the throne, made an opening for a more forward policy. The Emperor's greatest need now was for reliable, steady mercenaries.

Although the Crusades proper began in 1095 when, at the Council of Piacenza, the Emperor's emissaries appealed to Pope Urban II for mercenaries to help recapture the provinces of Asia Minor, the idea of a Holy War was not entirely foreign to western Europe. As early as the middle of the ninth century Pope Leo IV had ruled that a heavenly reward awaited those who died in defence of Christianity. The reconquest of Moslem Spain, begun early in the eleventh century, was strongly supported by the monks of Cluny, the leading religious community of the day. In 1064 Pope Alexander II offered indulgences to all who fought the infidel in Spain. Pope Gregory VII was particularly warlike. As a cardinal he had persuaded Alexander II to support Norman aggression against England. As Pope he wrote to the Emperor Henry IV in 1075 suggesting an expedition to restore the eastern Empire after Manzikert; he apparently intended to lead it in person, thinking perhaps that a successful campaign might lead to a settlement in his favour of his quarrel over supremacy with the Patriarch of Constantinople. He too encouraged expeditions to reconquer Spain.

The motives of the Church were mixed. Doubtless foremost was a genuine desire to spread Christianity, but an important consideration was the need to put the warlike instincts of western knights to some useful purpose, and to prevent the endless warfare, royal and baronial, which devastated Europe. A campaign to limit warfare between Christians had been started at the Council of Charroux in 989. In 1054 the Council of Narbonne had tried to combine the Truce of God, by which Christians did not fight on Holy Days, with the Peace of God which protected the possessions of the Church and of the poor in time of war. After consider-able initial enthusiasm it had met the fate of all subsequent idealistic movements to limit war, and within a few years was being ignored by some of its major supporters. Any plan to canalize belligerence away from central Europe was to be encouraged. A third motive can be seen in the arrange-ment by which newly conquered lands in Spain were held by their conquerors as vassals of the See of St Peter. This system was also followed on later crusades.

The motives of those who took the Cross were certainly as mixed. No doubt many truly felt a burning ardour to carry out the work of Christ as seen by the Church, to regain the Holy Places for Christianity and to kill the infidels whom they regarded as desecrators of churches and oppressors of their fellow Christians. This feeling was, however, by no means universal. The savagery of the foreign Crusaders towards the Moslems in Spain was in marked contrast to the toleration shown them by the native Spaniards. The Muslim Emir of Seville was an ally of Alfonso VI of Castille (died 1108), and El Cid Campeador, the hero of Spanish legend, compar-able to King Arthur in England, was in reality a mercenary ready to sell his sword to Muslim or Christian alike.

Other Crusaders no doubt took the Cross in the hope of gaining remission of their sins and of winning grace. Yet others, landless knights, younger sons, and soldiers of fortune joined in the hope of winning lands and position for themselves beyond the sea, and the Pope played on this hope quite openly in his appeal. Even some of the leaders of the First Crusade, like Baldwin of Boulogne, were landless. Love of warfare, or fear of justice, must have sent others out on the campaigns. Very few can have had any idea of the enormous distance to be covered, or of the difficulty of the task. No doubt, knowing that God would be on their side, they never questioned the outcome for a moment.

Urban II, one of the great diplomatists of his age, had healed the widening schism between the Churches of East and West. He eagerly accepted the idea of a Holy War to relieve the sufferings of the Christians in the East, and to reopen the pilgrimage routes to the Holy Places, closed, not by deliberate policy, but by the anarchic condition of Asia Minor and the Holy Land, fought over by rival bands of Seldjuks. Urban's appeal was made at the Council of Clermont on 27 November 1095 to a great multitude gathered in the fields outside the city. He described to them the sufferings of their fellow Christians and the difficulties encountered by pilgrims, and appealed to his hearers, rich and poor, to cease fighting each other and use their swords in the service of God alone. He offered them earthly rewards in a new land, and absolution for all those who fell in battle.

The Pope spread his appeal by synodal letters to all his bishops, and probably also by letters to the kings and princes of the West. The response was enormous and enthusiastic. While the Pope made his preparations, arranged that the Church should protect the land of all who took the Cross, looked round for a leader of sufficient standing to command the expedition, and organized a supply fleet from Genoa, promises of support poured in from all directions.

The most successful appeal seems to have come from itinerant preachers, like Robert of Arbrissel and Peter the

Hermit, who awoke the emotions of the peasants at a moment when life was particularly grim because of baronial oppression, land hunger due to a rising population, and a succession of disastrous harvests. The visionary preaching of such men seemed to offer the villeins, whose lot on earth appeared hopeless, a sure road to a better life and to ultimate salvation. The journey of Peter the Hermit through France and northern Germany gathered around him a great horde, almost completely undisciplined and disorganized, consisting mainly of the poorer classes, villeins and townsmen, many criminals eager to avoid judgement, and containing only a very few of the lesser German nobility. Many were accompanied by their families. The long and disastrous march through central Europe of this People's Crusade, its unexpected descent on the Eastern Empire which was preparing for Crusaders to arrive by the trans-Adriatic pilgrim routes, and its eventual crushing defeat shortly after entering Asia Minor were of no military importance. Nor was the so-called German Crusade which, after massacring all the Jews that could be found in the Rhineland and Moselle and in the towns along its route, did not penetrate much beyond the Hungarian frontier before being dispersed by Hungarian troops. However, both increased the apprehension at Constantinople at the approach of the Crusading armies. Experience of their western mercenaries both at Manzikert and later, and contacts with the Normans in southern Italy, had taught the Byzantines to distrust the Franks as faithless, greedy barbarians, fearless in attack but because of that more dangerous now that they were coming, not as the hoped-for mercenary bands, but as large armies commanded by important nobles.

The Emperor gave orders for the setting up of supply bases along the routes that the Crusaders were expected to take. He sent out high-ranking officials to welcome the leaders, and to bring them to the capital as quickly as possible under escort of the Imperial military police to prevent the Franks from pillaging the countryside they would have to pass through. Alexius realized that the main motive of the Crusader princes was to win lands for themselves, to which he had no objection so long as these formed buffer states between the Turks and the reconquered territories of the Empire. In order to be able to control their activities he decided to induce each leader as he arrived to take an oath of allegiance to him in western fashion, after which these dangerous and un-predictable allies were to be shipped across to Asia Minor before the temptation to plunder Constantinople overcame them, there to await the arrival of the other armies.

The effective portion of the First Crusade was led by princes and nobles with experience of war and prepared therefore to wait until the necessary preparations were completed before setting out. They were followed by their own vassals, and by volunteers, most of whom apparently financed them-selves by the sale or pledging of their estates. Bohemond, the Norman lord of Otranto, son of Robert Guiscard, Duke of Apulia, apparently financed all those that followed him. Robert, Duke of Normandy, pledged his Duchy to his brother, William Rufus of England, for 10,000 marks of silver to pay for his part of the expedition. The financing of the First Crusade, once it was under way, was by subsidies from the Emperor and by treasure captured on the campaign.

The first western leader to reach Constantinople was Hugh, Count of Vermandois, brother of Philip 1 of France, accompanied by a small army of French knights. His arrival at Dyrrhachium on the Adriatic coast was somewhat un-dignified since he was cast ashore by shipwreck, but he was re-equipped by the governor, John Comnenus, and sent on under a strict escort to the Emperor who received him warmly,

showering him with gifts. Hugh, in spite of being virtually
held a prisoner, was dazzled and flattered into taking the
oath of allegiance to the Emperor. The second arrival was
Godfrey of Boulogne, Duke of Lower Lorraine, who was
accompanied by his two brothers, Eustace III, Count of
Boulogne, and Baldwin, and an army including many
important knights from their sphere of influence in Flanders
and Lower Lorraine. They too chose to travel by the
traditional route for German pilgrims through Hungary.
Apart from a bad outbreak of pillaging as they neared Constantinople, discipline was maintained throughout the march.
Hugh of Vermandois was sent to secure Godfrey's oath of
homage to the Emperor. Godfrey, perhaps because he was
already a vassal of the Western Emperor, Henry IV, and perhaps because he had already heard highly biased accounts of
their treatment from surviving followers of Peter the Hermit,
refused even to visit the Emperor. He was allowed to camp
outside Constantinople and was supplied with forage and
food throughout the winter. It was only when spring came
and the arrival of other crusading armies was imminent that
Alexius tried to force Godfrey's hand by gradually reducing
the supplies sent to him. This led at first to foraging raids by
the Franks, and then on Thursday of Holy Week to an attack
on one of the city gates, which was not however pressed
home. On the following day, what began as a skirmish with
the military police developed into a pitched battle in which
the Crusaders were worsted as the exasperated Emperor flung
in more troops. Thereafter Godfrey and his chief followers
took the required oath, promising to hand over all the reconquered Imperial territory and to hold any new lands
as vassals of the Empire.

Thus it continued. It was only by the use of the greatest tact
and enormous bribes that Alexius was able to persuade the

Crusaders to take the oath. The Norman Bohemond was alone in taking it without question. After years of campaigning against the Empire he did not underestimate its military power and its resources, and he realized that without its co-operation the Franks could achieve nothing. Since he hoped also to be given command of the expedition he was unwilling to displease the Emperor. Alexius, probably very relieved that his most formidable and best equipped ally was so amenable, promised to revictual the Crusaders, pay all their expenses, and send Imperial troops with them, but at the same time made only a vague promise about the post of commander.

The most important of the French Crusaders, and indeed the first noble of any importance to take the Cross, was Raymond IV, Count of Toulouse. It was with him that Urban had first discussed the idea of the expedition, and, since he was accompanied by the Papal legate, Adhemar, Bishop of Le Puy, he hoped to be given command of the whole army. As this command could only be granted by the Pope, he was very unwilling to compromise his position by taking the oath to the Emperor, and he was also jealous of the obvious ascendancy gained by Bohemund. He was persuaded, only with great difficulty, to take a modified oath of non-prejudice; that is, that he would do nothing to prejudice the Emperor's rights or harm his person.

These preliminary dealings between the Crusaders and the Empire were far from leading to a feeling of mutual trust. The Byzantines' opinion of the Franks as rapacious barbarians was confirmed by the behaviour of the newcomers; their ill-discipline and pillaging. Their fighting in Holy Week, particularly, had disgusted them.

The Crusaders, although dazzled by the splendours of Constantinople, were also resentful of it, partly because it accentuated their own inferiority, their lack of polish and culture, and partly because they despised it as effete. This dual view is evident much earlier; for instance, in the reports of his two visits to Constantinople by Liutprand, Bishop of Cremona. In 949 he was well received and wrote enthusiastically of the magnificence of the court and its elaborate ceremonial. In 968–9, when he was rudely received, he wrote of the squalor of the great city and its discomforts, and of his scorn for the decadent, untrustworthy, and greedy Romans. The Franks were humiliated by the oath forced upon them and by their unsuccessful brushes with the Imperial forces. Later Crusader writers, like William of Tyre, show that they thought that the Empire had forfeited its rights as Protector of Christendom by its defeat at Manzikert. As the campaign began the gap was widened by the entirely different military outlook of the allies; the well-disciplined Byzantines, strategists interested in results even if obtained by diplomacy or by a ruse rather than a battle; the ill-disciplined Franks, scornful of what they considered underhand tricks not far from treachery and cowardice, and yet only too ready to forget their oath to the Emperor.

The numbers of actual combatants taking part in the First Crusade given by the different Chroniclers are quite irreconcilable, varying from the 100,000 of Raymond of Aguilers to the 600,000 of Fulcher of Chartres. Both men actually took part in the campaign. A letter written to the Pope after the capture of Jerusalem, reporting on the state of the army, gives their numbers as 5,000 cavalry and 15,000 infantry. The number of combatants at any one battle might be very much smaller; at the Crusader victory of the first battle of Antioch the whole force is said to have consisted of only 700 cavalrymen owing to the shortage of horses.

IO

Crusading Campaigns

The Crusaders wanted to march straight to Jerusalem but could only do so if the road through Asia Minor was first cleared of Turks. As this was exactly what the Emperor wanted, both sides could co-operate. At least at the beginning of the campaign the Crusaders were willing to take advice from the Greeks, and Anna Comnena states again and again that the Emperor, her father, warned them about the Turkish method of warfare and advised them on the best methods of dealing with it.

The first objective was Nicaea, the Seldjuk capital astride the Byzantine military road across Asia Minor, which must be taken before any expedition could set out. The Sultan Kilij Arslan I, contemptuous of the threat of the Crusader Army since his easy victory over the 'People's Crusade', was away on campaign. Before the Sultan's relieving force could arrive, the city was successfully invested by the greater part of the western army with the help of some Byzantine engineers under Manuel Butimites. When the Sultan reached the city he was beaten off by the Count of Toulouse and the warlike Bishop of Le Puy who led his troops in person, with the help only of Robert, Count of Flanders, since the remainder of the army was needed to contain any sorties made by the garrison. The great Byzantine fortifications of the city were attacked with vigour and with all the engines the allies could build. The defenders replied with equal vigour, rebuilding during the night the base of the undermined tower on which the attack was concentrated and undoing all that the miners could do. Supplies could still be brought in across the lake which lies under the western wall of the city, and the Crusaders were therefore obliged to ask the Emperor to send boats to complete the blockade. According to Anna Comnena, Alexius was hoping for some such appeal in order to prove to the Crusaders that they were dependent on him. He sent not only boats but several regiments of what the anonymous author of the *Gesta Frankorum* calls 'Turcopoles', that is, light cavalry, probably mounted archers. Meanwhile, to prevent the city being sacked and his future subjects antagonized, he had ordered Butimites to discuss terms of surrender secretly with the garrison. Seeing that further resistance was hopeless and the final assault prepared, they agreed, and on the morning on which the assault was to have taken place, the Crusaders saw the Imperial flag waving over the city. Robbed of the glory and the expected plunder and ransoms the Crusaders were understandably furious at the underhand methods of their ally, although in fact their leaders may have had some warning of the plan in advance. The Emperor succeeded in placating them by generous gifts of gold and jewels to the leaders and of food to the men; however, most of them were disgusted by his generous treatment of the more noble of his Turkish captives. The Sultan's wife was royally treated and returned to her husband free from any ransom.

With this great fortress no longer threatening their line of communications, the Crusaders were free to march southward across Asia Minor towards Iconium (now Konya) and Antioch (now Antakya near the southernmost point of modern Turkey). Meanwhile, Kilij Arslan had gathered together all his forces and those of the Danishmend Emir with whom he had hurriedly patched up an alliance. He was lying hidden by low hills near the point where the old Byzantine military road debouches through the mountains onto the plain near Dorylaeum (Eski-Sher), about 85 miles south of Nicaea. Here the road forks and this is the last point at which the Sultan could be certain of intercepting the Crusaders' march.

The Christian army was marching in two divisions, probably to lessen commissariat difficulties and to ensure sufficient water, as well as to make their huge train of non-combatants, priests, families, and camp-followers, less unwieldy. The first division, consisting of the French and Sicilian Normans, the northern French, and the Flemings, was commanded by Bohemond and was accompanied by some Byzantine troops under an officer called Taticius. Bohemond's division, having passed the night encamped near the southern end of the pass, was apparently just beginning the day's march when the Turkish horse archers swept down on it. Bohemond ordered his knights and sergeants to dismount and formed them up in front of the camp, which was hurriedly pitched on the edge of a marsh. He sent off messengers to bring up the second division under Count Raymond, and ordered his men to stand fast and await the Turks coming to hand blows. His infantry were told off to guard the camp, presumably as much because of the need to defend the helpless non-combatants as because of any doubt about their effectiveness in battle. The women were to carry water to the fighting line to quench the men's thirst. One knight alone apparently disobeyed Bohemond's order to stand fast, and charged out with his own men, only cutting his way back to the army with great difficulty. These tactics were quite useless against mounted bowmen who refused to come to close quarters but rode in circles shooting in an endless hail of arrows. Throughout the day, and as the heat increased, the Christian front was slowly compacted and driven back onto the camp by exhaustion, and by the rain of arrows to which they could not reply. The Turks broke into the camp and began to slaughter the non-combatants whose shrieks added to the despair of those fighting. Hope had almost been given up when the arrival of the cavalry of the second division reversed the day. The left wing of the Turks was caught between the new arrivals and Bohemond's division, and the Sultan himself was surprised and driven from the field by the sudden arrival over the hills to his rear of Bishop Adhemar at the head of his men. The Turks fled so far and so fast that the Crusaders found the bodies of horses ridden to death over a distance of three days' march from the battlefield.

The victory was one of chance, and no credit can be given to the Christians for the timely arrival of Raymond's troops. They had apparently set off a day behind Bohemond's force, but at the time they seem to have been marching on a parallel route. Fulcher of Chartres, an eye-witness, states that they had taken the wrong road, and the fact that Bishop Adhemar was apparently able to arrive in the rear of the Turks makes it unlikely that his division can have been behind Bohemond at the moment when his messenger found it. After this battle the Crusaders continued their march towards Syria in a single body.

The Turks lost their entire camp, including the Sultan's treasury, and for some time made no further attempt to obstruct the Crusaders' march, beyond laying waste the country in front of them to deprive them of food and forage. A generation of Turkish occupation had in any case devastated this once fertile countryside which was now largely barren. Bridges and roads were falling into ruins from neglect or deliberate destruction, and the all-important cisterns were broken. All knowledge of the routes was out of date; even the Byzantines could not know what conditions were like far into enemy territory, and the few surviving inhabitants were not always helpful. Several of the later expeditions seem to have completely ignored all advice and others set off over quite impossible routes against impossible targets, like the second expedition of Raymond of Toulouse which in 1101 tried to reach Baghdad over the mountains of Armenia. Most of these expeditions failed entirely because of thirst and starvation of man and horse. Exhaustion, due to the difficulty of crossing a rugged country affected by extremes of climate while encumbered by hordes of non-combatants, made them incapable of resisting the long drawn out attacks of a foe against whom they could not retaliate. Although the country and climate were unsuitable for keeping European chargers in good condition, the heavily armoured Christian knight, if well mounted, could overthrow any Saracen light horseman who would stand up to him, but if his opponent turned tail he could rarely catch up with him. The cavalry charge at this time was not the carefully disciplined affair that it became in the seventeenth century with the men riding knee to knee at a controlled speed, but a fierce, undisciplined dash at full speed, almost impossible to control once launched. Anna Comnena, deeply impressed, commented that a charging Frank would make a hole through the walls of Babylon. There was no tradition of efficient infantry in western Europe except in England, Normandy, the Low Countries and, under Norman influence, in southern Italy, and it was not until the infantry and cavalry were used in co-operation that it became possible to campaign successfully against the Turks.

Later Crusades were able to avoid the terrible land route

through Asia Minor because the Italian mercantile cities, Pisa, Genoa, and Venice, trading with the Levant, gained naval supremacy in the eastern Mediterranean, and after the Second Crusade the great majority of pilgrims and soldiers went to the Holy Land by sea. In the meantime the Byzantines used the opportunity of Kilij Arslan's defeat to reconquer the north-west coastline and the off-shore islands of Asia Minor, as well as the themes of Lydia and Phrygia. This opened up the coast road to Syria which could be kept open fairly easily by the newly rebuilt Byzantine navy.

The next major battle of the Crusade was outside Antioch in 1098. This city, one of the holiest in Christendom because it was here that the faithful were first called Christians, had been held by the Seldjuks since 1085. The Crusaders, exhausted by their long march through the mountains and with numbers badly depleted, sat down outside it for many months, prevented by the weakness of their force from completely blockading the city, and deterred by the strength and height of its wall and many towers from making an assault. During the winter of 1097/8 they had in fact nearly succumbed to starvation themselves, and deserters had been many, including even Peter the Hermit who had been brought back in disgrace. Early medieval armies almost always suffered from disease and starvation if they had to camp in one place for any length of time. No central organization for rationing either food or forage seems to have been developed, and similarly no sanitary organization existed. In this case, the army was only saved by arrival of the Genoese fleet which seized the port of St Symeon and made it possible for supplies to be sent in by the Orthodox Patriarch Symeon of Jerusalem, now in Cyprus, with whom Adhemar took great care to remain on good terms. It was only when spring came, after beating off a relieving army, and the arrival of engineers and materials from Constantinople, that the Crusaders were able to complete the blockade by building watch-towers outside each of the gates not covered by their own camp.

Bohemond, spurred on by the success of Count Baldwin in winning himself an independent county at Edessa, had determined to make himself lord of Antioch. He pressed his claim with the other Crusader leaders, using the departure of Taticius, the Emperor's representative, probably really on Bohemond's urging, to argue that since the Byzantines had deserted them the oath to the Emperor was no longer valid. He claimed that only thus could he afford to stay in the East while his affairs were going to ruin at home. Time was running out for him since Kerbogha, Emir of Mosul, was preparing a relief army, and by the summer the Emperor might arrive himself and then Antioch would have to be restored to him. Taking a leaf from the Byzantines' book, Bohemond, without telling any of his colleagues, opened negotiations with an Armenian officer of the garrison called Firouz, who was disaffected. He agreed to hand over to Bohemond his command which was the great Tower of the Two Sisters, the key to the south wall of the city. Secretly by night the Normans entered the tower, ran along the wall-walk to seize the adjacent towers, and opened two of the city gates to let in their waiting companions. A massacre of the Turks, men and women, followed, and an orgy of looting. Only the citadel, high on its hill overlooking the town, remained in Turkish hands.

Five days later Kerbogha lay outside the walls on the site recently vacated by the Crusaders who, although now protected by their walls, were too few to defend them and were desperately short of supplies since they had, of course, found none within the city. Several of the more important leaders, thinking the position hopeless, deserted, slipping through the enemy lines by night. The only hope now seemed to be the arrival of the Emperor who was known to be campaigning in Asia Minor, but he, advised by the deserters that Antioch must already have fallen and mindful of his responsibilities to his Empire, withdrew north to prepare for the inevitable Seldjuk counter-offensive which would follow their victory. When this news reached Antioch, although by then the danger was passed, it convinced the Crusaders that they had been deliberately betrayed and that the Emperor was a traitor to Christianity.

At a council of war it was decided that the only hope was to risk everything on a major sortie. The morale of the army had been raised by the miraculous discovery of a lance-head, believed to be that which pierced Christ's side, under the floor of the cathedral. Almost certainly the quarrels and rivalries of the Moslem allies were known to the Crusading leaders, if by no other means than by the embassy of Peter the Hermit to their camp when he was accompanied by a Frank speaking both Arabic and Persian.

So many of the Crusaders' horses had died that a large number of knights and sergeants were forced to serve on foot and these were apparently used to strengthen the infantry, who were to take an important part in the battle. The army was formed up in the streets of the city, with the exception of a few hundred men left to cover the citadel under the command of Count Raymond who was too sick to leave his bed. The Chroniclers are in complete disagreement about how the army was divided but probably it was in six corps grouped according to nation. The first consisted of the men of France and Flanders under Hugh of Vermandois and Robert of Flanders; the second, of the men of Lorraine under Godfrey; the third, of the Normans of France under their Duke; the fourth, of the southern French under Bishop Adhemar; the fifth, and the sixth, of the Normans of Sicily and southern Italy under Tancred and Bohemond respectively. Bohemond was in overall command on this occasion because of Count Raymond's illness.

The Crusaders marched straight out onto the plain to the north-west of the city across the River Orontes which runs close under the walls, in order to form a line extending from the river to the mountain to prevent themselves being outflanked. They had discovered the advantage of having both flanks covered at the first battle of Antioch some months before. The leading corps took up its position facing northeast with its right flank on the river bank; as soon as it had crossed, in order to cover the crossing of the army, the second corps took post on their left and so on. For the first time on the Crusade the infantry were drawn up in front of the cavalry, probably to keep the Turkish horse archers out of shot of the Crusaders' precious horses.

Apparently, Kerbogha was urged by one of his lieutenants to attack the Christians while they were crossing the river but he left it too late. In the event, Bishop Adhemar failed to reach the mountains before several thousands of the Turks got past the head of the column, but the corps of Tancred and Bohemond, together with a body of French under Rainald of Toul, formed a reserve and tackled this force before it could fall on the Christians' rear as they faced right to meet the main Turkish army. The Christian line advanced across the plain and the Turks, unable to outflank it or break through it, fell back in a retreat which soon became a rout as several important Emirs deserted at the critical moment. They covered their retreat by setting fire to the grass, making both a smoke-screen and a barrier of flames almost impossible to ride through.

Since Bohemond was in command on this day he is usually

given the credit of devising the new tactical co-operation of
infantry and cavalry, which later became standard practice
in the Latin Kingdom of Jerusalem. The Byzantines had used
cavalry and infantry in conjunction but had usually placed
the infantry in the second line behind which the cavalry of
the front line could reform if they were repulsed. However,
Bohemond's tactics seem to be foreshadowed in some of
his father's battles in Apulia and are certainly not unlike those
used by the Normans at Hastings.

Antioch was saved. The citadel surrendered to Bohemond
by a prior secret agreement, the commander refusing to
accept Raymond's standard and later entering the service
of Bohemond. This led to a long drawn out quarrel between
those, like Count Raymond and Bishop Adhemar, who
wished to keep faith with the Emperor, and those who for a
variety of reasons supported Bohemond. Unfortunately,
at this point Adhemar died, possibly of typhus. He had been
not only wise in council and courageous in the field but
diplomatic in his dealings with the Eastern Church, never
claiming any superiority over it for himself or for his master
the Pope. He had been looked upon as the unofficial leader
of the Crusade, not only because of his personal authority but
as the Pope's representative. The subsequent quarrels of
Raymond and Bohemond were only quelled by a general
mutiny of Raymond's forces eager to press on to Jerusalem.
Bohemond and Baldwin remained in possession of Antioch
and Edessa respectively, while the remainder of the leaders
passed on with Raymond.

From the military point of view the battle of Arsouf in
1191, during the Third Crusade, is an excellent example of
the successful employment of the fully developed tactics
of the Latin Kingdom. It was not apparently the crushing
victory for the Christians that it has sometimes been made

out, since Saladin was able to offer battle again next day, but
it gave a great boost to the morale of the Crusaders after the
terrible defeat at Hattin and the loss of the True Cross.
Coming after his failure to relieve Acre it was also a great blow
to the personal prestige of Saladin.

The feudal Kingdom of Jerusalem with the great Principal-
ity of Antioch and the Counties of Edessa and Tripoli, was
only successfully founded because of the division of Islam,
the breaking up of the Seldjuk Sultanate and the rivalry of
the Baghdad and Cairo Caliphates. As with all feudal states
it suffered from the complicated quarrels of closely inter-
related baronial families, in which disagreements the king
himself was also involved. The Kingdom was weakened by
a series of rulers who came to the throne as minors unable to
ensure the rights of the crown or coerce their baronage.
Because the kingship was elective the king was never able
to act without the co-operation of his powerful vassals. His
suzerainty over all the Frankish states of the East was only
effective when a king was strong enough to enforce it. In
addition the colonists, few in number in any case, were
divided by religion from their subjects, Syrians, Jews and
Armenians. Inter-marriage between the ruling classes and
the natives was extremely rare, although common among
the sergeants, the rank and file of the army. The natives,
except perhaps the Armenians, made poor soldiers. Finally,
the Eastern Empire was frequently antagonistic to the Latins.

The main strength of the kingdom lay in the Military
Orders who were, by the end of the twelfth century, its
greatest land owners and received a stream of recruits from
the West, men born in colder lands, not enervated by a childhood spent in an unhealthy climate and by contact with an
unwarlike and luxury-loving race. These men were sworn
to defend their religion and were not encumbered by the

strains of feudal ambition. They provided a body of regular soldiers, both knights and sergeants, with a continuity of service and a knowledge of warfare. They remained permanently in residence in the Holy Land, unlike the many pilgrims who stayed only for a campaign or two before going back to their homes.

The eclipse of the kingdom of Jerusalem began with the uniting of the Moslems of Syria with those of Egypt under Saladin (Salah ed-Din Yusuf), a Kurd, who started his career as an officer of Nur ed-Din, Emir of Aleppo, and rose to be principal Moslem ruler after his master's death while the heirs were quarrelling among themselves. He had risen on the shoulders of his uncle Shirkuh, who had captured Egypt and thus reunited the two great sects of Islam. By 1169 Saladin had made himself virtual overlord of Egypt, the young Fatimid Caliph being only a figure-head who, in any case, died leaving no heir in 1171. The death of his nominal master, Nur ed-Din, and the almost simultaneous death of Amalric II, the last great king of Jerusalem, left him the most powerful figure in the Middle East. In 1176 the Emperor Manuel was crushingly defeated at Myriocephalum by Kilij Arslan II, the Seldjuk Sultan of Rum, a blow which complemented the disaster at Manzikert a century before and virtually finished the Empire as a great power. While Saladin conquered the Syrian Moslems he was willing to make a truce with the Christians, but both in 1181 and 1186 this was broken by the greed of Reynald of Châtillon, lord of Outrejourdain. His barony stretching across the Negeb from the Dead Sea to the Gulf of Aqaba, was crossed by caravans specifically protected by the Treaty, and on both occasions Reynald, careless of policy, seized Moslem caravans and refused all appeals, even from his king, to release the captives or return the booty.

In 1187 Saladin, now master of Mosul, Damascus and

Aleppo, as well as Egypt, set out to punish Reynald for his outrages and for his great naval raid into the Red Sea. The two armies, the one the largest Saladin had ever commanded, the other almost the entire force of the Latin kingdom under King Guy, some 1,200 knights, numerous light cavalry, and nearly 10,000 infantry, met at the Horns of Hattin above the Sea of Gallilee. Here, almost the entire Christian force was destroyed, only some 200 knights cutting their way out. The King and most of the great barons of the realm were captured, as was the Holy Cross itself. All the members of the Military Orders captured were put to death by the order of Saladin. By the end of the year 1188 almost every fortress and city of the kingdom had fallen, defenceless and stripped of their garrisons to furnish the army lost at Hattin. In the south only the seaport of Tyre remained in Christian hands; and in the north only Tripoli and Antioch with its port of St Symeon, Le Krak des Chevaliers, and two other fortresses were held by the Military Orders.

When the news reached western Europe, particularly of the fall of Jerusalem and the loss of the Cross, it caused enormous consternation. The Pope, Gregory VIII, preached a new crusade. Aid sent almost at once by William of Sicily and the fortuitous arrival of a determined and inspiring commander of high rank in the person of Conrad, Marquis of Montferrat, saved Tyre to act as a bridge-head for those who would follow. Henry II of England and Philip Augustus of France patched up a truce and prepared to march side by side under the banner of the Cross. A special tax, the Saladin Tithe, was collected to pay for the expedition. In the event the English were led by Richard I since his father died before he could set out, and, in fact, since further fighting broke out between them, the two kings did not get under way until 1190, and their progress even then was by no means hurried.

They reached the Christian army besieging Acre, and itself besieged by Saladin, in the summer of the following year. Richard had come with an English navy of some 100 ships which had sailed round through the Straits of Gibraltar and picked up the English army at Marseilles and the King himself at Messina, where both he and Philip had overwintered. On his way thence to Acre, Richard avenged an insult to his betrothed by capturing Cyprus, which gave him much additional wealth to finance his campaign and later became a sure base for the Crusaders, thus prolonging the life of the Latin Kingdom. The vigorous personality of Richard put new life into the besiegers as soon as he landed, and by July Acre was once again in Christian hands. Philip of France returned home at this point, but left the greater part of his army behind under Hugh III, Duke of Burgundy, and Henry of Champagne, Count of Troyes, and thereafter the entire field army was commanded by Richard.

On 22 August Richard led his forces out of Acre along the coast-road towards the port of Jaffa, 80 miles to the south, where he planned to make his base for the advance inland to Jerusalem. The march seems to have been particularly well organized so as to avoid all the mistakes which had destroyed earlier expeditions, although how much of this was due to Richard's personal inspiration and how much to the advice of the experienced knights of the Latin Kingdom will probably never be known. No women other than washerwomen were allowed to accompany the army. To avoid the starvation which had been the downfall of so many of its predecessors the expedition was to be regularly supplied by the fleet, particularly as in this case the army was very short of pack animals and Saladin had carried out the usual scorched earth policy. The army was only to march for short stretches, starting in the cool of the morning and resting for a whole day every second day when supplies were to be landed. The longest single stretch seems to have been the thirteen miles between Athlit and El-Melat, and the entire march took 19 days. It was realised that the army would be under almost continuous attack all the way and that the order of march must also be the order of battle. The precious cavalry were to march in a single column divided into twelve squadrons, with the Royal Standard of England on a cart in the centre. In order to keep the enemy out of bowshot of the horses, this column was flanked on the landward side by a similar column of infantry also divided into 12 companies. These infantry included many crossbowmen. By hugging the shore the army made sure that it could not be encircled. These were the tactics of the second battle of Antioch adapted to the line of march. The two most dangerous posts, the van and the rear, were held on alternate days by the experienced regular cavalry of the Templars and Hospitallers. The shortage of baggage animals meant that a large part of the infantry had to carry loads and this group moved along on the seaward side of the cavalry. According to one Moslem eye-witness, the infantry columns took it in turns to march along the sea-side in order to give themselves a respite.

Saladin's army consisted not only of Turkish horsed archers but also of the forces of Egypt; large bodies of Nubian infantry archers, and a heavy cavalry which one Moslem observer tells us were armed and equipped so like the Crusaders that they were difficult to distinguish. His tactics were to keep the Christians continuously under attack by part of his force, while concealing the remainder in the foothills bordering the narrow coastal plain. The attack was concentrated on the rear of the column in the hope that the advance of the rear guard might be slowed down and a gap might open between it and the remainder of the army, allowing the Moslems to break in. Alternatively, the knights might be goaded into a charge and then, when separated from their infantry, surrounded and their horses shot down. Anna Comnena says that although invincible when mounted, the Franks were powerless if deprived of their horses.

Richard's unbounded energy and his commanding personality inspired such confidence in his men that, though of many races, they held together and repulsed every attack. Finally Saladin was forced to commit his entire army in a pitched battle at a point near the little town of Arsouf, where a thick oak forest stretched to within three miles of the sea and in which the Saracens could lie hidden until the last moment.

The Saracens, amid a terrifying din of war-cries and the music of kettle-drums, horns, and cymbals, swept down on the Crusaders, pressing most heavily on the rear, held on that day by the Hospitallers. The Christian army pushed slowly on; the Templars in the vanguard forcing their way towards the gardens and orchards around Arsouf; the rearguard constantly having to turn and beat off attacks, losing horses all the time, and sweating in the heat of the Syrian high summer. The Saracens had now closed in on the Hospitallers and come to hand-blows with them with sword and mace. Several messages were sent by the Master of the Hospital to Richard asking for permission to charge, but the King wanted to wait until Saladin's army was committed all along the line. Eventually, the Hospitallers could stand it no longer and under their Marshal and Baldwin de Carew they charged out. Their example was followed by their neighbouring squadrons in succession. Almost at the same moment Richard gave the signal for attack, the call of six trumpets, and the infantry opened gaps in their ranks to let out the squadrons of cavalry. The four left flank squadrons crashed into the Saracen ranks sending them reeling back, but because of

the premature charge the enemy in front of the remainder
of the line were able to escape before the Christians could
reach them. A Saracen eyewitness, Saladin's secretary, described the swift disintegration of the army.

The pursuit was brief and controlled. The Crusaders had
learnt their lesson and no longer pursued until they were
scattered and their horses blown. They drew back in orderly
array and charged twice more to clear their enemy from the
field.

Richard's brilliant defence of Jaffa, which he had recaptured
in the nick of time, brings us for the first time an example of
apparently new tactics for infantry. The king had with him
only some two thousand infantry, who were mostly Italians,
fifty knights, and fifteen horses. He drew up this force behind
a low fence of tent-pegs to break up charging cavalry, and
arranged his men so that each archer was accompanied by a
spearman. The enemy cavalry were held off by the levelled
spears of one infantryman while the other shot at them; both
were protected by the spearman's large shield set with its
point in the ground to form, together with those of his
neighbours, a wall along the front of the army.

Whether these tactics were of Richard's own devising or
were those normal in Italy is unknown. Certainly, the laws
of the city of Florence for 1259 and 1260 describe the infantry
of the town divided into companies of spearmen equipped
with large shields, and companies of crossbowmen and
archers. The officers of the spearmen were to see that the mules
carrying the shields were always to march close to the archers,
under pain of a minimum fine of 100 *solidi* for an officer and
10 for a man. This suggests a tactical combination very similar
to that used at Jaffa. Crossbowmen sheltering behind shields
held by other soldiers are shown in the *Maciejowski Bible* of
about 1250 (Pierpont Morgan Library, New York) (Plate 7).

Plate 7 A page from the *Maciejowski Bible*, French, about 1250.
Mr. 638, f. 10 v. The upper section shows a cavalry battle and the
assault on a city. The infantry are wearing what appear to be quilted
gambesons or aketons. (Reproduced by permission of the authorities
of the Pierpont Morgan Library, New York)

Richard, in fact, never reached Jerusalem, but his success at Arsouf seriously undermined Saladin's reputation, and his capture of Cyprus prolonged the life of the Latin Kingdom by giving it a base out of reach of the Saracens. Saladin died two years later and his empire broke up as his heirs quarrelled, and this gave the Crusaders a respite.

Appendix: Military Books and Tactics

Wace describes the precise technique of landing on a hostile shore used by the Normans at Pevensey in 1066. The archers came ashore first, each with his bow bent and his quiver at his side, and took up a position on the beach ready for immediate action. Only after they had carried out a reconnaissance and had reported that all was clear, were the men-at-arms, all in full equipment, allowed to disembark with their horses. The cavalry then apparently rode inland through the screen of archers. It would be interesting to know whether this manoeuvre had been rehearsed before the expedition set out. Although this may not be how it was actually done on that day, it could very well be the method used when Wace was actually writing. Possibly the landing in Ireland in 1169 had been carried out with this military precision.

In general however, the descriptions of medieval battles given by chroniclers and even in the letters of those who took part are rarely accurate enough to find even the precise battlefield, let alone the exact position of the troops. It is scarcely ever possible to work out beyond any argument the precise tactics employed or the reason for their employment, and even more difficult to be able to discern a logical development of tactics from one battle to another.

As far as tactics on the Crusades are concerned, it seems at least possible that Bohemond of Otranto profited from the advice given him by the Emperor and probably by Taticius. His management of the battles of Antioch does suggest a conscious attempt to follow precepts akin to those of the Emperor Leo VI in his *Tactica,* but this may, of course, be no more than the result of a common-sense appreciation of the battle of Dorylaeum. A number of Roman military books were still in existence, or were available in later copies; ninth- and tenth-century copies of Caesar's *Gallic Wars* still survive, as does a late Roman copy of part of Livy's *Historia,* which was to become one of the most popular of medieval books. The *De re militari* of Flavius Vegetius, written in the reign of Valentinian II (died AD 392), survives in no fewer than ten manuscripts of the seventh to twelfth centuries, and what was apparently a copy is recorded in the will of Count Eber-hard of Fréjus, about 867.[1]

Although any of these books could have affected tactics at this period it has not been possible to show conclusively that any of them did so. Even when an eye-witness account of a battle seems to show that tactics based on Roman ones were in use, this may be due more to the author's desire to show his scholarship than to his powers of observation. For instance, the author of the *Gesta Fredrici I,* who was apparently with the army at the siege of Cremona in 1160, based his description of it on a passage in *The Jewish War* by Flavius Josephus, a first-century writer.

In the same way, it is not even certain how much the tactics developed on the Crusades affected those in Europe. The idea that early medieval infantry were useless and that tactics combining infantry and cavalry developed gradually in the Holy Land, has recently been convincingly attacked by Mr

---

[1] C.C. Dehaisnes, *Documents et extraits divers concernant l'histoire de l'art dans la Flandre,* Lille 1836, p. 11.

R. C. Smail in his *Crusading Warfare*.[1] Cavalry massed behind infantry, typical of many Crusading battles, had already been used at Hastings and by the Normans in Southern Italy. Even the use of mounted archers at such battles as Bourg Théroulde in 1124, does not necessarily indicate Crusading experience, since mounted archers were common along the Hungarian marches long before the Crusades began.

[1] See the bibliography for this section at the end of the book.

11

Arms and Armour
of the Crusaders

The armour worn by the knights on the First Crusade must have been very much the same as that worn by the Normans at Hastings, to be seen in the Bayeux Tapestry (Plate 6). There they are shown wearing knee-length mail shirts, called hauberks, slit up to the fork of the legs so that the skirts hung down on either side of the saddle, and with sleeves reaching only to the elbow. The embroiderers used a number of conventional patterns to indicate the material of the hauberk, principally contiguous circles; occasionally trellis-work, sometimes with rings inside the trellis. Since, in some cases, more than one convention has been used on the same shirt, it is thought that the differences are of no great significance, and that probably all are intended to represent mail. In one place, however, Duke William's half-brother, Bishop Odo of Bayeux, is shown in what might be interpreted as a hauberk of overlapping scales. Although most of the hauberks have tight-fitting mail hoods, or coifs, made in one with them, a few appear to have coifs made of some material quite different from that of the hauberk, perhaps leather or cloth. In a few cases, riders are shown as wearing the coif without a helm of any sort, and this later became a very common practice until well into the fourteenth century.

In the Tapestry many hauberks are represented as having a rectangle outlined with bands of a different colour immediately below the neck. In one representation of Duke William this rectangle appears to have loose tags at the top corners, perhaps some form of tie. Another figure has these on the lower corners. It is not clear what this rectangle represents. It may be some form of reinforcement, perhaps an extra thickness of mail tied on or, on the other hand, it may be the ventail, the flap closing the neck opening.

The first interpretation is supported by a miniature in an Italian encyclopedia of 1023 at Monte Casino. This shows a solid green rectangle on a blue hauberk which is clearly made in one with its coif. On the other hand, an early eleventh-century Spanish Bible from the Monastery of Roda, now in the Bibliothèque Nationale, Paris (Ms. Lat. 6), and a closely related Bible in the Vatican Library (Codex Lat. 5729) both show the rectangle on the breast without a top-bar and as if an extension of the coif hanging over the breast. The lower part of the face is invariably uncovered. Something of this nature is much more clearly shown on a capital illustrating the *Psychomachia* in Nôtre-Dame-du-Port, Clermont Ferrand (Plate 14). With the exception of one figure, the faces are uncovered, the coifs are clearly made in one with the hauberk, and a large rectangle, apparently of mail, hangs below the throat. The face of the remaining figure is muffled up to the eyes in mail – presumably the rectangle drawn up over his mouth. If it were not frequently shown hanging down in battle one might presume that the embroiderers of the Bayeux Tapestry were representing this flap or ventail closing the face-opening. Furthermore, a similar rectangle is shown entirely without a coif on some figures in the Roda Bible, and on a figure in an early eleventh-century English Psalter at Oxford (Bodleian Library, Ms. Douce 296). In the Bayeux

Tapestry, in a few cases, there is only a single bar across the base of the neck, which could be interpreted as the lower edge of the coif if it was made separate from the hauberk. No certain illustration of a separate coif earlier than the next century has so far been discovered.

The part of the Tapestry where the bodies of the fallen at Hastings are being stripped and are shown as being naked under their hauberks, is a nineteenth-century restoration. It is extremely unlikely that mail could be worn in this way, since its weight would rub the edge of the rings harshly against the skin; in any case, an undergarment is shown at the wrists of most of the living figures. Robert Wace in his *Roman de Rou,* admittedly writing a good deal later, specifically tells us that Bishop Odo wore his hauberk over a white cloth shirt. Most other illustrations show long skirts of some soft material appearing under the edge of the hauberk. It may be that the coloured bands at the edges of the hauberks in the Tapestry represent some form of binding. They are also illustrated, for instance, in a Spanish manuscript of the *Commentary on the Pauline Epistles,* formerly in the Chester Beatty collection. A twelfth-century Saracen writer, Usāmah, refers to mail being lined with rabbits' fur.

The typical helm of this period had a conical skull with a nasal, apparently sometimes wide enough to make it difficult to identify the wearer, since Wace described how, at Hastings, Duke William had to raise his helm to dispel a rumour that he had fallen, an incident also recorded in the Tapestry. A helm of this type, found in the Priory of Olmütz, Moravia, is now in the Waffensammlung at Vienna. The skull and nasal are both worked out of the same piece of steel. On the other hand, some of the helms in the Tapestry seem to be made of many segments attached to a framework, like the Frankish helm already discussed. This construction, with particularly broad supporting bands, is still very clearly shown in the *Heisterbach Bible* of about 1240 (Berlin, Staatsbibliothek, theol. fol. 379). A helmet made up of several segments of iron riveted together but without a frame is in the Metropolitan Museum of Art, New York. Where, in the Bayeux Tapestry, the helms are shown on a cart being transported to the ships, it is clear that they are not made with a curtain of mail like the Frankish ones, but it is possible that they have some form of neck-guard. Nasal-helms with neck-guards are clearly illustrated, for instance, in a twelfth-century manuscript at Piacenza in Italy (Codex 65). A number of Norse ivory chessmen of about 1200, found at Uig on Lewis, have conical

Plate 8 Three of a group of Norse chessmen found at Uig in Lewis, about 1200. The one on the right wears a kettle-hat. The horseman has pendant ear- and nape-guards on his helm. (Reproduced by permission of the Trustees of the British Museum)

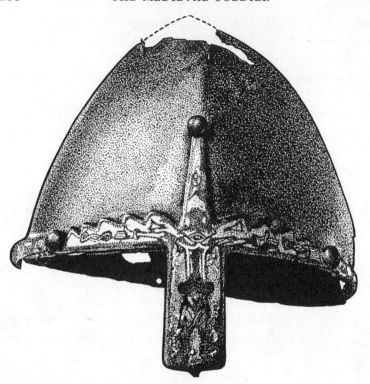

Figure 9 The helmet preserved in Prague cathedral as that of
St Wenceslaus (died 935). The applied nasal is decorated with the
figure of Christ crucified

helms with a pendant flap at the back of the neck, as well as
cheek-flaps (Plate 8). The helm of Duke William in the Tapestry has two short tags at the back like the *infulae* on a bishop's
mitre. It is not clear what these are, but many illustrations in
the next century show a long veil or scarf emerging from
beneath the helm at the back or, as in the first seal of King
Stephen of England (1135), two thin cords.

The *Chanson de Roland,* which is thought to be contemporary with the Tapestry, frequently refers to jewelled helms.
A stone capital in the Musée Granet at Aix-en-Provence

shows helmets with brow-bands apparently studded with jewels. The *Chanson de Roland* also mentions the Saracens lacing on their good Saragossa helms and, although no means of attaching the helm is indicated in the Tapestry, the statue of Roland outside Verona Cathedral shows a chin-cord worn over the mail of his coif, and the same thing occurs on a mid-twelfth-century capital from Nôtre-Dame-en-Vaux at Châlons-sur-Marne, now in the Musée du Louvre, Paris, and on another dateable to 1170 in the Museo Civico, Pavia, and on many other carvings.

An English manuscript of Pliny's *Natural History* at Le Mans (Ms. 263) illustrates Pliny's helm hanging up by means of its chin-cord beside his sword, spear and shield. Most representations show the strap branching at the top where it joins the helm, to give a two-point linkage and prevent the helm from waggling as the wearer moves.

A number of knights in the Tapestry are shown with their fore-arms protected by separate, wrist-length sleeves, apparently of mail, worn under the hauberk sleeves, and some have their legs similarly protected. As they are wearing shoes, one cannot be sure that the feet are also in mail. The fashion of wearing shoes with mail leg-armour is still found in the thirteenth-century *Alexander Book* at Trinity College, Cambridge (Ms. O. 9.34).

Although some of the Saxons at Hastings are illustrated with the old-fashioned round shield, most of the shields in the Tapestry are of the new long kite shape with a semicircular top edge, capable of covering the whole body from shoulder to knee. This type of shield was probably introduced about the last quarter of the tenth century for use by cavalrymen. One of the earliest illustrations of it is in a manuscript produced at Etternach between 983 and 991 (Gotha, Landesbibliothek, Cod. I. 19). The long point would protect the rider's highly vulnerable left side and leg far better than the old round shield which had to be moved to catch a blow. Since the shield hand also controlled the bridle it could not be moved rapidly. The right side was defended by the sword. The shield was held by means of various arrangements of straps approximately at the centre of balance. The boss, although still present, and occasionally represented even in the thirteenth century, no longer covered the hand-grip which was placed off-centre. The most common device was a saltire of straps which were grasped at the point of intersection. The Bayeux Tapestry, however, shows a number of more complicated methods. In one case, the saltire was augmented by two short straps below it through which the fore-arm passed to prevent the shield from flapping. A single additional strap of this type is shown on an early twelfth-century figure of Goliath on the west front of the Abbey of St Gilles, Gard, France. Others have a rectangle or diamond of straps, one side of which acted as the grip while the opposite side passed over the fore-arm. These straps were called 'brases'. An adjustable leather strap called the *guige* was attached to the shield near the brases. It could be used to hang the shield up in the hall, to sling it on the back if a two-handed grip was needed on a weapon, or to hang the shield round the owner's neck on his left shoulder in action, hence the conventional phrase '*Escu al col*' (*écu à col*) used to describe a knight ready for action. The surface of these shields was painted with a great variety of devices of which crosses and winged dragons are the commonest, but as yet there is no sign of any system of organized heraldry.

Probably as late as the Third Crusade (1189), some of the Crusaders were still dressed exactly like Duke William's Normans. For instance, a figure in the late twelfth-century English *Puiset Bible* (Durham Cathedral, Ms. A. ii.i) wears

Plate 9 The Joshua initial from the *Winchester Bible*, English, about 1160–70. The gowns are of unusual length and the sleeves of the hauberks leave only the fingers uncovered. (Reproduced by permission of the Dean and Chapter of Winchester Cathedral)

no other armour than a conical nasal-helm and a hauberk with elbow-length sleeves, very like those shown in the Bayeux Tapestry. His own men, and all but one of his opponents, are unarmoured except for shields and a few helms. The shields are unchanged from those used at Hastings.

Until about 1400, the conical nasal-helm is still illustrated occasionally, very often in the twelfth century, with the point of the skull slightly tilted forward. The helm, however, developed considerably during the period of the first three Crusades. Round-topped helms, with or without nasals, occur from early in the twelfth century as in the *Pembroke College Gospels* (Pembroke College, Cambridge, Ms. 120). *The Winchester Bible* of about 1160–70 also shows conical

Plate 10 Figures from the front of Angoulême Cathedral of about 1128, showing fluted helms, one drawn out at the back to protect the neck. (Reproduced by permission of the Cathedral authorities)

helms without nasals (Winchester Cathedral) (Plate 9). In order to protect the nape of the neck, the back of the helm was sometimes drawn out several inches deeper, like a sou' wester, as on the knights carved on the front of Angoulême cathedral about 1128, and another of about 1100 in the crypt of Modena cathedral (Plate 10). By the end of this century more or less cylindrical helms with flat or slightly domed tops, often with a nasal, became common; as in the *St Guthlac Roll* in the British Museum (Harl. Roll. Y.6), or in the seal of Philippe de Flandre et de Vermandois of 1162.

A German manuscript of the *Roulantes Liet* in Heidelberg University (Pal. Germ. 112) of about 1170 shows a short cross-bar, sometimes quite deep, on the end of the nasal, protecting the area of the mouth. In this manuscript, the ventail, the flap closing the neck of the coif, covers the whole face to just under the eyes, an arrangement found well on into the following century, as on the carved figures on the west front of Wells cathedral. A twelfth-century bible from Avila, now in the National Library at Madrid (Sign. Vit. 15–1), shows conical helms with a crescent-shaped plate on the end of the nasals, its points curving round to protect the lower part of the face opening of the coif. In the destroyed manuscript of the *Hortus Deliciarum* of Abbess Herrad of Landsberg, illuminated during the last quarter of the century, the ends of this crescent have reached up to join the edge of the skull, thus filling the whole of the face opening except in front of the eyes. This plate is pierced by many small holes to make breathing easier. By the early thirteenth century, the face-plate occasionally covers the whole front of the face, curved under the chin and pierced by two rectangular slits for the eyes, as in the Charlemagne window at Chartres cathedral of about 1210. Similar helms are shown on the Shrine of Charlemagne at Aachen cathedral, of 1200–7, and on the

Plate 11 Two knights from the West Front of Wells cathedral,
Somerset, English, about 1230–40. One wears a flat-topped,
cylindrical helm, and the other a specially shaped arming-cap.
(Reproduced by permission of the Dean and Chapter of Wells
Cathedral)

seal of Louis, son of Philip Augustus, of 1214, and in both cases they also have short neck-guards (Plate 13).

Two of the statues on the west front of Wells cathedral, of 1230–40, wear flat-topped cylindrical helms (Plate 11). Although they are made rather deeper at the front than at the back there is no longer a marked division into face-guard and neck-guard. The flat plate on top appears to have been made with a flange which fits down onto the top of the cylinder and to have been riveted to it all the way round. On one helm the sight is formed as a single slit serving for both eyes. On the other there is a vertical reinforcing bar down the centre of the front dividing the sight into two, which is very much the more common construction. On this sort of helm, the sight is always strengthened by a raised rib or bar running around the edge; the only surviving example is in the Zeughaus at Berlin (Plate 12). The upright reinforcing bar has two broad arms at right angles to it, each pierced with a rectangular slot, and these form the reinforces to the edge of the sight. This helm is pierced by numerous pairs of holes, presumably for the laces retaining a quilted lining. The Wells helms might have been similarly lined but the rather curious caps worn by some of the figures discussed below suggest that they may not have been.

The date of the Berlin helm is not at all certain. Very similar helms were still in use about 1270, as in the *Psalter of St Louis* (Paris, Bibl. Nat. M5. Lat. 10525).

Once the face was covered, some form of identification mark became essential. The organization, classification and description of these later developed into the science called Heraldry.

Several of the Norse chessmen found at Uig are wearing a new kind of headpiece, a broad-brimmed open-faced helmet called a 'kettle-hat', presumably from its resemblance to an

Plate 12 Helm, possibly of the mid-thirteenth century, excavated at Schlossberg bei Dargen, Pomerania, and now in the Museum für Deutsche Geschichte, Berlin. (Reproduced by permission of the Museum authorities)

inverted cauldron, then known as a kettle (Plate 8, page 199). This is probably the *vida stálhufa*, the wide steel-hat, of the Sagas. A resurrection page from a South German manuscript of about 1150 in the Metropolitan Museum, New York, shows the chin-straps dividing at the top to give a two-point linkage to the helm. By the middle of the thirteenth century, the kettle-hat was certainly considered suitable head-gear for a knight and one appears on the seal of Arnoul III, Count of Guines, of 1248. Although these are apparently made in one piece, many manuscripts, such as the *Maciejowski Bible*

Plate 13 A panel of the silver shrine of Charlemagne in Aachen cathedral, made between 1200 and 1207. It illustrates an arming-cap worn under the coif, helms with face and neck guards, and on the right the deep arson of the saddle. (Reproduced by permission of the Cathedral authorities)

of about 1250, show them as if constructed in the composite principle of earlier Frankish helmets but with a brim riveted on (Pierpont Morgan Library, New York) (Plate 7, page 192, and Plate 18, page 217).

The kettle-hat remained popular as long as armour was worn, and was the typical helmet of the seventeenth-century pike-man at the time when armour was falling into disuse. It was re-introduced as a shrapnel helmet for the British Army in 1915.

The Shrine of Charlemagne shows one of the knights with his coif flung back on his shoulders to reveal the tight-fitting quilted cap worn underneath as a shock-absorber to the mail (Plate 13). This cap is very common in thirteenth-century illustrations, like those of the *Maciejowski Bible*. Since, in this century particularly, the coif is very often worn without a helm, this padding must have been very important. The flat-topped coifs typical of the middle of the thirteenth century were apparently supported by specially shaped caps with a thick roll of padding around the top, as on one of the figures on Wells cathedral, of about 1230–40. A similar cap is shown on another of the Wells figures, worn over the mail, presumably as a support for the helm (Plate 11, right). It may be, of course, that additional protection was occasionally given by a steel cap worn under the coif. This is very difficult to prove but an effigy in Abergavenny church, probably of Lord John Hastings (died 1313), clearly shows the outline of a hard headpiece worn under his coif.

It is difficult to find illustrations of how the ventail was kept closed at this time, although a variety of differently shaped flaps are indicated in twelfth-century paintings and sculpture. However, a later effigy at Pershore Abbey, Worcestershire, has a long flap hanging down on the right side of the neck-opening of his coif, while a drawing by

Plate 14 A capital illustrating the *Psychomachia* in Nôtre-Dame-du-Port,
Clermont Ferrand. French, middle of the twelfth century.
It shows the ventail hanging down, and, on the left, covering the mouth.
(Reproduced by permission of the Church authorities from a
photograph taken by Mr James Austin, Cambridge)

Plate 15 A drawing by Matthew Paris or one of his followers,
English, about 1250, from British Museum Roy. Ms. 2. A. XXII.
Notice the unusual leg defences and what appears to be a shoulder
defence under the gown. (Reproduced by permission of the Trustees
of the Museum)

Matthew Paris of a kneeling knight of about 1250 in the British Museum shows a similar flap drawn tightly across the throat and laced to the coif above the left ear (Ms. Roy. 2. A.xxii) (Plate 15). An effigy at Shepton Mallet, and that of William Longspée the Elder, Earl of Salisbury, in Salisbury cathedral, shows a flap with a broad rectangular end held up by the brow-band of the coif which is laced through it.

In some cases, the ventail is formed by the face-opening being made so large and loose that the chin and throat are left exposed until action is expected, as in the *Codex Calixtinus* in the Archives of St James of Compostella. Later ventails of this type are shown either with a lining, as on a figure of about 1300 from Strasbourg cathedral, now in the cathedral museum, or unlined, as on the effigy of Landgrave Johann, died 1311, at Marburg. A group of slightly later English effigies, such as that of Sir Peter de Saltmarshe (died 1338) at Howden in Yorkshire, have a knotted lace on either side of the face perhaps holding up a ventail of this type.

During the twelfth century, long-sleeved hauberks became common and by about 1200 the hand was often protected by a mail bag-mitten, consisting of one bag for the thumb and another for the fingers, made in one with the sleeve, as in the Shrine of Charlemagne (Plate 13). A cord or strap round the wrist prevented the weight of the mail dragging on the gauntlet. When action was not imminent these gloves could be allowed to hang loose from the wrist, the hand emerging from a hole in the centre of the palm which, to allow a firm grip, was covered not in mail but in cloth or leather. The earliest illustration of a cuffed gauntlet made independently of the hauberk sleeve is in a drawing in Matthew Paris's *Chronica Minora* of about 1250 (Cambridge, Corpus Christi Coll. Ms. 16). The word 'haubergeon', a diminutive of hauberk, which occurs in writings of this time, presumably

Plate 16 A man at arms from the *York Psalter*, English, about
1170–75. The trellis worn over his hauberk has not yet been
satisfactorily explained. (Reproduced by permission of the Librarian,
The Hunterian Library, Glasgow University) (Ms. U. 3. 2. fol. 54v)

Plate 17 Figures formerly on the twelfth-century Porta Romana at Milan, now in Castello Sforzesco. One is wearing a complete hauberk of scale. (Reproduced by permission of the authorities of the Museo Civico, Milan)

refers to the brief mail shirts, sometimes with short sleeves, that frequently appear in paintings and sculpture.

An apparently unique representation in the *York Psalter* of about 1170–5 shows a series of white bands edged with red, forming a trellis over the hauberk through which the mail covering the body and arms is visible. It does not cover the coif (Glasgow University, Hunterian Ms. U.3.2). So far, no explanation of this has been put forward (Plate 16).

The coif is occasionally represented as if made separately from the hauberk, for instance, in the *Glossar von Salomon von Konstanz* of about 1150 (Munich, Bay. Staatsbibl. Clm. 13002), where the coif is apparently made of scales while the hauberk is clearly not.

Scale armour was clearly a popular substitute for mail at this time, for instance, a hauberk completely made of small scales is illustrated on the late twelfth-century Porta Romana at Milan (Plate 17). A Moravian manuscript in the Pierpont Morgan Library (Ms. 7739) probably made between 1213 and 1220, illustrates hauberks made of quite large scales, as does the early twelfth-century carving of Goliath on the west front of the Abbey of St Gilles. A German poem of the late twelfth century, *Wigalois,* mentions that the scales were sometimes made of cow-horn, a light but tough material very difficult to cut.[1]

Wace in his *Roman de Rou* mentions a new form of body armour, the *curie,* which from the derivation of the word was presumably made of leather, *cuir*. No illustration of this date is known, but Guillaume le Breton writing before 1225 indicated that it is armour for the breast, while the romance *Gaidon* of about 1230 shows that it was certainly made of leather, at least in this case, was sometimes reinforced with

[1] J. Hewitt, Vol. I, p. 133.

Plate 18 A page from the *Maciejowski Bible*. Ms. 638 f. 27 v. The
waistcoat of the man seated in the cart in the upper section is
probably some kind of body armour. (Reproduced by permission of
the authorities of the Pierpont Morgan Library)

iron, and was worn over the hauberk but under the gown. Although no illustration of this is known in the twelfth century, several mid-thirteenth-century manuscripts show waist-length sleeveless jackets made of some stiff material. For instance, a single figure in the *Maciejowski Bible* wears one over his ordinary tunic without any other armour, except his arming cap and a small hemispherical headpiece *(cervel-lière)* (Plate 18, top right). It appears to open down the sides under the arm and was presumably put on over the head like a poncho. A similar garment is shown, worn over a hauberk,

Plate 19 A miniature from an English *Apocalypse* of about 1250–75. The man with the sword, pointing, is wearing what appears to be a body-armour reinforced with four circular plates. (Reproduced by permission of the authorities of the Fondação Calouste Gulbenkian)

in an English *Apocalypse* at Lisbon (Gulbenkian Ms. L.A. 139) (Plate 19). In both manuscripts, the laces are clearly shown at two points under the arm. In the *Apocalypse,* the surface is possibly reinforced by a number of circular metal plates. The earliest recorded illustration of what is probably one of these body armours is a wall-painting of about 1227 in the baptistry of St Gereon's, Cologne. Something of this nature is shown more certainly, in this case under the gown, on the effigy of Hugo II, Châtelain of Ghent (died 1232), now in the Abbey at Niewen Bossche, Heusden, near Ghent.

In the second half of the thirteenth century, the gown is occasionally represented as if lined with plates, as on the figure of a sleeping guard on a reliquary at Wienhausen in Germany (Plate 20). The position of the plates is indicated by the rivet heads which secure them to the fabric, and often by a suggestion of the outline of the plates showing through the cloth. Nothing like this has been discovered for the early part of the century but very often gowns, clearly made of a soft clinging material, stand stiffly away from the point of the shoulder; as, for instance, on the statues on the front of Wells cathedral (1230–40). The drawing of a kneeling knight by Matthew Paris mentioned above, shows that this may be due to some form of stiff shoulder guard which, in this case, is clearly illustrated beneath the gown, and separate from it (Plate 15). One of the Wells figures, however, has a stiff up-standing collar to his gown, so that it is at least possible that the stiffening of the shoulders is also an integral part of the garment (Plate 11, page 206).

The characteristic body armour of the first three-quarters of the fourteenth century was the 'coat of plates', sometimes simply called 'plates'. It normally appears in paintings as a short, usually sleeveless, tunic, powdered with small circles or flowers which are, in fact, the large heads of the rivets

Plate 20 Sleeping guard from a reliquary at Wienhausen, Germany,
second half of the thirteenth century. His gown is apparently
reinforced by rows of narrow, vertical plates riveted to its inside.
(Reproduced by permission of the authorities of the
Niedersächsiche Landesgalerie, Hannover)

attaching the overlapping plates inside to their cloth covering. This type is characteristic of north Italian paintings, such as the series of the life of St George by Altichiero in the Chapel of St George, Padua, of about 1380–90. It is not clear when the coat of plates first appears, but tunics powdered with dots and circles, very similar indeed to those in the Altichiero paintings, occur in the work of Matthew Paris and his colleagues about 1250, and also in a Spanish *Beatus, Commentary on the Apocalypse* of very much the same date or even a little earlier (Paris, Bibl. Nat., Nouv. acq. lat. 2290). In the *Beatus* manuscript what appear to be nail heads are clearly shown in horizontal rows on the surface of the coat, as well as the vertical seams of the covering material.

Another form of body armour was apparently just beginning to come into use. Guillaume le Breton, describing a fight between William des Barres and the future Richard I of England, says that the lances pierced shield, hauberk and gambeson, and rebounded from a plate of worked iron on the breast, beneath all these.

The gambeson is first referred to by Wace as an alternative to the mail hauberk. Later references show that this was a coat, usually made of two thicknesses of linen, padded with wool, cotton, or old rags, and quilted like an eiderdown to keep the stuffing in place (Plate 7, page 192). The quilting was usually in parallel lines, sometimes crossing like a trellis. This resisted sword cuts quite well and deadened the force of a blow. It was the common defence of those unable to afford a hauberk. The Assize of Arms of Henry II of England in 1181 gives it as a minimum requirement of all burghers, and of freemen with goods and rents worth less than 10 marks a year. A similar garment was worn under the hauberk to prevent the rings from chafing the skin, certainly from the early thirteenth century when references first occur to lances piercing shield, hauberk, gambeson, and breastbone. However, no illustration of a quilted undergarment of this period seems to be known. An alternative name for this coat is the aketon, from the Arabic for cotton, *al-qutun,* with which it was stuffed. Later inventories differentiate between aketons and gambesons but the distinction is not at all clear.

A manuscript of the *Roman de Perceval* of about 1160 describes a warrior being armed in a gambeson of silk over which he puts a quilted aketon.[1] The *Maciejowski Bible,* which appears to show on many figures a sleeveless quilted garment worn over one with sleeves, perhaps illustrates this (Plate 18, upper left). A Saracen writer, Beha ed-Din ibn Shedad, describing the Christian infantry at Arsouf, says of them: 'Each foot-soldier had a thick cassock of felt, and under it a mail-shirt, so strong that our arrows made no impression on them. .... I noted among them men who had from one to ten shafts sticking in their backs, yet trudged on at their ordinary pace and did not fall out of the ranks.'

Although a good many knights still fought without leg-armour, there were two different kinds in general use. One consisted of long mail stockings (hosen), braced up to a waist-belt under the hauberk, and gartered under the knee to prevent the weight of the mail dragging. The other type consisted of a strip of mail covering the front of the leg and top of the foot only, held on by laces around the back of the leg. This type was also braced up to the waist-belt. An example of the first type is shown in the Shrine of Charlemagne, and of the second in an English Psalter of about 1200 in Leiden University (Ms. Lat. 76A). In the second type, it is quite clear that cloth hose were worn under the mail since they are visible, and in the first case it seems most probable that they were

---

[1] Gay, *Glossaire Archéologique,* I, 1887, p. 757.

Plate 21 'Pallas and Turnus begin the battle' from the German, early thirteenth-century manuscript of the *Eneid*. It illustrates early examples of free-standing crests and of thigh defences (cuisses) worn over the mail leg harness. (Reproduced by permission of the authorities of the Staatsbibliothek Preussischer Kulturbesitz, Berlin)

there, although unseen. In an early thirteenth-century manuscript of the *Eneide* at Tübingen University, two people are
shown putting on their mail hosen. It is clear that both are
wearing some form of cloth stockings underneath. The
drawing by Matthew Paris of a kneeling knight of about
1250 shows quite clearly that, at least in this case, the two mail
legs are not joined at the fork where part of the knight's shirt
or drawers appears (Roy. Ms. 2. A. xxii) (Plate 15, page 212).

The early thirteenth-century manuscript of the *Eneide*
shows for the first time some form of thick padding worn
on the thighs, over the mail hosen (Plate 21). An illustration
in the *Maciejowski Bible* shows a man sitting down to put
these thigh defences on. They consist of two separate
tapering tubes of some thick material, probably quilted, and
would presumably have had to be tied to the waist-belt.

In German lands quilted thigh-defences (cuisses) are frequently illustrated extending down to mid-calf. Below the
knee they often appear to be cut into vertical strips, the edges
of which seem to be laced together, presumably to give a
tight fit, as for instance in a Psalter of the first half of the
thirteenth century in the British Museum (Add. Ms. 17687).

A knight engraved on the reliquary of St Maurice (dated
1225) in the treasury of the Abbey of St Maurice, Switzerland,
has a saucer-shaped plate attached to his cuisse over the knee-
cap. The Trinity College Apocalypse, which illustrates a
similar small plate worn directly over the mail, has hitherto
been dated about 1230, but is now thought to be about 1245
to 1250 (Trinity College, Cambridge, Ms. R. 16.2). (The
Icelandic writer of the *King's Mirror,* which is thought to be
of about 1240–50, describes these knee-defences as being of
iron.[1]) In this case the knee-plate is cup-shaped but has a tri-

[1] L.M. Larson, *The King's Mirror, Scandinavian Monographs,* III, New York
1917, p. 219.

angular extension to protect the outside of the knee joint. On two folios there are, in addition, narrow plates on the front of the shin tapering towards the ankle. No method of attachment is shown but numerous later illustrations make it clear that they are held on by straps round the leg over the mail. In the *Maciejowski Bible,* Goliath wears rather broader steel shin-guards (schynbalds) strapped round the centre of the calf. Possibly a second strap at the top is concealed by the quilted cuisses which guard his thighs and knees and seem to cover the top edge of the schynbald (Plate 18, page 217).

Once the face was covered by the helm, some form of identification of friend from foe was essential. The second seal of Richard I of England, probably of the year 1194, shows a fan-like object attached to the top of his helm on which is depicted a lion like those on his shield. The *Liber ad honorem augusti* of Pietro de Eboli of about 1200 (Bern, Codex 120) shows the devices painted on the knights' shields repeated on the sides of their conical, or round-topped nasal-helms. Usually these are abstract, diagonals, chevrons, crosses, and circles, but the Emperor already has an eagle, and the Margrave Diopold von Schweinspoint has a wild boar. This is the first known example of a favourite contrivance of heralds, the canting arms, in which the device is a pun on the bearer's name (Plate 25).

The manuscript of the *Eneide* at Tübingen shows fantastic crests on the helms, birds and animals modelled apparently in the round, and flanked by little flags (Plate 21). In some cases, the device is painted on the side of the helm, a feature which seems to have been very popular, particularly in Spain where it was used on open helms as well as on fully enclosing ones. Some of the helms in this manuscript have long scarves wrapped round them with trailing ends, as if descendants of the scarves mentioned above, but these seem to be the veils of the Amazon warriors and are not found on the male figures.

During the second half of the twelfth century devices used on shields began to be adopted by the sons of the original bearers. The golden lions on the blue shield held by Geoffrey, Count of Anjou, on his tomb-plate of about 1150 at Le Mans, are the ancestors of the lions of the English royal arms borne by his Plantagenet descendants on a red ground. On the other hand, his illegitimate descendant William Longspée the Elder, Earl of Salisbury, bore the same arms as Geoffrey, as is shown by his effigy and a description of the arms in an early heraldic work called Glover's Roll.

From about the middle of the twelfth century a loose flowing gown was occasionally worn over the hauberk, as on the seal of Waleran de Bellomonte, Earl of Worcester, before 1150. This example has long sleeves with long trailing cuffs, but more usually, as in the Winchester Bible of about 1160–70, they have no sleeves at all (Plate 9, page 203). The gown did not become common until the early thirteenth century when, in manuscripts like the *Eneide*, almost all the knights wear it, usually sleeveless and reaching to mid-calf. It is normally split up to the fork of the legs, before and behind, to allow it to hang freely when the wearer was in the saddle. It had a separate belt or cord at the waist independent of the sword-belt. It may have been introduced to protect the mail from the heat of the sun on the Crusades or, as the poem of *The Avowing of King Arthur* and *The Buke of Knychthede* suggest, to protect it from the wet. More probably, it is in imitation of Saracen costume. All through history, armies have been prone to copy the dress or uniform of their opponents. Early examples of the gown are nearly always shown as white or self-coloured, and it is only later that the device on the shield is also painted or embroidered on it.

A loose cloth covering for the horse, called the housing,

also appeared before the end of the century, as in two seals of Alfonso II of Aragon, of 1186 and 1193 respectively. The second of these clearly shows the vertical stripes of the owner's arms. Housings were usually divided into two parts; one covering the head and withers, the other covering the crupper behind the saddle. In the manuscript of the *Liber ad honorem augusti* they have jagged edges reaching to within about one foot from the ground and bear the arms of the rider. In a few cases, only the front part was worn, as on the seal of Louis II, Count of Looz, of 1216. The seal matrix of Robert Fitzwalter (1198–1234) in the British Museum shows the horse's head covered in different material to the rest of the housing, and this may be defensive. There are a number of later references to *testiers* and *chanfreins,* the armour for a horse's head, in thirteenth-century documents. Illustrations of hoods similar to that shown on this seal, but made independent of any housing, are found in manuscripts towards the end of the century. Horse armour of iron *(fer)* is mentioned by Wace writing between 1160 and 1174 but, it has been suggested, only because of the need to find a rhyme for the name Osber. The first record of what are apparently horse armours, one of mail and one of linen, probably to be worn with the mail over the fabric, is in the inventory of Falk de Brauté made in 1224.[1]

Although the round-topped, kite-shaped shield continued in use down to about 1200, and was in fact used by spear-carrying infantry in Italy until the fifteenth century, it was largely superseded by a new type with straight top by about 1150, as on the seal of Robert de Vitré (1158–61). The removal of the arched top probably made it easier to see over the shield without reducing its protection. The boss still occasionally

[1] *Publications of the Bedfordshire Record Society,* IX, Aspley Guise 1924, p. 60.

appears even in the thirteenth century. The *Liber ad honorem augusti,* while still showing the older form of kite-shaped shield, indicates that it is comparatively smaller than before; and the *Eneide* manuscript shows it only some two-thirds the size of the Bayeux Tapestry shield, although still large enough to be used as a stretcher to carry off the wounded. Many illustrations show the shield horizontally curved so that it laps round the wearer's shoulders, as in the *Eneide* manuscript.

A single shield of this period has survived, although it has been altered to a more modern shape by cutting off the arched top at some date about 1230–50. It bears the arms of a member of the von Brienz family, probably Arnold who in 1197 founded the convent where the shield was found, and died in 1225. It is 15 mm thick, of wood covered in parchment on both sides, and on the front is a very stylized silver lion on a blue ground. The original length of the shield before it was altered must have been 95 to 100 cm, which means it would have reached from the shoulder to the knee. This is approximately the same proportion as the shield held by the earliest effigy in the Temple Church in London, that said to be of William Marshal, Earl of Pembroke, died 1219. Rather larger shields are held by two of the later effigies in this church. On the back of the von Brienz shield are traces of the guige and brases, as well as the pad for the fist, which is illustrated in the *Eneide* manuscript.

The older round shield did not entirely disappear; it is often shown in Spanish art and in illustrations of Saracens. A very small round shield called a buckler, held by a central grip usually behind a boss, was used throughout the Middle Ages, normally by infantry but occasionally by knights, as on an effigy in Malvern Abbey, Worcestershire, of about 1240. A small round shield held by means of a single central grip is shown on a portable altar of about 1160 in Augsburg.

At some time during this period, a new method of using the cavalry shield with the couched spear was adopted. In the Bayeux Tapestry and other sources of that period, the shield is grasped by the brases with the left hand, which is held level with the shoulder and also holds the knotted ends of the two reins. This method is still shown in the mid-thirteenth-century *Lives of the two Offas* in the British Museum (Ms. Cott. Nero. D.I.). On the other hand, the illustrations of Matthew Paris's *Chronica Maior,* also of about 1250, show the bridle hand held in the modern riding position just above the saddle bow, and not holding the shield which hangs from the neck on the guige (Corpus Christi College, Cambridge). It may be that a single brase was used over the upper arm only, as in the *Alexander Book* at Trinity College, Cambridge (Ms. 0.9.34). *Le Tournois de Chauvenci* of 1285 still says, 'L'escu au col fort embracié', implying that the arm was through the brases. This method is still shown in a Lombard drawing of the fourteenth century in the Pierpont Morgan Library, New York. By the late thirteenth century, however, the shield was apparently frequently hung on the guige with no other support when the spear was couched, and only when the spear was broken and the sword was used was the hand transferred to the brases.

Wace described the Norman archers at Hastings as wearing short tunics, and thus the Bayeux Tapestry shows them, with the exception of one in full armour who is presumably an officer. The quivers were hung either on the right side of the waistbelt or behind the right shoulder. Archers shown in the *Liber ad honorem augusti* of about 1200 are still without armour of any sort although some of the crossbowmen have conical nasal-helms (Plate 25). Although none is illustrated in the Tapestry, the anonymous author of the poem *Carmen*

de Hastingae Proelio, reports that many crossbowmen were
present in the Norman ranks.

The crossbow, or arblast, which was known certainly
from late Roman times, since it is mentioned by Vegetius
writing about the year 385 and is shown in a Roman carving
in the Musée Crozatier, Le Puy, consists of a short heavy bow
mounted horizontally at right angles to one end of a straight
stock, called the tiller. The bowstring was held in the spanned
position in a groove in a horizontally rotating, barrel-shaped
catch, called the nut, set into the stock. The nut was prevented
from rotating and allowing the string to snap forward by
means of a long, lever-like 'trigger', the forward end of
which engaged in a groove cut in the underside of the nut.
The arrow or bolt was laid in a groove along the top of the
stock with its rear end immediately in front of the nut. The
bow was aimed by holding the rear of the stock against the
cheek, and was discharged by pressing up the rear end of
the 'trigger'. Since the stout iron heads of the crossbow bolt
were often of square cross-section, they were usually called
'quarrels' from the French *carré*. The *Eneide* manuscript shows
a quiver of D-shaped cross-section with a narrow neck just
below the mouth, presumably to prevent the arrows or bolts
from rattling together. A similar quiver is also shown in the
early twelfth-century *Pembroke College Gospels*.

Anna Comnena, daughter of the Emperor of Byzantium,
describes this weapon in the hands of the Crusaders as something entirely new to the Byzantines. 'He who stretches this
war-like and very far-shooting weapon must lie, one might
say, almost on his back and apply both feet strongly against
the semi-circle of the bow and with his hands pull the string
with all his might in the contrary direction. ... The arrows
used with this bow are very short in length, but very thick,
fitted in front with a very heavy iron tip'.

By the early thirteenth century at the latest, because of the increase in strength of the bow, it was spanned by means of a hook attached to the centre of the bowman's waist-belt. The string was passed over the hook and the bow flexed by placing the foot in a stirrup lashed to the forward end of the stock and then straightening the leg. A stirrup of this type is illustrated in the *Trinity College Apocalypse* (see Plate 7, page 192).

Although the use of the crossbow was anathematized by Pope Innocent II at the second Lateran Council in 1139, and by many later decrees, it became one of the most important weapons of the Middle Ages, particularly in the hands of well-trained mercenaries. It was generally considered a judgment on Richard I that he died from a wound inflicted by a crossbow bolt, since he had employed the weapon so extensively himself.

The primary cavalry weapon was still the spear. In the eleventh century it was still normally wielded at arm's length and very often over-arm, as shown in the Bayeux Tapestry. In moments of great need, the spear might be thrown, as at Hastings, where it was necessary to make gaps in the Saxon shield-wall to allow the cavalry to break through. The new method of holding the lance couched, that is, tucked under the right arm with the hand held just in front of the shoulder, was becoming more popular. This gave much greater rigidity to the weapon, and the strength of the wielder's right arm was replaced by the speed of the horse carrying man and spear as a single missile. It is clear from descriptions in poetry that when action was imminent the spear was carried more or less upright with its butt end resting on the front of the saddle, and that the spear was not actually couched until immediately before the impact. In order to balance the weight of the spear, and probably also to keep the shield towards the enemy, the contestants, where possible, passed left-side to left-side, with the spear crossed over the horse's neck, as shown on the carvings on Modena cathedral of about 1099–1106.

The early twelfth-century *Châsse de Saint Hadelin* at Visé shows a spear with a small ring fitted over the haft at about the point where it is gripped. This was probably used to improve the grip on the lance and prevent the shock from forcing the weapon back through the wielder's hand. It was, apparently, a very rare feature until a much later date.

The cavalry spear now invariably had a plain leaf-shaped head with a very acute point, and the older winged spear was only used by infantry and by huntsmen.

In the Bayeux Tapestry the flags shown on cavalry spears are almost all square with three small triangular streamers on the outer edge. One is semi-circular with nine small triangles attached to its rim. The dragon 'standard' of Saxon England, on the other hand, is illustrated not as a true flag but as if made in the round, or cut out completely from the flat. Wace distinguishes between the *gonfalons* carried by barons and the *penons* carried by knights. The *Winchester Bible* of about 1160–70 shows flags exactly like those in the Tapestry, but the figures on the front of San Zeno Maggiore at Verona, carved about 1139, carry square flags laced to the spears at three points and with three long, rectangular streamers on their outer edge. A number of late thirteenth-century flags of this type have survived in the Abbey of Köningsfelden and are now in the Museum at Bern, Switzerland. The *Liber ad honorem augusti* illustrated the long triangular penons used throughout most of the Middle Ages. Another type of pennant, shaped like a long right-angled triangle with its second shortest side against the shaft and the right angle at the bottom, was also popular, as in a twelfth-century Spanish Bible at Amiens (Ms. 108).

Once the use of the couched lance became popular a steadier seat on the horse was required. The saddles of the Bayeux Tapestry have a breast-band and are slightly built up before and behind the seat, but by about 1200 a tall, protective back-piece, partially encircling the rider's hips, and a similar but narrower piece at the front had developed. These were called the arsons *(arçons)*. Occasionally these were painted with the owner's heraldic arms, presumably to identify him more readily to an infantryman who could not easily see the device on his helm.

To give the greatest possible support to the saddle at the moment of impact, the breast-band was sometimes, as shown in the *Maciejowski Bible,* strapped round the rear arson and the girths were often doubled, one sometimes passing over the top of the seat. In spite of this, girths sometimes broke, as described in the *Chanson de Roland* where both contestants crash to the ground simultaneously. The knight did not sit in the saddle so much as stand on his stirrups with almost straight legs, supported by the arsons in front and behind. The *Chanson de Roland* describes how Roland, al-though he had fainted from loss of blood, was supported in his saddle by the stirrups. In the twelfth century a deep saddle-cloth with long dagged lower edge was worn over the saddle with the arsons emerging through slots in it. The girth is sometimes shown passing over the saddle-cloth.

The bridle was normally fitted with a bit with long side-levers to the lower ends of which the reins were attached, and was presumably therefore some form of curb, although no firmly dated medieval example seems to be known earlier than the one found in the ruins of Schloss Tannenberg, Prussia, destroyed in 1399. A curb bit is, however, clearly illustrated in an Astrological Treatise of about the second quarter of the fourteenth century (British Museum, Sloane Ms. 3983).

The Romans had used curb-bits but the Barbarian cavalry used only snaffles. The bits found in Barbarian cemeteries from Lombardy to Scandinavia all have simple mouth-pieces, usually jointed, with side-rings and no side-levers.

Once his lance was broken by the impact of the charge, the rider drew his sword and, if necessary shifting his grip on the shield, attacked his opponent with mighty blows; according to the poets, cleaving him through jewelled helm, through skull and body, right down into the saddle.

Many of the swords used by the Normans had the same broad blade with a wide fuller as used by the Vikings; indeed, the blades in some cases are inlaid with the same name, Ingelrii, and are presumably from the same source. The average blade length is about a metre, and the broad fuller runs to within an inch or so of the rather sharp point. Many have inscriptions inlaid in large iron capital letters, but these are often of a religious nature; for instance, HOMO DIE, or IN NOMINE DOMINI, or a garbled version of one of these.

A new type of blade appeared about AD 1000, longer, more slender, and with a narrow and shallow fuller stopping about 20 cm from the point. The average length is about 13 cm longer than the earlier type. The earliest known example of this blade has runes of English, tenth-century type cut in its tang. The 'Sword of St Maurice' in the Treasury at Vienna, the Sword of State of the Holy Roman Emperors, which was probably refurbished for the Emperor Otto IV (1197–1212) since it bears his personal arms on the pommel, has a blade of this type. Some of these blades also have inlaid inscriptions but with smaller iron letters to fit the narrower fuller. A number include the phrase GICELIN ME FECIT (Gicelin made me). The majority of those with inscriptions, however, have them inlaid with widely spaced, beautifully formed letters made of thin brass or white-metal wire, as on a sword,

now in the Bury St Edmunds Museum, found on the site of
the Battle of Fornham fought in 1173. This has on one side
'+SESBENEDICA+ AS', and on the other '+IN OMINEDOM-
INI+.' Inscribed blades are quite often illustrated in manuscripts and in carvings. The statue of Roland outside Verona
cathedral has the name of his sword, Durendal, cut along the
blade, while Goliath in the *Maciejowski Bible* has 'GOLIAS' on
his.

Just at the end of this period, another new type of blade
began to appear, broad, evenly tapering, and with a sharp
point. It had a marked fuller running for about four-fifths
of the length of the blade. The taper meant that the blade was
less point-heavy, and the point of percussion was nearer the
hand, making the sword more wieldy than earlier ones, not
only for cutting but also for thrusting.

Although the vast majority of illustrations of swords of
this period show straight blades, long, slender, curved blades
occur in a wall painting of the Martyrdom of St Thomas,
about 1200, in St Mary's Church, Egara, Spain, in the early
eleventh-century Spanish Bible in the Vatican Library
(Codex Lat. 5729), and in a Salzburg *Antiphonar* of the late
twelfth century (Salzburg, Abbey of St Peter, Codex A.
XII.7).

The hilt also developed considerably during this period.
The most common forms of pommel were the brazil-nut and
the tea-cosy, discussed under the Saxons, or a form between
the two. These pommels no longer have the old divisions
marked on them in the way some late Saxon ones have.
Decoration of any sort is exceptionally rare. The disc-pommel
first noted in Ælfric's *Paraphrase of the Pentateuch* remained
rare in the eleventh century, became increasingly common
in the following century, and largely replaced the other
types in the thirteenth century. The Fornham sword presum-

ably made before 1173, for instance, has a plain disc-pommel; others are illustrated in *St Swithun's Psalter* before 1161 (British Museum, Ms. Cott. Nero C. iv). The *Bible of St Etienne Harding* completed before 1109 shows a trefoil-shaped pommel, a type particularly popular in the thirteenth century (Dijon, Bibliothèque Publ., Mss. 12–15).

The cross-guard was now longer than on Viking swords, usually of square cross-section, straight, and sometimes tapering towards the ends. A few late Viking hilts have this type of quillons but are quite exceptional. An excellent illustration of one of the new fashion of hilts, with brazil-nut pommel and long straight quillons, occurs in a *Sacramentary* from Bamberg cathedral of the first quarter of the eleventh century, (Munich, Staatsbibl. Clm. 4456, fol. 11^r). The Vienna 'Sword of St Maurice' has a stout brazil-nut pommel and a long straight cross-guard. Although straight cross-guards remained the commonest type, in the twelfth century the ends are sometimes turned sharply towards the blade, as illustrated in the mid-century *Lambeth Bible* (Lambeth Palace Ms. 3), or the whole cross is gently curved towards the blade as in the late twelfth-century *Munich Psalter* (Munich, Staatsbibl. Clm. 835). Cross-guards with tightly curled ends are illustrated in the *York Psalter* of about 1170–5 in the Hunterian Museum, Glasgow. On one surviving sword of the twelfth century, with the second type of blade and a tea-cosy pommel, the ends of the cross-guard are turned sharply towards the blade and are carved as small animal heads.

Since the majority of surviving swords of this period are excavated, often from river beds, there is rarely any trace of the grip. Representations in art are not usually clear enough at this period to tell us anything about the style of binding but they consistently show a grip tapering evenly towards the pommel. An early twelfth-century *Commentary on the*

Psalms at St Scholastica near Subiaco in Italy (Ms. CXXI 124) shows a grip apparently bound with interlaced thongs or ribbons. In some cases, the grip is bound with a fairly thick thong interlaced to form a trellis over the grip binding to make the sword less likely to slip in a sweaty hand. This is shown in a twelfth-century manuscript of the *Etymologie* of Isodorus (St John's College, Cambridge Ms. 214) and on the figure of St Theodore on the front of Chartres cathedral of about 1225–30, and is found on surviving swords of later date (Figure 10).

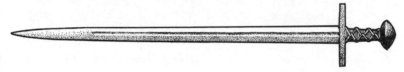

Figure 10 A reconstruction of a sword of the second half of the eleventh century or the first half of the twelfth, based on an example in the Nationalmuseet, Copenhagen

The only surviving everyday scabbard of this period is on a second 'Sword of St Maurice' in the Royal Armoury at Turin. This is of thin wood covered with parchment and has an openwork metal guard on the tip, consisting of a U-shaped strip protecting the edge with its upper ends linked by a chevron-shaped bar. The sword on the effigy of Henry II of England (d. 1189) at Fontevrault Abbey in Anjou has a simple tall U-shaped guard to its scabbard tip. There is no metal mount at the mouth to the Turin St Maurice scabbard but near its upper edge are remains of the belt and the holes by which it was laced to the scabbard. The portion of the belt nearest the top came round the front of the wearer, the portion fixed some inches down the scabbard passed right round the wearer's back to join up with the other portion at the centre of the front. The two parts being at different heights caused the sword to hang with its point slightly to the rear, where it was not so likely to trip up the wearer. The upper part of the belt was laced firmly to the scabbard and linked by laces to the lower part of the belt to prevent the two parts sliding apart.

Although the Bayeux Tapestry shows sword-belts with buckles, the great majority of illustrations show the ends of the belt knotted together, as, for instance, on the guards of the Sepulchre on a capital of about 1140–50 in the parish church at St Nectaire, Puy-de-Dôme. A belt of this type has survived in Bamberg cathedral. The front portion has two parallel longitudinal slits near the end, the other portion is cut into two long narrow ribbons. These are each threaded through the appropriate slit from behind and then knotted together in front. Quite often, presumably to prevent it from being cut, the sword-belt was worn under the hauberk. The hilt appeared through a slit in the hip of the hauberk and the end of the scabbard emerged from beneath the hauberk skirts. This is shown, for instance, in the Bayeux Tapestry, the *St Swithun's Psalter* (illustrated before 1161) and the *Winchester Bible* of 1160–70.

The coming of Christianity may have taken away some of the sword's magic, but replaced this with its own religious significance. Oaths were still taken on sword hilts as formerly, and their sanctity was probably reinforced by the symbolism of the cross-shaped hilt. Relics were, apparently, occasionally concealed in the pommel to give the wielder the saint's protection, as in Charlemagne's Joyeuse. The inscriptions on the blade were probably for the same purpose. The sword, although carried by all ranks of the army, was considered peculiarly the symbol of chivalry. It was laid on the altar during the vigil before knighthood, girt on the knight's side at the climax of the ceremony of knighthood, and hung over

Plate 22 The so-called Sword of Charlemagne in the Musée du Louvre. Probably actually of twelfth-century date it was used for many centuries as the Coronation sword of the kings of France. (Reproduced by permission of the Museum authorities)

Plate 23 Sword of a type common in the second half of the thirteenth century. Found in the River Witham near Lincoln, it is now in the British Museum. (Reproduced by permission of the Trustees)

Plate 24 Bronze mace-head found on Mattas farm, Finby, Sund,
Åland, Finland; now in the Museum of Mariehamn, Finland. It was
probably made in the second half of the twelfth century, possibly in
the Rhineland. (Reproduced by permission of Dr Mr Dreijer, Curator
of the Museum. Photograph copyright National Museum Helsinki)

his tomb when he died. In the *Chanson de Roland,* the dying hero desperately tries to break the blade of Durendal on a stone rather than allow his famous weapon to be used by an infidel after his death. If a knight disgraced the order of chivalry his sword was broken in front of him by a menial.

The sword was also a symbol of justice and was carried point upwards, sheathed and wrapt in its belt, whenever a king or great lord appeared ceremoniously. The scabbard of the Vienna St Maurice Sword is covered with gold plates decorated with figures intended to be looked at when the sword is held in this way. In early times, particularly, kings seated on their thrones are often represented with their sheathed sword lying in their laps. At other times, it is carried by an officer of the court, a marshal or constable, who in the case of a king or emperor would be one of the great nobles. The arms of the Hereditary Marshal of the Holy Roman Emperor are crossed swords, while the arms of the Heredit- ary High Constable of Scotland include a hand grasping a sword.

The Bayeux Tapestry shows Duke William and his half- brother Odo both carrying clubs, perhaps as a sort of baton of command. The lightly-armed English troops have clubs with quatrefoil heads, one of which is seen flying through the air. Wace mentions a weapon called a *gibet* which also appears to be a form of mace. Maces illustrated in twelfth- century manuscripts have heads of a variety of shapes and are often supplied with numerous long, sharp spikes (Plate 24).

Wace describes the troops as carrying axes and *gisarmes.* The latter was apparently an axe with a very large crescentic blade, the lower point fixed to the shaft. Such an axe is illus- trated in the only surviving manuscript of *Sir Gawayne and the Grene Knight* and is there called both an axe and a 'giserne'.

This linking of the lower point of the cutting edge with the shaft, either by means of a secondary socket at this point or by twisting an extension of the point round the shaft, took the strain off the point immediately under the head where the shaft was most likely to break. A second method of doing this was to make the head with a tubular socket extending several inches down the shaft below the head, a feature illustrated in a late twelfth-century *Bestiary* in the Bodleian Library, Oxford (Ashmole Ms. 1511) and in the *Apocalypse* of Trinity College, Cambridge. About 1190, the Normans are described in the *Chroniques des ducs de Normandie* as carrying 'Haches danesches', the Viking axe under its new medieval name.[1] Crescentic bladed axes of Norse descent occur, for instance, in the *Bible of St Etienne Harding* before 1109, in the *Pembroke Gospels* of the early twelfth century, and in the Trinity College *Apocalypse*. The effigy at Malvern Abbey, mentioned above, is armed with a small pick-like war hammer, and many thirteenth-century manuscripts illustrate small tomahawk-like axes with a sharp spike on the back of the head.

Many peasants and small townsmen who set out on the First Crusade with Peter the Hermit would not normally have had weapons of their own, nor probably could many of them afford to buy them. These people probably took with them any implement they had which could be used as a weapon. Certainly, manuscripts of the mid twelfth century, like those of the School of Matthew Paris, show infantry armed with hay-forks, flails, the great mallets used for breaking clods in the fields, and the blades of hedging bills or scythes fixed on long shafts. No doubt the huntsman took his spear, and the woodman and carpenter their axes. These simple

---

[1] Gay, *Glossaire Archéologique,* I, 1887, p. 59.

arms were the ancestors of whole families of weapons used by later infantry. In the sixteenth century highly decorated ones were made to be carried by guards on ceremonial occasions only.

The early twelfth-century *Pembroke College Gospels* show a straight, parallel-sided, apparently single-edged blade with a narrow finger-like point, mounted on a shaft about one metre long. A similar weapon is illustrated in the *Codex Calixtinus*. It is possible that this is the weapon referred to occasionally in English and French documents from the twelfth century onwards as a *fauchard,* a word related to the old French *faus,* meaning a scythe. A Spanish Bible at Amiens (Ms. 108) of the twelfth century shows a man armed with a hedging bill on a long shaft.

12

Crusader Ships

Those of the northern Crusaders who sailed round into the Mediterranean came in double-ended clinker-built ships, the descendants of the Viking long-ships, but by then apparently normally propelled by the wind and only rarely equipped with oars. Earl Harold's ship in the Bayeux Tapestry is shown being rowed out of harbour; and it, or another English ship, is being rowed as it prepares to drop anchor. A row of holes in the top strake of many of the ships in the Tapestry may represent ports for oars, like those on the Gokstad ship. Mr E. H. H. Archibald has recently suggested that the break amidship in the level of the gunnel on the English ships shown in the Tapestry and the absence of oar-ports at this point may indicate the presence of a deck in this area, perhaps to act as a fighting platform. Although illustrations of oared vessels are rare in the northern countries thereafter, it is known, for instance, that Henry II of England kept a galley or *esnecca* (serpent) at Southampton, presumably for Channel crossings. This had a crew of sixty, three times that of a normal trading vessel, and so was probably propelled by oars. There is a reference in 1295 to a London ship said to have 70 pairs of oars. Circular ports for oars appear on two ships in a mid-thirteenth-century *Life of St Thomas of Canterbury* in a Belgian private collection. In this case, the ports are of precisely the same shape as those on the Gokstad ship, with a slot at one side to allow the blade of the oar to pass through. The early fourteenth-century *Holkham Bible Picture Book* in the British Museum (Add. Ms. 47682) shows one ship still reminiscent in shape to the Viking long-ship. It has a lion's head carved on top of the stem- and stern-posts, a stern rudder, and is still being rowed by sweeps in round ports in the top strake. A smaller boat in this manuscript has rowlocks made of two pegs projecting upwards from a block fixed on the gunnel.

The thirteenth-century seals of the ports of Winchelsea and Sandwich show double-ended ships of this type but without oars and with a small turret or castle, supported on arches, built inside the hull at each end. Both these seals show what are apparently the ends of deck beams projecting through the planks of the ship's sides. The single mast is supported by shrouds attached to the ship's side. Two groups of three shrouds straining the mast forward and back are shown in a Mosan *Dialogues of St Gregory* of the twelfth century (Brussels, Bibl. Roy., Ms. 9916). They are attached to the top strake on the outer side. There are no ratlines – the small ropes fastened across the shrouds like ladder rungs – which apparently do not appear until the fourteenth century; as on the seal of San Sebastian (Spain) of 1335. The *Dialogues* also show the ropes, known as sheets, tied to the lower corners of the sail and attached to a horizontal cross-bar fixed between two upright posts immediately in front of the steersman, presumably some form of windlass; also attached to this bar is the halyard by which the sail was raised and lowered. The yard has no braces, but the sail of this apparently rather small ship could probably be manoeuvered by means of the sheets alone.

An early seal of the town of La Rochelle shows several rows of reefing points on the lower part of the square sail. These were used to tie up the lower edge of the canvas in a bundle to reduce the area catching the wind. This is very clearly shown in an astrological manuscript of the second quarter of the fourteenth century in the British Museum, which actually illustrates the sail reefed (Sloane Ms. 2983). The seal of Sandwich shows a top-castle at the mast-head to act both as a look-out post and as a place from which missiles could be hurled onto the deck of an enemy ship.

By 1284 the seal of the port of Dover shows a ship with the castles supported on two arches and built onto and over-lapping the stem and stern-post, thus becoming an integral part of the ship rather than merely something built into it. As time went on the fore-castle was made smaller than the after-castle and was given a triangular plan to adapt it to the shape of the bow. The Dover seal also shows a bow-sprit passing through the fore-castle. This is a spar sloping forward beyond the bow to carry the bowlines which keep the edge of the sail drawn forward when sailing close to the wind.

In smaller ships without castles the stern-post was sometimes divided at the top to form a crutch or fork, called the 'mike'; as shown in the *Dialogues of St Gregory* mentioned above. This probably acted as a support for the spars and the mast when unstepped. In a late twelfth-century Psalter from Canterbury a coil of rope is shown hanging on one arm of the mike (Paris, Bibl. Nat., Ms. Lat. 8846).

The manuscript of *La Estoire de Seint Aedward le Rei* of about 1250 shows a small sailing ship with a mike at the stern on which the anchor is hung and against which the sweeps have been stacked. A monster's head on the bow-post sup-ports a bow-sprit. The whole fore-end of this ship has a castellated bulwark built above the top strake, supported by brackets where the ship narrows towards the bow (Cambridge, University Library, Ms. Ee. 3. 59).

The steering-oar, like its Viking predecessor, still had a tiller fitted at right angles at the top to make it more manageable. Judging by an illustration in a twelfth-century *Life of St Cuthbert* at Oxford, (Bodleian Ms. 165), the bottom of the oar was sometimes shod with metal. An early thirteenth-century drawing, scratched on the walls of Fide Church in Gotland, shows the earliest certain representation of a true rudder hung on the stern post. The same thing is shown on the seal of the town of Elbing of 1242, while in 1252 the Port Books of Damme distinguish between ships with 'a rudder on the side' and those 'with a rudder astern.' The *Holkham Bible Picture Book* shows the tiller, operating on the top of the rudder and divided to pass on each side of the stern-post. The necessity of hanging the stern-rudder by two or three hinges probably encouraged the adoption of a straight stern-post, in place of the curved kind. The planking of the sides was still curved round to join the stern-post as on Viking ships, and the square-ended stern apparently did not appear until the fifteenth century. The advantage of the stern-rudder is that it does not lift out of the water when the ship heels as does a steering oar.

A drawing of a ship in the early thirteenth-century *Eneide* manuscript for the first time illustrates a loading door in the side of the hull. The seal of Sandwich shows a ship's boat carried on deck amidships.

The ships hired in Mediterranean ports by the Crusaders to carry them to the Holy Land derived from an entirely different tradition from those of the north. The *Liber ad honorem augusti* of the late twelfth century shows ships not unlike those painted on Greek vases (Plate 25). Apparently square-rigged, they have in addition a single bank of oars and an open rail running along the side. The high prow curves back and has a fish-tail terminal, and there is a long ram pro-

Plate 25 Men at arms, archers, crossbowmen, and warships of about 1200, from the *Liber ad honorem augusti* of Pietro de Eboli, now in the Burgerbibliothek, Bern (Codex 120, fol. 131). (Reproduced by permission of the Librarian)

jecting from the bow just above water-level. The curved line of the stern is continued upwards by two tall tapering beams, one on each side, curving forward over a small stern cabin. The purpose of these two beams is unknown but it has been suggested that they were to support the yards when they were lowered, since these were often longer than the ship itself. Other ships in this manuscript are without sails but have a second bank of oars emerging from a row of ports below the gunnel on which the other bank rests. These rowing galleys nearly always carry two or three very large flags on short staffs. Both types of ships, in common with all Mediterranean craft, have a steering-oar on each side of the stern, which ensures that, however much the ship heels over, one of the steering oars will still reach into the water. Southern ships were 'carvel-built'; that is, the planks of the hull were placed edge to edge to give a smooth outer surface, and not over-lapped as on northern ships.

The triangular sail carried on a yard set fore and aft, known as the lateen (latin) rig and typical of Mediterranean ships, is illustrated in the early mosaics in St Mark's Cathedral, Venice. It probably developed over a very long period, from a square sail, by gradually swinging one end of the yard forward and down. The other end of the yard eventually rose high above the top of the mast. As time went on, the square sail would have been modified into a triangle to suit this setting. Since a fore-stay would have obstructed the manoeuvering of this type of sail, it was dispensed with and, instead, the mast was raked forward. The fact that the shrouds were fitted astern of the mast, and therefore strained it backwards, made an after-stay unnecessary. The lateen sail was hoisted from a point well above where the shrouds met the mast and, when set, was outside the shrouds on the leeward side. The shrouds could be loosened by means of pulleys when sailing on different tacks. The mosaics of St Mark's already show ships with two masts; while in 1191, Richard 1 of England, on the way to the Holy Land, encountered a three-masted ship.

The specifications for the ships built for the crusade of Louis ix in 1268 have survived. Those ordered in Venice were to be 17·7 metres long in the keel, 26 metres between stern and stern-post, 6·5 metres wide, and 6·7 metres deep from keel to bulwark amidships. The stern and stern-post were to rise 8·8 metres above the keel. They were to have two decks, with a half-deck above from midships to the bow, and two or three extra decks at the stern to form cabins. Those built at Genoa, on the other hand, were to be smaller, only 23 metres overall, and for these the specifications for the masts and yards also survive. The fore-mast was to be 23·3 metres and the after-mast 18·4 metres. The length of the yards was to be 29·3 metres and 25·6 metres respectively, allowing for the overlap of the two timbers from which each was made. In this case the main yard was 6·4 metres longer than the hull.

The St Mark's mosaics show the stern built up to form an after-castle in the manner specified by Louis ix. There are apparently top-castles but no fore-castles. A small fore-castle is shown on the tomb of St Peter Martyr in the Church of St Eustorgio, Milan, of 1339. This carving also shows the ends of two rows of deck beams projecting through the planking of the side, a relatively high after-castle, probably two decks high, and, for the first time, a hawse-hole for the cable of the anchor, which is secured by one fluke so that it hangs with its shank parallel to the bulwark. The rope ladder up the mast is visible as are the pulleys for adjusting the shrouds. The lower part of the steering-oar is also supported by ropes and pulleys.

Conclusion:
The Decline of
Feudalism and Chivalry

The fourteenth century saw a great revolution in medieval society: particularly in England the stratification of society became much less rigid. The purely feudal bonds of society based on homage and tenure of land were gradually replaced by personal contracts at all levels, from the villein renting a part of the manor in return for a small cash payment, to the earl or great captain serving under contract to the king for a daily wage and with a stipulated force of men.

The feudal summons to the tenants-in-chief was not finally abandoned in England until 1385, but the normal method of raising troops throughout the fourteenth century was by indentures. The earliest recorded English contract for knightly service is one of 1213; Robert, lord of Berkeley, in order to repay a debt of 500 marks to the Crown, agreed to serve with ten knights at his own expense with the king in France. The next is a sub-contract made in 1287 between Edward Mortimer and Peter Maulay. The latter agreed to serve the former with ten covered (i.e. armoured) horses for the duration of the royal campaign against the rebellious Welsh. His horses were described and valued so that, if any were killed or died on the campaign, Maulay could be fully compensated. The variation of values suggests that his retinue consisted of three other knights and seven sergeants which would have been typical of sub-contractors' retinues at that period. If successful such a leader would be employed again on later campaigns and might eventually become a banneret and be given land to support his title. It is typical of the social revolution of the fourteenth century that by the middle years successful bannerets are occasionally found with larger retinues than some earls, while others commanded field armies or acted as King's Lieutenant in large areas of France.

During the first half of the Hundred Years War, the need to organize numerous complicated campaigns in France led to the widespread use of complex contracts. Royal officials had already begun the process of standardizing the form of agreement. Generally the area of operations and the period of service were stipulated, the number of men to be supplied and their ranks – knights, sergeants, and archers mounted or on foot – and their rates of pay. At the end of the stated period, or if pay failed to be forthcoming, the indentee was free to go, but many contracts mention the possibility of an extension on similar terms. Pay was normally granted in advance and included a 'regard', a payment to the captain over and above his wages as an inducement to serve. Compensation was granted for horses lost on campaign. Finally, the conditions governing the 'advantages of war' were stated; these included such things as loot, captured lands and castles, and the ransoms of prisoners. The men would be mustered and inspected on the specified day, often at the port of embarkation, and their horses inspected and described on the horse valuation roll to prevent substitution. Commanders failing to produce the full number of their retinue were occasionally brought to book. No feudal bond was involved in such a contract, the relationship of the parties was purely commercial.

In 1257, for the first time, the English shire levies were offered royal pay from the moment of leaving their own county, and this soon became customary. The loss of their unpaid service was undoubtedly a blow to the Crown. The infantry of fourteenth-century English armies were drawn from the lower ranks of those sworn to arms for the keeping of the peace by the Assize of 1242, as restated by the Statute of Winchester of 1285. All those with income of between 2l. and 5l. a year were to provide themselves with bows and arrows. It was this group which was to form the formidable archers of Edward III and his captains. Before campaigns the *jurati ad arma* were mustered in their own shire or hundred by Commissioners of Array appointed by the king, who then selected those most suitable for the service required. Since English tactics during the fourteenth century depended on the co-operation of archers with dismounted men-at-arms, it was essential that the infantry did not fall behind the cavalry on the march. As the Hundred Years War progressed an increasing proportion of the archers were mounted on cheap nags, but they invariably dismounted to fight.

In France there was among the lower ranks of society increasing disillusionment with the feudal hierarchy. The century that opened with the crushing defeat of the flower of France's chivalry by a force of Flemish burgher infantry at Courtrai (1302), saw the gradual discrediting of a knighthood incapable of carrying out its side of the feudal bargain – the protection of the people against the murdering and pillaging of English, and later their own, mercenary bands. The loss of influence by the nobility can be seen in the acts of the Estates which met in Paris in 1357 in the aftermath of the disgrace of Poitiers, in the appointment of a commission of thirty-six by the Estates to replace the ministers of the Crown, the forbidding to the nobles of private wars and their subordination to the local authorities, and in the grant of maintenance for 3,000 men-at-arms to be paid by the Estates and not by the Crown.

Rather less is known about the development of contractual forces in France during the fourteenth century, but a written contract, the *lettre de retinue* was in use, and differed only in form from the English indenture. The different war aims of the two countries led to differences in national organization. While English armies were, on the whole, only required to serve for a limited time to carry out swift raids deep into enemy territory, the French had both to provide numerous small garrisons and a field army to intercept the raiders. The problem of garrisons was partially solved by the organization of a corps of crossbowmen in each of the major towns. The feudal summons to tenants-in-chief *(ban de l'ost)* continued to be used in France more frequently than in England, particularly for major campaigns under royal leadership. On the other hand a determined attempt was made to maintain organized companies paid at regular intervals, with a clear chain of command, and officers responsible for the actions of their men. A royal *Ordonnance* of 1351 and a letter to the treasurers of wars written shortly afterward tell us a little about the organization of the French army at that date. The army consisted of two main groups; first, the cavalry consisting of knights, esquires, and sergeants *(valets);* second, the infantry crossbowmen and the spearmen who carried the large shields, called pavises, behind which the crossbowmen operated. The cavalry were to be grouped in squadrons *(routes)* of a definite number, and a strict system of muster and review by royal officers was instituted in order to ensure that each squadron was always at full strength and properly armed on its own horses. The name of each man was to be recorded on the muster roll with a list of his equipment and a description of his horse to prevent captains borrowing from other squadrons on the day of the review. The infantry were to be similarly organized in companies of 25 or 30 each under a constable who was to have a *pennoncel à queue* (tailed pennant), with such arms or device as pleased him. Crossbowmen were to shoot several times at musters, presumably to ensure that they really did know how to handle their weapons. The necessary armour was stipulated only for the *valets,* crossbowmen, and pavisers, presumably because the knights and esquires could be relied upon to equip themselves fully. During the second half of the century the infantry were often mounted, presumably so as to be able to overtake and bring to action the highly mobile English flying columns. It is not apparently known at present whether the crossbowmen and pavisers were mixed together in companies or, as in the Florentine army, marched in separate companies until immediately before battle commenced.

In both England and France the growth of the contract system in the army meant that the greatest captains did not necessarily come from noble families. Du Guesclin came from a relatively obscure Breton family, and, because of the past experience of the great offices of the Crown falling into the hands of over-powerful nobles, was able to rise to become Constable of France. In England some of the best known leaders of the Hundred Years War were simple knights like Sir Thomas Dagworth, Sir John de Chandos, Sir Hugh Calveley, and Sir Robert Knollys, to name only a few. Sir John Hawkwood, the leader of the 'White Company' whose memorial portrait by Paolo Uccello is in the Cathedral at Florence, is said to have been the son of a tanner and to have been apprenticed to a tailor.

The lowly origin of Hawkwood, perhaps more than anything else, shows how far real life had moved from the ideal of chivalry; the thought of a man of lowly birth receiving knighthood was still ridiculed in the romances. The decline of chivalry, which parallels the decline of feudalism, was in part due to the impossibility of reconciling its high ideals with the facts of everyday life. In time, chivalry became a matter for poets and heralds, very much more in evidence during court festivities, at banquets and tournaments, as the subject for tapestry, painting, and sculpture with which to decorate the houses and palaces of the rich, than on the field of battle, or in the court of law, or in government. The duty of every knight to protect women, particularly those of gentle birth, did not prevent Lord Molyns from sending his men to besiege Margaret Paston in her house at Gresham, Norfolk, in 1449. Chroniclers like Froissart proclaimed the nobility of their heroes and their knightly virtues without, apparently, noticing how far they fell below their ideal. Edward III did not hesitate to hang young Thomas Seton before the eyes of his parents who were standing on the walls of Berwick, in order to induce the father to surrender the town. Nor did he hesitate to put to death the Scots taken at Halidon Hill (1333), not in hot blood but on the day following the battle. Froissart's lament for the dispatch of the prisoners after the battle of Aljubarotta (1385) was for the loss of prospective ransoms, not for the loss of noble lives.

The whole idea of fighting for gain, whether in the form of pay or booty, was entirely against the principles of the chivalric code, and yet the main wars of the fourteenth century were fought very largely by mercenaries. The chances of plunder were held out openly as an inducement to enlist. There was, in fact, a very marked decline of chivalry in warfare, due to the growing commercialism of even the greatest nobles, and the rise of professional captains of lowly birth, untrained in the tenets of chivalry and with their way to make in the

world. Many fortunes were in fact made by war; Caister
Castle in Norfolk was built by Sir John Fastolf, traditionally
with the ransom of the duc d'Alençon whom he had captured
at Verneuil. Thomas Holland, scion of an obscure North
Country family, who captured the comte d'Eu at the fall of
Caen in 1346, and achieved a romantic marriage with Joan,
countess of Salisbury, the Fair Maid of Kent, was himself
created Earl of Kent. In fact, ransoms were a form of status
symbol, and it was not unknown for a knight to decline to
be ransomed for a sum he considered too modest, lest by doing
so he lost face.

The outward form of chivalry flourished. Tournaments
became more elaborate, designed to resurrect the golden
age of Arthur and Charlemagne, and even of those more
ancient courts, of Alexander the Great and of Julius Caesar,
from which chivalry and knighthood were thought to
descend; an age when it was felt that all knights had been
true and brave and all ladies beautiful and loving. The tournament gave an opportunity for the display of knightly prowess
and personal finery. In the lists could be found the glamour
and excitement of war without the acute discomfort and
inconvenience of campaigning.

The etiquette of court became stricter and more elaborate.
Knighthood itself was encouraged by kings like Edward
III, by the foundation of personal Orders (in his case that of
St George, or the Garter), in order to gather round them a
brotherhood of the most illustrious captains, both to increase
their own glory and to set an example to their subjects of
military prowess. Writers of the time began to attach elaborate symbolic meanings to each part of the knight's equipment
and dress.

One must be careful not to bury chivalry too soon. The
Hundred Years War saw many 'adventures' by small groups

of knights undertaken for the love of fighting and to win renown, like the famous Combat of Thirty held in Brittany in 1351. In 1349 Edward III and the Black Prince set off from England with the greatest secrecy to take part in the ambushing of Geoffroi de Chargny, who was planning to surprise the castle of Calais in time of truce. Both of them, together with the Earl of Suffolk and lords Stafford, John Montacute, John Beauchamp, Berkley, and de la Ware served under the command of Sir Walter Manny, a simple banneret. The warcry used on that frosty December morning as the English sallied out of Calais gate and fell on Chargny's force was 'Manny to the rescue'. It is clear that during the action the King was not wearing his coat armour with the arms of England on it, since none of his opponents recognized him. After the fight was over the King gave a feast at which he and the Prince waited on their captives. Each was presented by the King with a new robe. To Sir Eustace de Ribeaumont, who had struck him to his knees twice on that day, he also gave a chaplet of fine pearls from off his own head, praised him most highly and set him free without ransom. Similarly, after Navarette the Black Prince with chivalric generosity released du Guesclin, although politically it would have been better to keep prisoner such a capable and inspiring commander. In 1352 Henry of Lancaster, although one of the most successful and most feared of English commanders, was royally received and entertained at the French court where he had gone to answer the challenge of Otto, Duke of Brunswick, a mercenary in the French service.

Bibliography

Part I: The Beginnings of Feudalism

1 THE LOMBARDS

GWATKIN, H. M. and WHITNEY, J. P. *The Cambridge Medieval History*, I, *The Christian Roman Empire and the Foundation of the Teutonic Kingdoms*, Cambridge 1911.

HEJDOVÁ, D. 'Der sogenannte St Wenzels-Helm', *Waffen- und Kostümkunde*, IX, 1967, pp. 38–41.

OMAN, C. *A history of the art of war in the middle ages*, I, London 1924, Bk. II, Chap. I and II, and the authorities cited therein.

PARIBENI, R. 'Necropoli barbarica di Nocera Umbra', *Monumenti Antichi*, XXV, 1919, pp. 136–153.

SERGI, G. and MENRELLI, R. 'La necropoli barbarica di Castel Trosino', *Monumenti Antichi*, XII, 1902, pp. 146–343.

2 THE FRANKS

ARBMAN, H. 'Les épées du tombeau de Childeric', *Bulletin de la Société Royale des Lettres de Lund*, 1947–8, pp. 7ff.

BÖHNER, K. 'Das Grab eines fränkischen Herren aus Morken in Rheinland', *Führer des Rheinischen Landesmuseum in Bonn*, No. 4, Graz 1959.

BÖHNER, K. 'Das Langschwert des Frankenkönigs Childerich', *Bonner Jahrbücher*, Heft 148, 1948, pp. 218–48, pls. 37–42.

BOULANGER, C. *Le cimetière Franco-Mérovingian et Carolingien de Marchélepot (Somme)*, Paris 1919.

DE LOË, A. 'Découverte d'un casque dans un tombe franque a Trivières (Province de Hainaut)', *Annales de la Société d' Archéologie de Bruxelles*, XXIII, 1909, pp. 469–75.

HEJDOVÁ, D. 'Der sogenannte St Wenzels-Helm , *Waffen- und Kostümkunde*, VIII, 1966, pp. 95–110; IX, 1967, pp. 28–54; X, 1968, pp. 15–30, and the sources cited therein.

LOT, F. *L'art militaire et les armées au moyen âge* I, Paris 1946, cap. II, and sources cited therein.

OMAN, C. *A history of the art of war in the middle ages*, I, London 1924, Bk. II, cap. I, & Bk. III, cap. I.

PAULSEN, P. 'Alamannische Adelsgräber von Niederstotzingen (Kreis Heidenheim)', *Veröffentlichungen des Staatlichen Amtes für Denkmalpflege Stuttgart*, Reihe A. Vor- und Frühgeschichte, Heft 12/1.

★SALIN, E. *La civilisation Mérovingienne*, 4 vols, Paris 1949–59, and the works cited therein.

TACKENBERG, K. Über die Schutzwaffen der Karolingerzeit und ihre Wiedergabe in Handschrift und auf Elfenbeinschnitzerein', *Frühmittelalteriche Studien, Jahrbuch des Instituts für Frühmittelalterforschung der Universitat Münster*, III, Berlin 1969, pp. 277–88, Pls. XV – XIX.

WERNER, J. 'Frankish royal tombs in the Cathedrals of Cologne and Saint-Denis', *Antiquity*, XXXVIII, 1964, pp. 201–16.

3　THE VIKINGS

ARBMAN, H. *The Vikings*, London 1961, and the publications cited in its bibliography.

BRØGGER, A.W. and SHETELIG, H. *The Viking ships, their ancestry and evolution*, Oslo 1951.

OAKESHOTT, R.E. *The archaeology of weapons*, London 1961.

SHETELIG, H. *Viking antiquities in Great Britain and Ireland*, I–IV, Oslo 1940–54.

STENTON, F.M. *The Oxford History of England*, II, *Anglo-Saxon England, c. 550–1037*, Oxford 1947.

WHEELER, R.E.M. *London Museum Catalogues: No. 1 – London and the Vikings*, London 1927.

★ This work is the principal source for this chapter.

4 THE SAXONS

BLAIR, P.H. *An introduction to Anglo-Saxon England,* Cambridge 1962.

DAVIDSON, H.R.E. *The sword in Anglo-Saxon England,* Oxford 1962.

EVISON, V.I. *The fifth-century invasions south of the Thames,* London 1965.

HOLLISTER, C.W. *Anglo-Saxon military institutions on the eve of the Norman Conquest,* Oxford 1962.

STENTON, F.M. *The Oxford History of England,* II, *Anglo-Saxon England, c. 550–1037,* Oxford 1947.

WILSON, D.M. *The Anglo-Saxons,* London 1960.

These foregoing titles all have useful bibliographies.

GAMBER, O. 'The Sutton Hoo military equipment – An attempted reconstruction'. *Journal of the Arms and Armour Society,* v. No. 6, June 1966, pp. 265–89.

Part II: Feudalism and Chivalry

ARCHIBALD, E.H.H. *The Wooden fighting ships in the Royal Navy AD 897–1860,* London 1968.

BLAIR, C. *European and American arms c. 1100–1850,* London 1962, and the sources cited therein.

————. *European armour circa 1066 to circa 1700,* London 1958, and the sources cited therein.

BLOCK, M. *Feudal society,* London 1961.

CRIPPS-DAY, F.H. *The history of the tournament in England and in France,* London 1918, and the sources cited therein.

GANSHOF, F.L. *Feudalism,* London 1966.

GAUTIER, L. *Chivalry,* London 1965.

HARVEY, R. *Moriz von Craûn and the chivalric world,* Oxford 1961.

HEWITT, J. *Ancient armour and weapons in Europe,* 3 vols. Oxford and London, 1855 and 1860, Reprinted Graz 1967.

HOLLISTER, C.W. *The Military organization of Norman England,* Oxford 1965.

HUSSEY, J. *The Cambridge Medieval History,* IV, *The Byzantine Empire,* Oxford 1967.

KIMBALL, F.G. *Sergeanty tenure in medieval England,* New Haven 1936.

LOT, F. *L'art militaire et les armées au moyen âge,* I, Paris 1946, Cap. IV–V.

MOLLET, M. 'Problèmes navals de l'histoire des croisades', *Cahiers de civilization médiévale,* x, July–Dec. 1967, No. 3–4, pp. 345–59.

OAKESHOTT, R.E. *The archaeology of weapons,* London 1960.

———. *The sword in the age of chivalry,* London 1964.

POOLE, A.L. *Obligations of society in the XII and XIII centuries,* Oxford 1946.

———. *The Oxford History of England,* III, *From Domesday Book to Magna Carta, 1087–1216,* Oxford 1955.

POWICKE, M. *Military obligation in Medieval England,* Oxford 1962.

———. *The Oxford History of England,* IV, *The thirteenth century, 1216–1307,* Oxford 1962.

RUNCIMAN, S. *A history of the Crusades,* 3 vols., Cambridge 1951.

SANDERS, I.J. *Feudal military service in England,* Oxford 1956.

SMAIL, R.C. *Crusading warfare (1097–1193),* Cambridge 1956.

TANNER, J.R., PREVITE-ORTON, C.W. and BROOKE, Z.N. *The Cambridge Medieval History,* v. *Contest of Empire and Papacy,* Cambridge 1927, and VI, *Victory of the Papacy,* Cambridge 1929.

THOMPSON, J.W. *Feudal Germany,* Chicago 1928.

Conclusion: The Decline of Feudalism and Chivalry

The best general book is undoubtedly J. Huizinga's *The waning of the Middle Ages,* Penguin Books, 1955. A good summary of the development of contractual forces in England and France, with a list of source material, will be found in K. Fowler's *The age of Plantagenet and Valois. The struggle for supremacy 1328–1498,* London 1967.

Index

Note: Figures in italics refer to illustrations.